Brexitspeak

Were we talked into Brexit? And who is 'we'? It's impossible to do politics without words and a context to use them in. And it's impossible to make sense of the phenomenon of Brexit without understanding how language was used – and misused – in the historical context that produced the 2016 referendum result. This interdisciplinary book shows how the particular idea of 'the British people' was maintained through text and talk at different levels of society over the years following World War II, and mobilised by Brexit propagandists in a socially, economically and culturally divided polity. The author argues that we need the well-defined tools of linguistics and language philosophy, tied in with a political science framework, to understand a serious, modern concept of demagoguery. Written in an accessible manner, this book is essential reading for anyone who wants to probe the social, political and ideational contexts that generated Brexit.

PAUL CHILTON is Emeritus Professor of Linguistics at Lancaster University, and currently an associate member of the Faculty of Linguistics, Philology and Phonetics at the University of Oxford and the Centre for Applied Linguistics at the University of Warwick. His notable publications include *Security Metaphors* (1996), *Analysing Political Discourse* (2004) and *Language, Space and Mind* (2014).

Brexitspeak

Demagoguery and the Decline of Democracy

Paul Chilton
University of Warwick

CAMBRIDGE
UNIVERSITY PRESS

CAMBRIDGE
UNIVERSITY PRESS

Shaftesbury Road, Cambridge CB2 8EA, United Kingdom

One Liberty Plaza, 20th Floor, New York, NY 10006, USA

477 Williamstown Road, Port Melbourne, VIC 3207, Australia

314–321, 3rd Floor, Plot 3, Splendor Forum, Jasola District Centre, New Delhi – 110025, India

103 Penang Road, #05–06/07, Visioncrest Commercial, Singapore 238467

Cambridge University Press is part of Cambridge University Press & Assessment, a department of the University of Cambridge.

We share the University's mission to contribute to society through the pursuit of education, learning and research at the highest international levels of excellence.

www.cambridge.org
Information on this title: www.cambridge.org/9781108840811

DOI: 10.1017/9781108892681

© Paul Chilton 2025

This publication is in copyright. Subject to statutory exception and to the provisions of relevant collective licensing agreements, no reproduction of any part may take place without the written permission of Cambridge University Press & Assessment.

When citing this work, please include a reference to the DOI 10.1017/9781108892681

First published 2025

A catalogue record for this publication is available from the British Library.

A Cataloging-in-Publication data record for this book is available from the Library of Congress

ISBN 978-1-108-84081-1 Hardback
ISBN 978-1-108-74402-7 Paperback

Cambridge University Press & Assessment has no responsibility for the persistence or accuracy of URLs for external or third-party internet websites referred to in this publication and does not guarantee that any content on such websites is, or will remain, accurate or appropriate.

Every effort has been made to contact the relevant copyright-holders for the images reproduced in this book. In the event of any error, the publisher will be pleased to make corrections in any reprints or future editions.

To Tricia

Contents

List of Figures		*page* ix
Acknowledgements		x
	Introduction: Populists, Demagogues, Language	1
	Brexitspeak	2
	Populism	5
	Demagoguery	8
	Post-truth Politics	10
	A Closer Look at Language	13
1	**Identity**	22
	The Idea of Identity	23
	Identitarianism	26
	Immigration	31
	Blame the EU	34
2	**We**	43
	Monolingual *We*	44
	Cameron: British *We*	49
	Farage: British *We*	54
3	**The People**	61
	The People, Ancient and Modern	62
	The People and Sovereignty	66
	The Common People	73
	From *the Common People* to *Ordinary People*	80
4	**The British People**	85
	Nation and Empire	85
	The Will of the People	91
	The Mandate of the People	94
	So Who Was the British People in 2016?	99
5	**Fear of Foreigners**	103
	Xenophobia, Racism, Ethnocentrism	103
	Sources of Brexit Xenophobia	106
	Enter Enoch	109

vii

viii   Contents

    Powellism   113
    The Path to Brexit   118

6   Fear of Foreigners Mobilised   126
    The Rise of UKIP   126
    Anti-migrant Propaganda   131
    Invasion   136

7   How Demagogues Do It   147
    What Words Do to the Brain   147
    Vehicles of Untruth   153
    Breaking Point   158
    The Fear of Losing It   164

    Conclusion: Brexitspeak, Demagoguery, Decline of Democracy   170
    Identity   172
    Sovereignty   173
    Foreigners   174
    Demagoguery and Propaganda   176
    Lies and Post-truth Politics   178
    Undoing Democracy   180

Appendix A   185
Appendix B   186
Appendix C   187
References   188
Index   206

Figures

1.1	Scattergram for low-immigrant areas voting more strongly for Leave.	*page* 33
1.2	Relationship between immigration and Europe in 1975 and 2015.	35
2.1	Nationalist monolingualism post-Brexit.	45
3.1	Frontispiece to *Leviathan*.	68
5.1	'Rivers of blood' speech, 20 April 1968.	111
5.2	Neo-Nazi Powellism.	118
5.3	UKIP Powellism.	124
6.1	'Are you thinking what we're thinking?'	134
6.2	A 'go home' van.	135
6.3	Invasion arrows (Operation Sea Lion).	143
6.4a	Invasion from Turkey.	143
6.4b	Border with Syria and Iraq.	144
7.1	Response to threat words: activation of the amygdala.	148
7.2a	Taking voters for a ride.	153
7.2b	Variation on the theme with Boris Johnson.	154
7.3a	UKIP's 'Breaking point' poster.	159
7.3b	Nazi propaganda film.	160
7.4a	Take Back Control.	165
7.4b	Control of what?	166

Acknowledgements

Books are never totally the work of one individual, and this one would never have been completed without the intellectual input and professional eye of Patricia Chilton, my wife, nor without her moral support and love. Among the many colleagues, students and friends who have influenced and encouraged this project, I am particularly grateful to Ruth Wodak, Sally Tomlinson, Bill Downes, Monika Kopytowska, Bertie Kaal and Andy Roberts. For their suggestions and advice, I also wish to thank Bernhard Forchtner at the University of Leicester, Mikhail Ilyin and his graduate student Anastasia Butakova at the Russian Higher School of Economics, Majid KhosraviNik at Newcastle University, Manuela Perteghella of the Liberal Democrats and the European Movement, Tony Simpson of the Bertrand Russell Foundation, and Franco Zappettini at the University of Liverpool.

I am very grateful to the anonymous reviewers who scrutinised the drafts and gave invaluable advice on content, presentation and style, as well as support for the project itself. Thanks are due also to Dorothy Lawrenson, who expertly copy-edited an earlier draft, weeding out many errors and infelicities. My editors at Cambridge University Press have backed this project and kept it on track from the start. Special thanks go to Helen Barton who commissioned this book and has given encouragement through all its ups and downs. Isabel Collins has provided indispensable advice and expertise, and Laura Simmons has skilfully guided the production of the book through to its public appearance. I thank also Adam Bell for his scrupulous copyediting and Narmadha Nedounsejiane at Integra Software Services for overseeing the final stages. All remaining errors and omissions are, of course, my responsibility.

This book contains numerous illustrations and tables and I want to thank a number of people who have guided and advised me along the tortuous path of contacting copyright holders. Among them are Mary Andrews of *The Independent* and *Evening Standard*; Andy Boyd of the parliamentary Department for Culture, Media and Sport; Vega Elvira at *The Guardian*; Verity Manning, Digital Archivist at the BBC; Chris Morrison, Copyright and Licensing Specialist at the Bodleian Libraries; Mary Reid of *Liberal Democratic Voice*; Alexandre Reingatch at the Bundesarchiv; Martin Shaw

Acknowledgements   xi

of the University of Sussex and the Institut Barcelona d'Estudis Internacionals; Olivier Sykes at the University of Liverpool; and Matt Ward at BBC Sales and Operations Support.

For permission to reuse their graph for Figure 1.1, I thank Chris Lawton (Nottingham Trent University) and Rob Ackrill (Nottingham Trent University). For Figure 1.2, I thank Geoffrey Evans (Nuffield College, University of Oxford) and Jonathan Mellon (Nuffield College and University of Manchester) for permission to reuse their bar chart. Specific acknowledgements are due to the following: The German Bundesarchiv for Figure 7.3b; The Department of Culture, Media and Sport, for Figures 6.4a and 6.4b; The Communication Directorate, Home Office, for Figure 6.2; The *Proceedings of the National Academy of Sciences*, Copyright (1999) National Academy of Sciences, USA, for the reuse in Figure 7.1 of the illustration in Nancy Isenberg et al. (1999), 96(18), p. 10457.

For access to many publications used in writing this book, I am indebted to the Bodleian Libraries' online facilities. Like all scholars of the internet age, I have frequently depended on search engines, image banks, internet media, online organisations, websites and bloggers, and I am thankful for the existence of all those that ensure the diffusion of knowledge by open access.

Introduction: Populists, Demagogues, Language

> ... one ought to recognize that the present political chaos is connected with the decay of language, and that one can probably bring about some improvement by starting at the verbal end.
>
> George Orwell, *Politics and the English Language*

'Language', in the sense of the general human capacity for language, does not decay. What Orwell means, of course, is that it is the way politicians *use* language that had 'decayed', in the sense of no longer following certain ethical standards, such as telling the truth, giving information needed, giving answers when asked for them, being clear rather than ambiguous or obscure, and so on. To put it another way, the faculty of language decays when one's brain decays, but the use of language, judged by some ethical norms, can 'decay' under particular social, political and cultural circumstances. And the relationship is reciprocal: the ethical 'decay' in language use also brings about the process of ongoing decline. The basic assumption is: language use is part and parcel of doing politics.

Orwell, as is well known, had the nightmare, written up in his novel *Nineteen Eighty-Four*, that a political regime could develop its own vocabulary and that political words could constrain and direct political thinking and acting – in *Nineteen Eighty-Four* this language was called 'Newspeak'. Orwell was not trained in linguistics or the philosophical analysis of language, although he did contribute articles to the magazine *Polemic*, alongside the philosophers Bertrand Russell and A. J. Ayer. He was a journalist and novelist who insisted on truth and accuracy and persisted in opposing power. In language matters he was an astute observer of political abuses of language (but capable of being misled by the linguistic prescriptivism of his social class and Etonian education). While all journalists are necessarily embroiled in language, Orwell seems to have been particularly conscious of the fact that the practice of politics was inseparable from language use. He was able to stand back and make judgements about the effects and implications of words and what politicians were doing with them. He wielded no special tools of analysis – just the ordinary ability of the human mind to be linguistically vigilant and to apply ethical norms to acts of speech just as much as to any other social act. He was pessimistic about the extent of that ability.

When he wrote *Nineteen Eighty-Four*, Orwell, and his contemporaries, had witnessed decades of totalitarian propaganda and its effects. In the Soviet Union, millions were to do so for another forty years. Today still, mass indoctrination continues, and not only in the Soviet Union's successor state. The term 'propaganda' is useful for referring to any abusive deployment of language by, or on behalf of an organisation, especially a political one that is targeting a mass audience. The prototypical example is that of totalitarian regimes, as was the case in Orwell's day. In our own time, the developments in communication technology have gone far beyond the communication resources of Orwell's day. Today's technology has created the conditions for a new communicative culture and for a new kind of demagoguery. It is a kind of demagoguery that appears not only in the public forum and in the traditional press but also in social media and the dark web of extremists and disinformation activists.

The role played by the new social media channels has been of central importance in the spread of populist ideas and sentiments, and in the rise of the Brexit movement. Social media performed this role not just through the ideas and sentiments themselves, but through the dissemination of demagogic uses of language, images and other discourse devices. Contrary to what is sometimes claimed, social media technologies have actually contributed to the erosion of democratic deliberation.[1] Such communication systems are beyond Orwell's imaginings and are capable of consolidating destructive ideas and forms of talk among citizens and politicians alike.

Brexit was in large part a product of these processes, but political language and communication emerge in contexts with a history. Brexit was a product of Britain's problems of historical identity in a context where the world had changed structurally and was producing new national-populist ideologies. To grasp more clearly what happened around the UK's European Union (EU) membership referendum of 2016, we need not only the analytical tools of history and political science but also those of language philosophy and the language sciences.

Brexitspeak

This book draws on a variety of academic perspectives in an attempt to understand Brexit, its historical roots, and the means by which it was brought about. The Orwellian perspective has its limitations but its central ideas point the way to an analysis. Political behaviour is largely a matter of using language

---

[1] Cf. KhosraviNik (2019), Geoghegan (2020).

in particular ways. The accumulation of political power is not only a matter of physical force, but of controlling public discourse and the means of public communication in order to control a population. That means attempting to use language, among other weapons, to control thoughts, behaviours and feelings. And it means getting round whatever critical watchfulness people may be exercising. Orwell's linguistic dystopia – complete thought-control – may not be possible, precisely because of the potential of human vigilance. But effective propaganda can at the very least lay hold of public opinion and can produce turning points of historic significance – such as Brexit.

So this book will have a good deal to say about what certain influential and powerful political actors were *saying* and *writing* that led to the way people voted at the 2016 referendum. Brexit was an irrational decision and explaining it needs many different approaches. Economic, social and demographic explanations are certainly essential parts of the picture. But they leave out a key element. Given that there were indeed sections of British society who were economically and socially vulnerable, and susceptible to anti-EU rhetoric, we still need to explain the nature of the final shift in public opinion that produced the referendum result – by a narrow margin. Propaganda in favour of leaving the EU was decisive, especially in the final stages. In order to get to a more comprehensive understanding, and possibly an explanation of Brexit, not only is a macro-analysis of the contemporary context needed but also a micro-analysis of campaign propaganda.

Brexitspeak was a regular way of talking designed to direct people's attention to the EU and infuse a negative stance towards membership of it. This was done by way of constant repetition of words and phrases that sought to constrain thoughts about Europe and the EU in the desired direction – Brexitthink. Seeking to influence ideas alone is insufficient. Brexitspeak sought to trigger emotions and to re-activate latent feelings and attitudes – it was also Brexitfeel. The easiest emotions to activate are fear, hostility and hatred, and the easiest way to stimulate them is to talk up alleged dangers and threats. Brexitspeak stirred up latent xenophobia, directing it towards immigrants, and blaming increased immigration on the EU.

Micro-analysis enters the explanatory framework in order to explain how Brexitspeak pushed Brexitthink and Brexitfeel to the point that it sufficiently influenced pro-Brexit voting behaviour. After all, doing politics of any kind is primarily a matter of linguistic activity. To advance this type of explanatory goal, the book focuses partly on existing patterns of thought and feeling that Brexiters could exploit, and partly on the micro-mechanisms of their deployment of language to influence political behaviour. The book therefore backtracks in history, in order to trace the threads of discourse that produced the contexts of meaning in which Brexit was forged. And, in order to explore the details of pro-Brexit communication, I draw widely on the language sciences combined with related disciplines. Overall, the approach is interdisciplinary, crossing the boundaries of history, political science, philosophy and psychology. In particular, importing linguistics into political inquiry may be unfamiliar, even controversial. The risks involved in crossing disciplinary boundaries sometimes have to be taken, and the reasons for such risks lie in the nature of the complex questions that the extraordinary Brexit decision poses.

Brexit was not an isolated outburst peculiar to Britain but part of the 'new populism' that emerged in the 1990s and the early twenty-first century.[2] Donald Trump's election to the presidency of the United States in 2016 is the most obvious example, but closer to hand geographically was the rise of far-right populist movements in Europe.[3] Their ideological emphasis was on identity, often involving the invention of a political 'other'. Chapter 1 of the present book explores this identitarian context and how Europhobia and anti-immigrationism came to be combined. In effect, what the pro-Leave campaign did was project a new British identity. Chapter 2 examines how this was done linguistically by the Conservative Party's prime minister, David Cameron, under political pressure both from the UK Independence Party (UKIP) and from the nationalist and populist right within his own party. Appeasing the Brexiters was not just a matter of announcing a referendum but of simultaneously adopting a degree of Brexitspeak, thus undermining Cameron's own Remain stance. As the pro-Brexit movement grew in political strength, so its discourse developed an ideational coherence around the notion of 'the people', a notion that entailed a cluster of other words and political notions that were endlessly repeated in campaign propaganda. In a rough and ready way, and doubtless unwittingly, this put Brexitspeak in line with a long tradition of European political thought, which is considered in Chapter 3. But of course the populist ideas had to be spun out in a British context.

Chapter 4 therefore shows how the UK's national identity problem arose, and how a 'British people' was assumed to exist and to express its 'will' in a supposedly incontrovertible 'mandate' to leave the EU. Anti-immigration attitudes, mixed in with racism, had been endemic in the UK, and their manifestations on the domestic scene continued into the post-imperial period after World War II. They were not always explicitly expressed in the public sphere but were capable of being brought into the open by demagogues when the time was ripe. Chapter 5 examines how Enoch Powell's interventions in the 1960s persisted over time. Existing British ethnocentrism with a racist tinge was easily stoked up both before and during the pro-Brexit campaigns. Conservative Party policy became openly aggressive towards immigrants in the 2000s, and the Conservative-Liberal government set in motion the policy of 'hostile environment'. The United Nations later stated that the policy was

---

[2] Canovan (2004), pp. 1–2.   [3] Cf. Pelinka (2013, 2018).

'entrenching racism' in the UK. As Chapter 6 seeks to show, the 'hostile environment' fed into the Brexiters' narrative. The Leave campaign propaganda pushed the idea that being hostile to immigrants was part and parcel of being hostile to the EU. The language became increasingly deceptive, and dishonest to the point of blatantly denying known facts. All of the political manoeuvres, the deceptions and distortions, the stoking up of negative emotions, and the efforts to arouse an ethnocentric patriotism – all this and more depended on demagogic communication that primarily, but not entirely, involved the strategic deployment of language. Is it really possible to use language in such a way that it affects the minds of voters and leads them in a desired direction? And what exactly are the mechanisms of such language? Chapter 7 approaches such fundamental questions by taking some of the most notorious examples of Brexitspeak and focusing in on their workings with instruments of linguistic analysis. It is by this kind of close investigation that one comes to see how words, and images too, were designed to sway a public that was in fact divided on the referendum question. This happened in the context of the new populism and by means of the devices of the new demagoguery.

Populism

Brexit – or Brexitism – was a manifestation of populism. The term 'populism' has had numerous uses and definitions. Various forms of populism have been the subject of attention since the 1960s and have been increasingly discussed by journalists and academics since the turn of the century. There is at least a family resemblance among the variations, and arguably a shared conceptual and attitudinal core. Although it is still argued by some that the term unhelpfully groups together very diverse kinds of political orientation,[4] I adopt the label 'populism' to refer to a recognisable historical phenomenon found across the Americas and Europe, one that is made up of internationally shared ideas, attitudes and emotions.[5] This does not mean that 'populists' always brand themselves with that label, though in some instances they do so in order to lay claim to a term that has been standardly used in a pejorative sense. Nor is populism typically formulated as an ideology, theory or philosophy, since rejection of such 'elite' discourse is one of its professed characteristics. An exception is the left-wing theorist Ernesto Laclau, who viewed populism as emancipatory.[6]

---

[4] Art (2020).
[5] See for example: Canovan (1981, 2004, 2005), Taggart (2000), Mény and Surel (2002), Mudde (2007), Albertazzi and McDonnell (2008), Müller (2016), Mudde and Kaltwasser (2017), Eatwell and Goodwin (2018), Urbinati (2019), Rosanvallon (2020).
[6] Laclau (2005).

There are several ways of characterising the new populist wave. The socio-economic approach to populism enquires primarily into the impact of economic conditions on vulnerable sectors of the population. It is therefore also concerned with the economic policies of governments. For instance, the term 'macroeconomic populism' has been used to refer to the economic policies pursued by some South American countries during the 1970s and 1980s.[7] In general, this perspective focuses on the policies of large-scale spending, often followed by inflation, hyperinflation and subsequent austerity measures. This is sometimes called the 'supply side' approach since it concentrates on government seen as supplying economic resources to 'the people', whether to promote or appease demand. The economic term 'supply side' is also extended to the socio-political processes that produce populist actors who respond to demand. 'Demand side' approaches concentrate on the nature and sources of popular demand.[8] This includes examining socio-economic factors in the demand for populist policies, and the spread of attitudes such as xenophobia, ethnocentrism and disillusionment with established politics.

There is also an approach that treats populism as above all a 'style', what has been described as a 'folkloric style'.[9] Populism's 'style' tries to demonstrate solidarity with 'ordinary people' in order to mobilise a population or part of one. This 'style' may involve a maverick party politician or figure from outside established politics, and the adopting of untypical mannerisms, simplified diction and deliberately provocative turns of phrase. Talk of 'style' may give the impression that populism is no more than that and has no underlying set of ideas. However, the populists' way of communicating does integrate ideas, ideas that are expressed repeatedly in their use of language.

Rather than applying the term 'ideology' to populism, it is more accurate to describe it as 'discourse'. That is, discourse in the formal linguistic sense of cohesive communicative exchanges based on a common ground mutually accepted by participants as true. Populist discourse does not generally express clear and distinct ideas. The lack of conceptual precision and explicit formulation is actually one of populism's chief defining characteristics. This does not mean that populist discourse does not communicate any ideas at all. Most of the ideas that get conveyed are simply vague or very general. Often they are not stated at all but conveyed indirectly. One of the properties of language is that it can communicate ideas without stating them explicitly – by presupposition, association, the triggering of particular conceptual frames, and other kinds of implication and hints. It does not matter if those being addressed do not attach any clear idea to the much-repeated phrases of populist discourse, including 'the people', 'the will of the people', and numerous others. In populist

---

[7] Dornbusch and Edwards (1992). [8] Mudde and Kaltwasser (2017), pp. 3–4, 97–116.
[9] Ibid. pp. 3–4. Cf. Hidalgo-Tenorio et al. (2019).

discourse it is the relations among these notions that are important, the most obvious one being antithesis – for example, the opposition between 'the people' and 'the elite', not to mention 'the people' and 'Europe'. Conceptually, populist discourse deals predominantly with pairs of opposites.

In populism generally, the appeal to emotions outweighs appeal to reason and evidence. Brexitfeel dominates Brexitthink. Most of the key notions produced by populist discourse are essentially emotion triggers, and the emotions that are fired up have an overall negative force. However, there is one central idea that carries positive affect – identity. Conceptually, identity is binary: the Self is antithetical to an Other. This implies a border, separation, and more. The boundaries of personal identity have fundamental emotional aspects. In the social and political domains, individuals belong to groups, which are also conceptualised in terms of a containing boundary, insiders and outsiders. This conceptual structure carries both positive and negative affective force – insiders are good, outsiders bad. Positive feelings include desire for social homogeneity, collective belonging and bonding, and nostalgia for an imagined national greatness. Negative feelings include resentment and anger about perceived social and political exclusion, together with hostility and fear of the foreign, the outsider, the unfamiliar.[10]

Populism cannot be thought about without an initial notion of democracy. This is the case both for analysts of populism and for populist discoursers themselves. Analysis of populist notions of democracy also carries value attitudes and preferences, which should be rationally justified.[11] For populists, the understanding of the concept 'democracy' is characteristically binary. Their preferred form of democracy is simply the opposite of what 'the elite' or 'the establishment' accepts and practises, depending on the political culture they are operating in. When this is spelled out, what populism is rejecting is those institutions that are representative. Implicitly, it opposes theories of rational deliberative democracy, whether combined with representative democracy or not. Representative institutions and processes do not suit populists, because they are too indirect and provide no sense of personal control in a cultural environment that demands the immediate and the individualistic. This is not to say, of course, that supposedly representative governments do not have disadvantaged segments of the population.

An additional reason why democratic deliberation of any kind doesn't suit populist politics is that deliberation and deliberative processes take time. Such processes are, at least in principle, rational and evidence-based, and they do not necessarily mobilise the emotions that populism favours. Furthermore, they require relevant information that can be trusted by the community, as well as

---

[10] Cf. Browning (2019).
[11] Cf. the points made by Urbinati (2019), Rosanvallon (2020), and others.

some analytical insight and critical ability – capacities that need to be fostered by liberal civic education.[12] If there is a lack of critical vigilance in the general population, there is plenty of opportunity for a demagogue-leader with personal charisma to emerge. If such an individual does turn up as a populist leader, as they frequently do, then so may an idea of the 'embodiment' of 'the people' in that individual – 'the people' identifying itself with a 'man of the people'. This idea is able to yield yet another – that processes of representation and deliberation can be reduced or replaced, for example, by referendums. This is a path to placing a leader alone in the role of decision maker, as European history can demonstrate.

Demagoguery

The terms *demagogue*, *demagogy* and *demagoguery* are not much used in contemporary academic analysis of politics. But to fully understand the nature of populism the category of demagoguery is essential. From classical Athens to the Enlightenment authors of *The Federalist Papers*, legislators and philosophers have looked for both a satisfactory definition of demagoguery and constitutional solutions to democratically avoid it. The concept of the demagogue faded from academic attention in the nineteenth century and further in the twentieth-century era of ideologies. A notable exception was Theodor Adorno, who wrote about and analysed 'fascist demagogues'.[13]

However, several thinkers are bringing the category of demagoguery back into the serious study of politics. The historian Iván Berend has closely connected demagoguery with populism, and sketched the transition of demagogue to dictator and the destruction of democracy during the twentieth century. He also suggests this line is continued in the new populism of the present century – amply illustrated not only in Donald Trump, but across Europe in Silvio Berlusconi, Jörg Haider, Jean-Marie Le Pen, Marine Le Pen, Geert Wilders, Viktor Orbán, Jarosław and Lech Kaczyński, Nigel Farage, and Boris Johnson.[14] The political theorist Nadia Urbinati rightly insists that demagoguery must be understood in its institutional context.[15] She notes that '[i]n ancient direct democracy, demagoguery had an immediate law-making impact because the assembly was the unmediated sovereign'.[16] Modern populist demagoguery, however, exploits the context of modern representative democracy, of which it is, to use Urbinati's expression, a 'disfigurement'.[17]

---

[12] Cf. d'Ancona (2017), pp. 69–70, 114, Cassam (2019), p. 120. [13] Adorno (1950).
[14] Berend (2020).
[15] Urbinati (2019), pp. 8–10. On modern demagoguery, see also Ceaser (2007), Patapan (2019).
[16] Urbinati (2019), p. 9. [17] Urbinati (2014, 2019).

Philosophers of language have again begun to examine the fine details of political speech and the ethical problems raised by it.[18] Jason Stanley uses the term 'demagoguery' as a label for kinds of propaganda that are problematic both politically and morally. Modern demagoguery goes well beyond the individual orator in the agora. It is generated by organisations as well as individuals, uses many different channels of mass communication, and thus includes propaganda. However, an abstract general definition of 'demagoguery' has proved difficult to formulate. A better approach is to view demagogues as exhibiting a set of traits, some subset of which qualifies an individual to be labelled 'demagogue', though further refinement is needed. Well-known traits of demagogues include the disposition to:
- exploit democratic institutions and freedom of expression
- present themselves as one of 'the people' and an 'ordinary' person, even if they are wealthy and expensively educated
- stir up fears of an oppressive Other that may be an ethnic out-group, an institution or another country
- emphasise supposedly superior characteristics of the in-group
- ignore evidence and counterargument, equivocate, and lie.

The list can be extended, but the essential criterion is that demagogues use language, and other signals, to manipulate feelings and thoughts. The overlap between the definition of populism and of demagoguery is significant, in theory and in practice.

Training in public speaking – rhetoric – became an important feature in the development of Athenian democracy, and probably a beneficial one in that it fostered deliberative modes of decision making in the assembly and in the courts. The required verbal skills were taught by individuals known as 'sophists' (wise persons), some of whom could command high fees. The driving motive behind the teaching and learning of persuasive techniques was to win one's case. In this was the germ of rhetorical abuse and the modern pejorative meaning of the term 'sophistry'. The Greek sophists can be seen, *mutatis mutandis*, as the forerunners of the modern public relations experts, the spin doctors and the political consultants who appeared and rose to great heights in the twentieth and twenty-first centuries. Today's sophists have a huge range of technologies that include polling, data analytics of all kinds, including speech analytics, personal profiling, and lexical analysis of social media. In the Brexit context, as in all modern political campaigns, the rough equivalent of the sophists are not just the demagogic actors themselves, but the campaigning organisations behind them (especially Vote Leave and Leave.EU), along with their technical communications specialists and their wealthy backers.

---

[18] Mills (1995), Saul (2012, 2018), Stanley (2015), Cassam (2019).

Within city states, it was possible for political communication to be primarily face to face; in republics and empires, communicating with mass publics had to be done over long distances and by transcription. The medieval Christian Church used proxy preachers and scribal copying, and later the printing press; its highly organised *Congregatio de propaganda fide*, formed in 1622, was in many respects the forerunner of twentieth-century totalitarian propaganda machines. The twentieth century's cinema, newsreel and subsequently television again extended and changed the nature of mass communication, demagoguery and propaganda. The emergence of electronic communication technology and the devices and practices that were developed with it were a change that produced radically new forms of interpersonal communication. At the same time the new technology transformed communication between organisations and individuals, including communication between the state and individuals. We have a pseudo-agora, with individuals appearing to be co-present and able to address one another directly. What we actually have is an entirely new communication reality, the implications of which are not yet fully understood.[19] The pro-Leave campaign was able to exploit this new demagogic potential, investing more financial resources than Remain in sophisticated – and sophistical – campaign techniques. One of the aims of this book is to demonstrate the specific workings of some of the linguistic mechanisms involved in the new forms of mass political communication.

Demagoguery is integral to the practice of democracy, because of the centrality of the principle of free speech. Originally, the terms demagogue, demagogy and demagoguery did not necessarily imply a critical stance on the part of the user of these words.[20] Plato and later philosophers, especially Plutarch, wrote of 'demagogues' critically and used the term 'statesman' (*politikos*) as its normative opposite. In *The Politics*, Aristotle said that demagogues can bring about the type of direct democracy that would today be called populist – a type of democracy in which 'the multitude is sovereign and not the law'.[21] He also understood demagoguery as a problem of language, or rather of the use of language in public communication, that is, rhetoric. It is a short step from a utilitarian view of rhetoric to a rhetoric that relativises truth or disregards it altogether. Post-truth politics is not a recent phenomenon; it has been inherent in demagoguery all along.

Post-truth Politics

Writers who were spurred into action by the election of Trump and the Brexit referendum in 2016 applied the label of 'post-truth' to a new era in politics.[22] It may well be the case that the intensity, extent and apparent acceptance of

---

[19] KhosraviNik (2019). [20] Cf. Ceaser (2007), Signer (2009), Lane (2012), Patapan (2019).
[21] Book IV, 1292b39. [22] E.g. Oborne (2021).

political deception of all sorts surged around 2016, but the basic phenomenon is not new, and neither is philosophical concern about it. In the post-World War II period, the scale of US government lies during its involvement in the Vietnam War was exposed by Daniel Ellsberg and various *New York Times* journalists. Hannah Arendt published the essays 'Truth and politics' in 1967 and 'Lying in politics' in 1971. After several decades of public deception at the top of government, the philosopher Harry G. Frankfurt wrote *On Bullshit* (first published in 1986), which inspired James Ball's account of politics around 2016, and has influenced continuing efforts by thinkers such as Quassim Cassam (2019) to analyse the apparently increasing disregard of truth in political discourse.[23]

Frankfurt's analysis of bullshit was one of the first to base the distinction between bullshit and simple lying on whether a speaker cares about the truth in the first place. Cassam develops this further, introducing the concept of 'epistemic insouciance' – a concept particularly suited to understanding the speech behaviour that seems to predominate in the political language culture of the Brexit campaign and beyond. Cassam analyses in detail some specifically relevant features of epistemic insouciance. Epistemic insouciance is a type of attitude that he calls a 'posture', rather than a deliberately adopted 'stance'. A 'posture' in this classification is not deliberately selected, and, importantly, it has an affective element. This does not, I think, mean that such a posture with regard to truth is not used strategically in political discourse. Cassam says that: '[lack] of concern about what the evidence shows is one element of epistemic insouciance but another element in many cases is contempt. There is contempt for the truth, contempt for experts, and, in the case of politicians, contempt for the public.'[24] Contempt in turn involves, as Cassam notes, feelings that include arrogance and superiority. But such feelings do not come from nowhere. The sense of superiority in question is the kind that comes from a generalised social sense of 'being above' that is simply, as it were, a given. Feelings of this sort are acquired from social conditioning and certain kinds of education – for example, from inherited wealth, and from the purchased conditioning provided by the so-called public schools of the UK. Such characteristics are manifest, as it happens, among some leaders and funders of the Brexit populism.

'Post-truth' can be considered a label for a phenomenon appearing in parts of Western society around the turn of the twentieth century. It covers the doubting of objective truth in general, and the blurring of fact and fiction, as well as dishonesty in public communication.[25] A generalised epistemic indifference is capable of becoming a culture, or subculture, on lesser or larger scales. Its adoption by

---

[23] E.g. Ball (2017), d'Ancona (2017). For a comprehensive review of work on post-truth, see Harsin (2019).
[24] Cassam (2019), p. 85.   [25] Cf. Harsin (2019).

a governing elite implies also a calculation that it is widely shared by the public at large. It is intrinsic to the promotional commercial culture that grew and became normalised after World War II. Mass advertising did not concern itself with facts or fact-checking, and abandoned truthfulness.[26] In parallel, and as a consequence of such cultural changes, there grew up an interpretation of the principle of free expression in which all opinions were equal, and in which evidence and rational argument were also simply treated as opinion. In such an environment, politicians are only too ready to woo their voters in the way that many of these voters expect. Politicians of a certain stripe just do not need to *care* whether their assertions are consistent with facts, evidence or reason. Alongside mass advertising, and intertwined with it, has been the rise of so-called 'reality' television, 'infotainment', and virtual reality devices in entertainment and in news reporting. Because these genres mix traditionally separated categories of factual reporting and fictional entertainment, some commentators argue that they adversely affect attitudes towards and performance of political behaviour. And it is possible, though again hard to demonstrate, that this cultural climate contributes to people's distancing from established politics. Both alienation from politics, and cognitive instability around fact and fabrication, are promoted and exploited in populist demagoguery.

The concept of 'post-truth' raises philosophical questions centring on epistemological relativism. But the focus here is on the fact that being truthful or untruthful concerns language – or, more accurately, speech practices, which are rooted in the ethical norms of society, culture and politics. The truthfulness of a speaker or writer is often difficult to pin down, and this is because untruthfulness comes in various linguistic guises. These are not purely linguistic, but are tied up with states of mind, and perceptions of a speaker's state of mind. Lying is an ethical-linguistic concept that varies, depending on what is individually or communally believed to be true. To tell a lie means that the speaker believes they know the truth but decides to make an explicit assertion that is counter to what they know. One cannot always know for sure what truths a speaker believes they know; nor can a speaker be sure they know what their hearer knows or does not know. To accuse someone of lying involves the same issues. In practice, statements about facts can generally be fact-checked, and a critic can reasonably estimate what a speaker is likely to know, and what they ought to know, given a particular context. There is no point in ignoring these complexities, for they are real. They can be exploited by demagogues. When it comes to the linguistic substance of untruthfulness, it is not just a matter of uttering an explicit proposition. An untruthful utterance may *imply* an untruth, by means of hints, dog whistling, and being economical with the truth – that is keeping quiet over awkward facts, and other devices. There is a lot more to this

---

[26] Cf. Crouch (2020), p. 145.

A Closer Look at Language

perspective, since untruths in political demagoguery are always accompanied by substitute narratives and other constructed realities, which have their own linguistic vehicles.[27]

A Closer Look at Language

Use of language is the stuff of politics. Without it humans would not have the societies and political behaviours that they do have. This why looking closely at language use is essential to understanding political institutions and political behaviours.

Brexitspeak is discourse. In this book, I use the term 'discourse' primarily in the way it is used in linguistics.[28] Discourse is language in use in real situations, and sometimes it creates or changes situations. In form, it is a level of linguistic structure larger than the sentence. Discourse researchers are interested in the details of how sentences cohere to produce a larger coherent unit we can call a 'text', written or spoken – a conversation, a political manifesto, a speech, a newspaper article, a billboard, a message on the side of a bus, and so on. These are localised texts with their own internal coherence – grammatical links, relations between word meanings, repetitions, paraphrases, and so forth. Texts at this level can be called 'micro-discourse'. How individual speakers and spokespersons set up their text can reveal a lot about what they are up to politically, including what they do not mention overtly.

Participating in a localised verbal exchange, written or spoken, means mentally processing utterances in real time for a limited time. There is an additional temporal dimension, however. Verbal events can relate back to earlier relevant verbal events, which may be recent or temporally remote, or passed on by hearsay (or 'read-say', so to speak). Present discourse therefore has multiple continuities, some of which can reach back over generations. This is why it is relevant to consider traditions of talk and thought – for example, the concept of 'the people' or 'British'. As such historical chains are established, selections, modifications and misinterpretations occur. Importantly, present speakers are generally not aware of them.

Understanding any kind of text, written or spoken, involves much more than recognising individual words and somehow adding them up to make a whole. Linguistic cues do not just signal dictionary meanings. We know from neuro-linguistic studies that understanding sentences involves partial processing, using salient word meanings, drawing on knowledge frames ('cognitive frames') stored in memory, and, above all, making inferences about the intended meaning.[29] Consider a leaflet reading 'Vote [name], Vote [name of

---

[27] Meibauer (2005, 2014, 2018).   [28] Schiffrin (1984, 1994), Tannen et al. (2015).
[29] Baggio (2022), p. 35.

political party]'. Its linguistic form conjures up a cognitive frame concerning political systems and the roles of politicians and voters, as well as the political ideologies involved. More abstractly, it rests on prior knowledge of the concept of democracy, even if this is only sketchy. Hearers make use of the triggered knowledge to infer a relevant meaning for the input discourse. Conversely, speakers produce discourse with the intention of affecting the hearer's mind – perhaps to get the hearer to add new information to memory, to receive orders and act on them, or to prompt them to think in a certain way about some issue. The list is long.

Discourse is a form of action containing 'speech acts'.[30] An example that stands out is promises. In politics, 'promises', so-called 'pledges', and 'commitments' are notorious.[31] Speech acts of this type, in the theory developed by the language philosopher John Searle, are called 'commissives'. They played a major role in Brexitspeak. All types of speech act have their own 'felicity conditions' – the 'conditions under which words can be used properly to perform actions'.[32] In Searle's theory, there are four kinds of condition that underpin speech acts: *propositional content*, *preparatory conditions*, *sincerity conditions*, and *essential conditions*. With regard to the speech act of promising, the first of these conditions is that an utterance predicates a future action by the speaker (propositional content). The second condition is that the speaker believes that the hearer prefers the promised action to be carried out, an action that neither party would have expected to be done as a matter of course (preparatory condition). The next two are particularly interesting for political contexts. The third condition is that the speaker does genuinely intend to carry out the action (sincerity condition). And the fourth condition is that the words of the utterance count as an undertaking to execute the promised action (essential condition). These formulations may sound moralistic, but the act of promising cannot work without them, and people are likely to be morally outraged if the conditions are infringed.

The different types of speech act encountered in language use can be put into five types:
- *assertives* make claims to truth
- *directives* try to get the hearer to do something (commands, requests, etc.)
- *commissives* commit the speaker to an action (promises, pledges, threats, etc.)
- *expressives* convey emotions and attitudes (regretting, apologising, blaming, etc.)
- *declaratives* bring about change in particular institutionalised settings (judging an accused person guilty, opening or proroguing a parliamentary session, etc.).

---

[30] Austin (1962), Searle (1969, 1995, 1998, 2010). For a summary, see Huang (2007), pp. 93–128.
[31] Cf. Ball (2017), pp. 21, 44–5, 49, 63–4.
[32] As Huang puts it (Huang 2007), p. 99. The term was introduced by John Austin and was developed further by John Searle and others.

All these types of speech have their role in political discourse, but assertives, like commissives, play a particular role in Brexitspeak. In politics generally, they raise serious ethical problems if the felicity conditions for assertives are breached – the crucial one being the *sincerity condition*. This comes out even in discussions that are intended as purely theoretical:

Perhaps assertions are acts of expressing beliefs or aiming to utter truths. But these proposals face the problem of insincerity. One needs to talk, rather, of *representing oneself* [italics in original] as intending to utter a truth or express belief. That is because assertions can be insincere. The insincere asserter does not express belief or aim at truth. Rather there is only the semblance thereof.[33]

However, there is also the theoretical possibility that there exist sincere asserters of presumed facts that are not believed by others. Using a different terminology, these would be 'true believers' who make 'truth claims' that they believe relative to some ideological or religious system of ideas. In Brexitspeak there are insincere asserters as well as asserters who are 'true believers' – it is often difficult to distinguish between them.

An extension of speech act theory involves the notion of 'face-threatening acts' – examples are speech acts like complaints, disagreements, criticisms, accusations, and insults.[34] 'Face', one's public self-image and private self-esteem, can be thought of as positive or negative. Positive face refers to the self's (perceived) desire to be accepted within a social group. Negative face refers to an individual's desire not to be imposed upon. Both kinds of face are 'addressed' by way of linguistic 'politeness strategies'. In positive strategies, speakers make linguistic choices that reflect 'common ground'. A politically important example, as will be seen in Chapter 2, is the pronoun *we* used inclusively. In negative politeness strategies, expressions are selected that 'hedge' intrusive or threatening speech acts such as commands and requests.

Inferencing is the principal way in which the brain makes sense of linguistic input. The hearer rapidly and unconsciously works out a relevant meaning, given the words and the context. This is the way language has evolved and it makes communication flexible and economical. But it also means speakers can insinuate ideas indirectly, the receiver processing them unconsciously. There are several ways in which language relies on inferred meanings. Some of these are set off more automatically than others.

Semantic presuppositions are a case in point. For example, in both the sentence 'the people decided the result' and the sentence 'the people did not decide the result', there is a presupposition that 'the people' exists.[35] If the hearer does not already have the assumption that 'the people' is an existing entity, then they may be induced to add it to their memory bank of things that exist. Another

---

[33] Barker (2011), p. 787.   [34] Goffman (1967), Brown and Levinson (1987).
[35] For an introduction to presupposition, see Huang (2007), pp. 64–90.

common type of presupposition trigger is 'factive verbs'. Take, for example, the verb *realise* in the sentence 'John realises that there are too many immigrants in the country' and in the sentence 'John doesn't realise that there are too many immigrants in the country'. There is a presupposition that there are in fact too many immigrants, whatever John thinks. Small words can trigger important presupposed meanings. In a phrase such as *give back*, the presupposition is that what is 'given back' was previously in the possession of the receiver. Semantic presuppositions can serve useful functions in communication. And despite being automatic, they can be cancelled, or suspended, in particular contexts. The hearer may have contrary information that they trust, or the hearer might be vigilant enough to question the presupposed content. But we can never be sure when we have the relevant information, or when we need to be on our guard, and in some situations any of us can be influenced by clever use of presupposition.

The type of inferencing necessitated by what is termed 'implicature' is fundamental in comprehending almost any use of language.[36] The classic theory formulated by the philosopher Paul Grice, much discussed and developed since, seeks to explain how it is that a hearer spontaneously figures out a meaning from some utterance. Grice postulates a shared 'cooperative principle' as the basis of human communication.[37] After all, linguistic communication could not work at all without this overarching assumption, even though some individuals might not be cooperative. Grice divided the cooperative principle into more detailed 'maxims' grouped under the terms Quality, Quantity, Relation and Manner:

- Quality: Try to make your contribution one that is true – do not say what you believe to be false and do not say that for which you lack adequate evidence.
- Quantity: Be as informative as required in the context, and not more informative.
- Relation: Be relevant.
- Manner: Be perspicuous – avoid obscurity, avoid ambiguity, and aim for brevity and order.

These maxims may sound schoolmarmish, but something like them is logically required to account for various language phenomena. It is reasonable to assume that human communication does need this normative element for language to develop in the first place. Furthermore, most language users express moral objections if somebody breaks the Quality maxim, and may object also to the breaking of the other maxims, depending on the situation. Implicatures are enabled by the cooperative principle and its maxims, and implicatures are a basic ingredient of linguistic communication. We seem to have them because they make communication faster and easier. There is

---

[36] Grice (1975, 1989). While there have been numerous theoretical developments since Grice, his work remains particularly relevant to this book.

[37] Grice (1975), p. 45.

nothing inherently nefarious about them, but in social situations, especially in political ones, they are easily exploitable for individual purposes and advantage. Duplicitous communicators would not be able to operate unless everyone was expected to be communicatively cooperative in the first place. On that basis, we are all susceptible to manipulation.

Of course, given stereotypical politicians' behaviour, Grice's maxims are an almost comical list of the norms that are routinely infringed. There are two ways in which the maxims can be infringed. They can be 'flouted' or 'violated'. In flouting a maxim, speakers and hearers are assuming the cooperative principle is in force, and if a speaker infringes a maxim, then the hearer will infer a relevant (to them) meaning. The meaning they come up with is an 'implicature'. Suppose for example, that someone says, 'The minister *always* tells the truth!' If the assertion is contrary to shared background knowledge, but the speaker is nonetheless taken to be following the cooperative principle, then the speaker can be taken to be 'flouting' the Quality maxim, the hearer being intended to interpret the intention as an ironic negation of the sentence uttered.

In violating a maxim, one is violating the entire cooperative principle. A politician may violate one or more of the maxims knowingly, while taking it that the hearers are presuming they are following the expected cooperative principle. In that case, the politician will be lying.[38] If the hearer is making the cooperative assumption, they will calculate an implicature and be taken in. If a hearer is on critical alert, they will still generate the implicated meaning but not accept it. If they proceed to challenge the implicated meaning, the political speaker knows the escape route. They will insist that 'that was not what I actually said'. Despite the deniability of implicatures, they enable a political speaker to get a message across without accepting responsibility for it.

Manipulating linguistic interaction in the ways just outlined goes hand in hand with the manipulation of mental representations. Particular language choices on the part of a speaker can steer the way in which hearers mentally 'view' one and the same object, situation or process. Such choices can affect what the hearer focuses attention on, what they leave out, and what perspective they adopt. The terms 'cognitive frame' and 'framing effects' refer to these conceptualising phenomena.[39]

The structure of sentences in all languages reflects cognitive frames. For example, the transfer of an object from one individual to another is conveyed in the verb *give*, which calls up roles of *giver*, *receiver* and *object*, and foregrounds the giver as the agent. The verb *take* reverses the direction of the transfer, foregrounding the receiver as the agent. The verb *donate* seems at first sight to be a synonym of *give*. In the abstract, the role frame is the same. However, its semantic frame adds socio-cultural concepts over and above the basic frame for

---

[38] Cf. Fallis (2012). [39] Fillmore (1977, 1982), Croft and Cruse (2004), pp. 8–22, Ziem (2008).

18   Introduction

give. In the case of donate, the object donated may be either money or a valued object. In most contexts, the *donor* is likely to be a wealthy individual and the receiver to be an individual or institution perceived as relatively less wealthy. In a political situation at a particular historical moment, the *donor* frame might be closely linked with the frame for *politics* and *political party*. Some verbs and frames are even more detailed. For example, *vote* is highly culture- and context-specific. It minimally involves a voter, a person voted for, and an office or issue *on* or *for* which the voter is voting, within an institution of some kind. But this is far from everything in the relevant mental frame that socialised individuals acquire. When *vote* is used in real situations, it evokes knowledge not only concerning the individual voted for but also knowledge of a specific political culture. A cognitive frame like this can be very rich, and can include links to other frames, such as historical knowledge, political ideologies, concepts of democracy, values and wishes. This is in addition to fundamental spatial frames for places and related objects: voting booths, ballot papers, pencils, and so forth.

Apparently minor tweaking of a grammatical construction can create a framing effect by leaving a slot unfilled, which enables the speaker to suppress information. An instance might be: 'the party received a donation'. Here the passive construction and the nominalised form *donation* makes it possible to avoid mention of the source of the donation. Frames are stored in memory, but they are flexible, can be adapted to context, and can be updated over time. This makes the more complex frames cognitively unstable, with the consequence that significant elements can be forgotten, overlooked, and manipulated. The concept *referendum* had details in its frame relating to the particular 2016 referendum on membership of the EU – for example, the proposal itself, voting age, and the advisory function of the vote. But speakers can deliberately fail to mention some part of the relevant knowledge frame, one that they themselves do know. Omissions may well not be noticed, and specific details can easily disappear from view. This is yet another way in which we are all vulnerable to being misled.

More stable than frames, and more fundamental, are 'image schemas', which play an important role in the meaning structure of many vocabulary items that have developed in human societies over time. Hardwired in the brain's cognitive system, they are condensed representations of the bodily interaction of humans with their physical environments.[40] Unsurprisingly, a BODY schema (conventionally written in small capitals) is fundamental in many linguistic expressions. Particular schemas deriving from bodily experience of the physical world include PATH, CONTAINER and FORCE. The PATH schema is present in linguistic expressions of direct motion from one point to another.

---

[40] Johnson (1987), Lakoff (1987, 2008), Talmy (1988), Fauconnier (1994), Fauconnier and Turner (2002), Rohrer (2005), Oakley (2010).

CONTAINER consists simply of a boundary (border), an inside and an outside. In discourse one's perspective may be from the inside or the outside. The combination of PATH and CONTAINER is behind the meaning of *enter* and *exit*, being *in* or *out*. Many different sorts of object, physical or not, can be represented as containing spaces – for example, states of mind, organisations and professions, not to mention sovereign nations and the EU. The FORCE schema underlies everyday literal uses of words such as *pressure*, *pressurise*, *stop*, *prevent*, *push*, *invade*, and many others. In discourse, image schemas create coherence by repeatedly triggering particular schemas in ways that can shape meanings that depend on them. These were important elements in Brexit propaganda.

Image schemas play an important role in metaphorical expressions. In cognitive linguistics, a metaphor is defined as a transfer (or 'mapping') of elements from a 'source domain' to a 'target domain', consistent with the semantic characteristics of the target.[41] Metaphors can play a sometimes useful role in thinking about an abstract or complex target domain – for example, progress is a PATH, or a whole society is a CONTAINER. In political thought, there are recurrent cases that offer metaphorical entailments as a way of reasoning about problematic entities.[42] An example is A COUNTRY IS A PERSON (or A STATE IS A PERSON), which metaphorically entails that a country (or state) has a head, a body (body politic), and can behave and act in certain ways. Metaphor can be deployed for the purpose of influencing or consolidating the ways in which people think and feel about the social and political world.

The linguistic phenomena described so far, entirely normal and natural as they are, afford demagogues the means of disrupting cooperative group reasoning based on available evidence. Rational cogitation, however, is obviously not the only factor in any political discourse. An emotive element is essential to it. In the case of populist discourse in particular, and of Brexitspeak, the prime objective is to arouse emotions and to override evidence-based reasoning. This is done by focusing attention on simplified, emotion-laden concepts such as 'the people', and by encouraging antithetical thinking in terms of Self and Other.

Research in neurolinguistics, using brain-imaging techniques (PET, fMRI, etc.), is beginning to uncover the ways in which emotive language impacts human brain processes, particularly with regard to fear, anger and perception of threat. Attention has centred on the role of the amygdala, a crucial organ in the human brain's emotion system (the limbic system). In both sides of the brain, it is involved in emotional responses to environmental triggers, including those provided via speech. Memory for perceived dangers, including threats from other humans, has been important in human evolution for the survival of social groups – hence the

---

[41] Lakoff and Johnson (1980), Fauconnier and Turner (2002).   [42] Cf. Musolff (2016, 2017).

potential effectiveness of fearmongering in political behaviour.[43] The neuroscientist Nancy Isenberg notes that imaging research suggests 'conservation of phylogenetically older mechanisms of emotional evaluation in the context of more recently evolved linguistic function'. She points out also that '[f]ears that are simply imagined and anticipated [...] have a profound impact on everyday behavior'.[44]

Although the brain reacts to emotive words even under laboratory conditions, in actual discourse both context and existing mental frames support more focused reactions. A fear response can be induced by isolated words that denote danger, and the surrounding context can be used to specify a source of that danger. Demagogues have an intuitive grasp of how to use language to perform such effects. Emotional responses are hard for subjects to resist. Moreover, they have the potential to interrupt rational processing of speech input. The processing of the perception of emotional stimuli is complex, however, and humans do have the ability to critically evaluate verbal as well as non-verbal stimuli.

'Cheater detection mechanisms' is a term used by experimental psychologists to refer to an evolved cognitive ability to detect cheaters in social exchanges. Without such an ability, the interaction needed to create societies could not have got off the ground.[45] Linguistic communication itself is a kind of social exchange, so language also would be expected to be linked with a cheater detection mechanism. In this approach, both cooperative maxims and what has been called 'epistemic vigilance' would be safeguards against misinformation and misrepresentation, whether intended or not.[46] But vigilance does not always seem to be activated. Why? One reason could be that vigilance is cognitively costly and will not be activated unless there is an obviously relevant benefit. Another reason could be that for social cohesion it is most efficient to rely on commitment to trust and trustworthiness. But a further possible reason is that, especially in political contexts, the very diverse techniques of language manipulation can get round epistemic vigilance and the detection of cheaters.

When the UK formally left the EU in 2020, the Conservative government was still unclear about what Brexit meant, what its benefits were if any, and where the country was heading post-Brexit. On the day after the 2016 referendum, even ardent Leavers were surprised at the result and had no specific plans for the long-term future of the UK outside the EU. Many Remainers were in shock and have searched ever since for explanations of what had happened. Academics and journalists have offered economic, political and social

---

[43] Wodak (2015).   [44] Isenberg (2011), p. 96.
[45] Cosmides (1989), Cosmides and Tooby (1992, 2000).
[46] Sperber and Wilson (2002), Sperber et al. (2010); cf. Hart (2011a).

analyses. These analyses have exposed the damaging effects of quitting the EU under Boris Johnson's 'hard Brexit', and are essential to any explanation. But in most attempts to explain Brexit there is an explanatory gap. One of the motivations for this book was the thought that the British had in some sense talked themselves into Brexit or had let themselves be talked into it. That is not the only way to look at what happened, but the interaction of language with many other elements of society, politics and history cannot simply be taken for granted. People can only do politics by using language, and we need to be more aware about what this means, especially for the understanding of crisis moments such as the referendum of 2016. This obvious fact has been the guiding thread through the constructing of this book.

1 Identity

Who do the British think they are? In the aftermath of the vote for Brexit, numerous commentators argued that the whole dispute around membership of the EU reflected a British identity crisis. After World War II the UK did not come to terms with its loss of empire and loss of world leadership. The Brexit process, furthermore, revealed deep divisions bearing on the self-image that British citizens held. The very idea of 'identity' is not as simple as it seems at first sight, however. And the ways in which identity manifests itself in the mind, in society and in politics are many and various, appearing in complex combinations. Individual identities interact with social experience and political input. But identities are not only an individual matter – they are also collective, the two aspects interacting and changing over time. They are only partly 'natural', and often are imposed by cultural norms or political constraints.

The focus in this chapter is primarily on national identity. Integral with this type of identity is the mental division of those perceived as belonging to the national body and those perceived as not belonging. Immigrants are frequently seen as those who don't belong and much of this book therefore probes the role of anti-immigration attitudes, their overlap with racism, and the part played by immigration issues in pro-Brexit propaganda. Brexit itself can be seen as an identity problem specifically framed in terms of whether Britain 'belonged in' the EU, and whether 'immigrants', European or not, belonged in Britain.

Believers in Brexit think of the British as unique in almost all respects, indeed as a unique race. But they were not unique in their obsession with national identity.[1] They were just one manifestation of an identitarian ideology that ran across Europe and elsewhere around the turn of the century. The ingredients of identitarianism included distrust or fear of multiculturalism and global interdependence, instead preaching the separateness of sovereign nation states, essentially along ethnic lines. Commitment to this kind of political thinking involves an alien 'other' perceived as a threat, if there is no genuine threat. In the case of Brexit devotees, the 'other' was built up as

---

[1] Šarić and Stanojević (2019), Ashcroft and Bevir (2021).

a twofold conflation made up of invading immigrants threatening British borders and an oppressive EU stifling British sovereignty.

By what means do ideas of national identity, such as those exhibited in Brexitism, establish themselves, spread and become powerful political forces? The answer proposed in this chapter and in the rest of this book is: by means of language and its deployment by demagogic political actors. The first section below examines the conceptual components of national identity. In the second section we survey the identitarian movements that provide the context for Brexit ideas and policies. The third and final sections examine closely the part played by attitudes towards immigrants in the 2016 referendum, and how it was that negative attitudes were mobilised.

The Idea of Identity

Philosophical discussions around identity stem from an intuition that individual objects do not change in some fundamental respect over time. Perhaps this is an intuitive assumption that is necessary for humans to function in their environments. There is a concomitant concept which has to do with how objects and creatures are different from one another. Logically this leads to the concept of categories – that is, the grouping together of entities sufficiently similar to be regarded as 'identical'. This is a cognitive operation that can be regarded as part of human mental architecture. It is flexible and dynamic. Whether something belongs to a category with similar members in it depends on your perspective, or whether your viewpoint is close or distant. That is the case for physical perception, but physical perception in physical space transfers to the mental operations of abstraction and generalisation.

There is another human cognitive operation that will bring us to our main concern in this chapter: the consciousness on the part of an individual that they are both different from and similar to other individuals in various ways. The extension of this is that whole clusters of individuals can become mutually conscious of similarities that differentiate them from other groups that they identify. In Pelinka's words: 'In any society, there is a strong urge to define the self, to be a specific self, to seek an identity. The search for identity implies the exclusion of others – or better – of social segments defined as others.'[2] In this search for collective self-definition, it is characteristics such as skin colour, religion, costume and language that become the focus of attention. Intra-group discourse can reinforce or weaken concentration on such details. Human languages play a crucial role in the formation of identity awareness at the level of the social, and political, group, distinguishing the self's group from that of others and producing bonding. Further, identity

---

[2] Pelinka (2018), p. 624. Cf. Enos (2014).

formation is accompanied by a strongly felt need for self-preservation and group-preservation, resulting in increased vigilance and anxiety vis-à-vis other individuals and groups.

All the above tendencies can be selectively focused and promoted by individual actors via various channels of communication. Discourse centred on collective identity can become politicised, as happened in the twentieth century, with disastrous consequences. In *The Concept of the Political*, the Nazi philosopher and jurist Carl Schmitt asserted that the ideas of political identity, sovereignty and autonomy are grounded in the opposition of friend and enemy. The 'enemy' can be anyone or any institution regarded as alien, as an 'other' that is threatening to the self.[3] This binary self–other pattern of political thinking reared its head once again towards the end of the twentieth century, associated with the rise of new right-wing movements across Europe.[4]

It may well be the case that, psychologically, it is entirely normal for there to be an 'other' in relation to which personal and group identities are formed. Such identities are not necessarily negative: benign others play an important role in personal identity development (in childhood, for instance). It is under certain socio-political conditions, and in nationalist and national-populist rhetoric, that the 'other' must be negative (evil, oppressive, invasive, powerful, etc.), while the self is a victim. In other words, in-group mutual recognition can be bolstered by antipathy towards, and also fear of, out-group others. This kind of mindset is the hallmark of nationalist and anti-immigration discourse. It is important to note that such a mindset does not always originate in the minds of the individuals of a group. It is just as likely, if not more so, to originate in demagogic leaders with their own particular interest in power. Such leaders present themselves as 'the voice of the people'. This is not to say that disadvantaged, 'left behind' and alienated individuals do not have authentic needs, something that the demagogues may not even seriously care about.

Perceptually and cognitively, identity is sameness. But sameness is not always easy to detect, and there are always different ways to draw boundaries around clustered entities. Difference is easier to detect, so this is often what human individuals and collectivities tend to look for, picking out different sorts of features or characteristics upon which groups can be based. Integral to this human habit of selective focus of attention are two processes involved in constructing identities. One is the drawing of boundaries around collections of selected things; the other is the ascribing of naturalness to such collections. As social scientists frequently note, communities are constructed, and identities are constructed. The construction processes themselves are essentially mental and conveyed by way of language.[5]

---

[3] Schmitt ([1932] 2007), on whom see Müller (2003), Sedgwick (2019). Cf. Musolff (2011).
[4] Wodak et al. (2013), Wodak (2015), pp. 25–6.   [5] De Cilia et al. (1999), Wodak et al. (2009).

The Idea of Identity

Drawing on cognitive linguistics, we can delve further into the details of how minds operate in constructing identities. There is a particular cognitive-linguistic process that is at the core of identity construction – the activation of the CONTAINER image schema. Image schemas, as outlined in the Introduction, are cognitive structures that arise from the interaction between human bodies and their environment. These structures provide the building blocks of many kinds of conceptualisation, which in turn provide the base for linguistic meaning. Thus the CONTAINER schema emerges from experiencing our bodies as enclosures, as themselves being inside enclosing spaces, as entering and exiting enclosed spaces (e.g. buildings and rooms).[6] Further, it is natural to project CONTAINER onto more abstract non-spatial entities, such as social groups, political parties, social organisations, nations, and supra-national entities such as the EU. You can be 'in' or 'out' of such containing 'spaces', you can 'enter' or 'exit' them. Thinking and talking in this way can trigger various socio-psychological and emotive effects. For example, being 'in' (or 'inside') can mean protection and security, or it can mean being imprisoned; being 'out' (or 'outside') can mean freedom, or it can mean exposure and insecurity. The meaning of expressions of this type depends on, and also evokes, the schema CONTAINER. Verbally embedding this schema in Brexit discourse was a powerful propaganda device, perhaps all the more powerful for being under the surface.

Self-containing identities proliferate in contemporary societies. In many cases they are liberating, but they generate complexity and can yield new divisions. The social world has to a large extent accommodated hitherto unimagined kinds of identity complexity. But there are individuals who find such complexity difficult to accept – and such individuals can turn themselves into identity groups that seek simplification. That is often the case with national populist movements, for the members of which the concept of 'nation' may seem to provide a simplifying and thus reassuring solution. Something of this kind played a part in the lead-up to the Leave campaign among those sections of British society that Sobolewska and Ford call 'identity conservative', as opposed to 'identity liberal'.[7] The authors show that 'identity conservatives' – those people who find social and cultural change intimidating and resist it – were likely to vote for leaving the EU. They were also likely to feel intimated by, and to oppose, immigration. Part and parcel of populist pro-Leave discourse was the deployment of notions of 'foreigner' and 'immigrant'. Such categorisations are cognitively rooted in the CONTAINER schema. It provided resonances that were easy to activate by demagogues who see their political interest in doing so. As will be seen, the combination of anti-EU identitarianism and anti-immigrationism was decisive for Brexit.

---

[6] Johnson (1987), pp. 21–3. On containment, see also Lakoff and Johnson (1980), Lakoff (1987), Chilton (1996), Charteris-Black (2006).
[7] Sobolewska and Ford (2020), pp. 43–8. Compare Goodhart's (2017) 'Anywheres' and 'Somewheres'.

Identitarianism

The UK was not alone so far as national identity movements were concerned. There exists a group within the European Parliament since June 2019 calling itself 'Identity and Democracy' (Identité et démocratie), which consists of national populist parties from across the EU. These are: the Freedom Party of Austria (Freiheitliche Partei Österreichs (FPÖ)), Belgium's Flemish Interest (Vlaams Belang (VB)), the Czech Republic's Freedom and Direct Democracy (Svoboda a přímá demokracie (SPD)), Denmark's Danish People's Party (Dansk Folkeparti (DF)), Estonia's Conservative People's Party of Estonia (Eesti Konservatiivne Rahvaerakond (EKRE)), Finland's Finns Party (Perussuomalaiset (PS), formerly known as 'True Finns'), the French National Rally (Rassemblement national (RN), formerly known as the Front national), Germany's Alternative for Germany (Alternative für Deutschland (AfD)), and Italy's League (Lega Nord, or more fully, Lega Nord per l'Indipendenza della Padonia). Spain's Vox party and Italy's Fratelli d'Italia maintain links with these and similar groups. And Britain's UKIP and Brexit Party (later rebranded as Reform UK) belonged to the predecessor of the Identity and Democracy group, the Europe of Nations and Freedom (Europe des nations et des libertés).

The whole Brexit movement in the UK reflected the central themes of this set of parties in the European Parliament. Their common ground consisted of various kinds and degrees of Euroscepticism – an insistence on national sovereignty, the idea that European culture was being eroded, tight controls on immigration, and opposition to the possible accession of Turkey to the EU. Whatever the specific differences among the various elements in the Identity and Democracy group, the overarching concept was 'identity'. It provided a general concept that could be made the focus of attention and could be linked with other national-populist frames, such as 'the people', 'the British people', and so forth. These patterns of thought could be communicated rapidly throughout different segments of a population. In fact, the patterns of thought found in Identity and Democracy and in the Brexit movement were part of the rise of right-wing and far-right movements across Europe. These had their own political actors and political theorists, who impacted institutions of representative democracy and produced extreme forms of identity ideology.

The aggressive mobilisation of the idea of 'identity' is most explicit in the declarations of the pan-European far-right movement that includes various groups adopting 'ethnopluralism'. This term does not mean what it might appear to mean at first sight. It is not the same as 'ethnic diversity' or 'multiculturalism' but denotes an ideology advocating the segregation of homogeneous ethno-cultural entities on a global scale. It is a product of far-right thinking that began in France in 2002 under the name Les Identitaires (Identitarians), becoming a political party in 2009.

The movement is an umbrella for a network of national groups: Austria has an Identitäre Bewegung Österreich (Identitarian Movement Austria, started by Martin Sellner, who was refused entry to the UK in 2018). Germany and several other European countries have equivalent groups. There is also a 'Generation Identity United Kingdom and Ireland', launched on Facebook the year after the referendum on EU membership. This offshoot of the identitarian movement is linked with the anti-Islam activist Stephen Yaxley-Lennon, publicly known as Tommy Robinson, who was prominent on the far right in the two decades leading up to the referendum. Robinson was a member of the British National Party (BNP) from 2004 to 2005, and of the British Freedom Party in 2012. More influentially, he was co-founder in 2009 of the anti-Islamist English Defence League (EDL), of which he was also leader until around 2013.[8] In 2015 he was involved in the formation of Pegida UK, which was an attempt to found a British branch of the prominent German anti-immigration movement Pegida (Patriotische Europäer gegen die Islamisierung des Abendlandes (Patriotic Europeans against the Islamisation of the West)). The UK branch was launched in 2016 under the leadership of Anne Marie Waters and Paul Weston, with Robinson as advisor. Anne Marie Waters also founded and heads the anti-Islam group For Britain, as well as Sharia Watch UK, founded in 2014. Weston had been a member of UKIP and had stood as one of the party's parliamentary candidates in the 2010 general election. He later left UKIP to join the briefly existing British Freedom Party along with members of the EDL and BNP, before moving on to yet another far-right outfit, Liberty GB.

Across Europe, identitarian movements and parties were developing in ways that enabled them to enter existing democratic institutions and change them, or attempt to do so. Their activity either brought them to power as governments or put them in a position to challenge governing parties and significantly shift their policies. This is what happened in the former Soviet nations of Eastern Europe. In Poland, the right-wing populist party Law and Justice had its roots in the anti-Soviet Solidarity (Solidarność) movement of the 1980s and was part of the 1990s coalition that had been led by Solidarity. Law and Justice left the coalition in 2001, advanced through the political system, won the parliamentary and presidential elections in 2005, and again in 2015. With a majority in the parliament, its policies became increasingly authoritarian and illiberal. A similar development marks Hungary's Fidesz movement. Formed in 1988, the Fidesz activists stood for human rights and democracy, challenging Soviet domination. After registering as a political party under the leadership of Viktor Orbán, Fidesz entered the National Assembly in 1990, and shifted step by step to its present national-populist, anti-human rights, anti-immigrant and authoritarian position.

---

[8] MacDonald (2013), Alessio and Meredith (2014), Busher (2018), Pilkington (2016).

The right-ward shift was not confined to Eastern Europe. A salient example is the rise of Matteo Salvini in Italy. Salvini moved through local politics as leader (from 2013) of the Lega Nord and became a member of the European Parliament in 2004. He was a Eurosceptic, in line with UKIP's Nigel Farage, who was already a Member of the European Parliament (MEP) representing the radical anti-EU position. As one of the most prominent leaders of the national-populist surge of the 2010s, Salvini disseminated an ideology centred around xenophobia, nativism and authoritarian governance. He networked widely with the other European populist leaders, cooperating for example with Marine Le Pen of the far-right French Front national. Le Pen's party was to significantly increase its hold over the French electorate under its new name, National Rally, gaining 42.5 per cent of the votes in the second round of the 2022 presidential elections.[9] In the UK, UKIP, as will be seen throughout this book, managed to challenge the governing Conservative Party, shifting it significantly to the right and reinforcing its existing anti-EU tendencies.

The UK's Brexit movement and the post-Brexit Conservative government of Boris Johnson were a constitutive part of the spread of national populism across Europe. Its various strands were widely networked and riven with disputes. Nonetheless, it was a dynamic vehicle for a set of ideas whose conceptual core was identity. The internet, with its capacity to coordinate like-minded activists, is central to Generation Identity and similar networks across Europe. In 2019, Generation Identity Europe had 70,000 followers on X (at that time known as Twitter), 11,000 on Facebook, 30,000 on Telegram and 140,000 YouTube subscribers.[10]

The new identitarian ideology originates in France, notably in the early twentieth-century writing of Maurice Barrès and Charles Maurras.[11] Barrès and his followers propounded the idea that nations are natural entities that have undergone a course of evolution and a struggle for survival. They take it for granted that certain nations have reached a stage of stability, with a cultural essence that should remain stable and be preserved in perpetuity. The concept of nation is not analysed as a collection of individuals with certain characteristics, nor as a legal construct, nor as Rousseau's concept of *le peuple*.[12] Rather, it is imagined as an entity with its origin in 'the earth', its varied natural members consciously living in the light of their history, culture and traditions. Changes brought about by external influences disturb and can destroy the nation, so should be prevented. Internal changes in social and cultural values should also be rejected and prevented, including changes in, for example, the roles and status of women, foreign influences in the arts, and liberal attitudes relating to

---

[9] Beauzamy (2013). [10] Ebner (2020), chapter 12.
[11] De Orellana and Michelsen (2019a, 2019b). [12] Krulic (2007).

Identitarianism

race, sexuality and marriage. Barrès was an ethnic nationalist, linked culture with race, and was openly anti-Semitic.

These kinds of ideas were present in the French Nouvelle Droite and the Groupement de recherche et d'études pour la civilisation européenne (GRECE) organisations, founded in 1969 with a resurgence in the 1990s and 2000s. The founders, Alain de Benoist and Guillaume Faye, have influenced not only the French far right but also their British and American counterparts. Among the earlier themes of Barrès and Maurras, they promoted the idea of 'organic democracy'. This included opposition to the mixing of ethnicities, to multiculturalism, and to the presumption of human equality. In contradistinction to the traditional conservative right, there was opposition to capitalism, and also to Christianity. It was de Benoist who introduced the term 'ethnopluralism', which carried the implication that ethno-culturally homogeneous white people could lay exclusive claim to European territories.

New Right tendencies in general reject liberal representative democracy, instead favouring direct democracy best exemplified by referendums. Certain currents also eschew populism and assert the role of elites in spreading the claim that Europeans possess a distinct ethnic identity. Some members of the New Right movements espouse the conspiracy theory of the 'Great Replacement', most recently and starkly formulated by the French writer and extreme-right presidential candidate (in 2012) Renaud Camus. In his 2011 book, *Le grand remplacement*, Camus claimed that European liberal activists are conspiring to replace existing European populations with Muslim populations. The word 'replacement' now evokes its own conceptual frame, developed within the extreme right's discourse network. It is now used by politicians on the right who have entered mainstream politics, including, for example, Heinz-Christian Strache of Austria's Freiheitliche Partei and Dries van Langenhove of Belgium's Vlaams Belang. In 2017, Camus started the National European Council of Resistance (Conseil national de la résistance européenne), with all the historical associations that 'Resistance' has for the French and other Europeans. This organisation has been supported by the Bloc Identitaire (now Les Identitaires). Camus claims as one of his influences Enoch Powell, to whom we return in Chapter 5.

One of the catchwords in replacement conspiracy theory is 'Eurabia', encapsulating a set of ideas about the supposed domination of Europe by Islam.[13] These ideas merge with a strand of thought revolving around the idea of 'clash of civilisations', found among both French- and English-language writers, of whom the most cited are Daniel Pipes, Bernard Lewis, and Samuel Huntington. Huntington's 'clash of civilisations' theory was taken up by Guillaume Faye in his *The Colonisation of Europe: Speaking Truth about*

---

[13] Eatwell and Goodwin (2018), pp. 143–4.

Immigration and Islam, where one of his arguments is that immigration should be resisted in order to preserve what he regards as separate biological and cultural groups, for instance, on the two sides of the Mediterranean. The book was disavowed by de Benoist.

Continuing this current of thought, the word 'Eurabia' was popularised in English by the British author Bat Ye'or (pen name of Gisèle Littman) in her 2005 book *Eurabia: The Euro-Arab Axis*, which has led to numerous publications in the same vein. Examples are a much-read *New York Times* article ('The way we live now: 4-4-04; Eurabia?') by the historian Niall Ferguson and the 2017 book *The Strange Death of Europe* by Douglas Murray. In this kind of discourse, the term 'Eurabia' is often used to refer to what is claimed to be the gradual penetration of Europe by Islamic people and culture. Proponents point to increased immigration in the 2010s, demographic trends favouring immigrants of Arab and Berber origin, terrorist atrocities, and a passive stance on the part of the West. Bat Ye'or used the term 'dhimmitude' in the 1980s and 1990s, and in her 2001 book *Islam and Dhimmitude: Where Civilizations Collide*. The word is supposed to denote a state of surrender and dependency under which the Islamic world has held the Judaeo-Christian world since the eighth century.[14] Geert Wilders, like Marine Le Pen, supports the 'Eurabia' and 'dhimmitude' thesis, both claiming to preserve the Judaeo-Christian tradition of Europe. Across Europe extreme-right politicians and activists have deployed such ideas. The supposed threat of Islamisation hovered in the background to much anti-immigration rhetoric during the Brexit campaign.

Establishing a polarity between self and other, more concretely between some inclusive group 'we' and certain contextually understood 'others', is fundamental in identitarian thought – as it is in Brexitspeak. In 2004 de Benoist, influenced by the writings of Carl Schmitt, published an article titled 'Nous et les autres: problématique de l'identité', translated into English as 'On identity'.[15] One of de Benoist's central ideas is a distinction between an individual's 'objective' identity and their 'subjective' identity. The first is presented as determined by ethnicity, religion, family and nationality. The second is supposed to be freely chosen over time. But de Benoist contradicts himself when he states that an individual's identity is 'dialogical', always under evolution. If this is so, then it should be difficult to claim that identities are fixed by birth and birth culture, thus in need of protective separation from other identities – unless one ideologically insists on the priority of birth identity over free choice of identity or particular identities. Such an insistence is often

---

[14] The word 'dhimmitude' is a lexical blend of Arabic *dhimmi* and the ending *-tude*. *Dhimmi* is a legal term used historically for non-Muslims living within an Islamic state.

[15] This essay was published by de Benoist in the monthly journal *Éléments* in 2004. The English translation, by Kathy Ackerman and Julia Kostova, appeared in *Telos*, also in 2004. It was published in French again in 2006, in *Krisis*, a publication of which de Benoist is the director.

derived from rigidly opposing in-group to out-groups. According to de Benoist, the distinction between 'we' and 'others' is the foundation of all collective identities, and dialogue between them as separate equals is the natural order.[16] True, he does declare that exclusionary non-egalitarian attitudes towards the 'other' are 'pathological'. But again this is not consistent with his statements, or with the inferential drift that brings users of his work to think of 'we' as superior. It is not clear that he escapes the 'pathology' he describes.

De Benoist concludes his article, 'Nous et les autres', with remarks on language. 'Certainly, language is not an absolute marker of identity', he writes, since one can speak a European language without being European and 'a people' can keep its identity even if it loses its language. 'Nevertheless', he continues, 'language has functioned as a major sign of recognition. In providing a tool for mutual understanding, it has created a connection from the outset.'[17] In other words, he wishes to retain some firm connection between a language and 'a people'. Further, he has the idea that languages express 'categories' of the world and values that are unique to those who speak them. These are ideas that echo those of Romantic nationalists like Herder and Humboldt, and the later language relativism of Benjamin Lee Whorf. As in much of de Benoist, there is an element of truth in this, but it contains an unspoken assumption – that the normal or natural condition is for communities to speak one unifying language. He does not mention the fact that many communities the world over are bi- or multilingual, and have been for millennia, so far as we know. What is more, though bi- and multilingual speakers do report that they switch between (slightly) different views of the world, the fact is that underlying all languages are universal patterns of structure and meaning. Such observations show it *is* possible to grasp other people's world views, and because this is so, monolingualism is not a precondition for community.

The important point is that Brexit and its ideology are not isolated phenomena. They are part of the far-right identitarian movement that spread across Europe as well as other parts of the world. It took various forms. Brexit was the UK's version. Central to asserting a national identity is the construction of a foreign other, and it was hostile xenophobic attitudes, specifically towards immigration, that the Brexit campaigns deliberately activated.

Immigration

The objective facts concerning increased migration into the UK over the past thirty years are now well known from reliable polls and surveys that are much quoted by social scientists.[18] At the end of World War II, the UK, like other

---

[16] De Benoist (2004a, 2004b, 2006). [17] De Benoist (2004b).
[18] E.g. Eatwell and Goodwin (2018), Mounk (2018).

32   Identity

European nation states, had emerged with high ethnic homogeneity. In the 1950s, the UK's ethnic minorities were counted in tens of thousands. A University of Warwick report found that from 1966 to 1980, the minority ethnic population of the UK more than doubled in size, increasing from 886,000 to 2.1 million.[19] The report cites more data indicating a further growth of over half a million during the 1980s, with minority ethnic groups forming nearly 5 per cent of the population by 1989–91 (and the report notes that this could be an underestimate). In the present century, the 2011 UK Census found that from 2001 to 2011, the percentage of the population of England and Wales identifying as white British decreased from 87.4 per cent to 80.5 per cent.

In certain places, an increase in non-white numbers had greater psychosocial impact than elsewhere. These were places that had previously been used to much greater white British homogeneity. The best-known example is Boston in Lincolnshire. Analysis of the 2011 Census by the Lincolnshire County Council Research Observatory, which reports socio-economic trends, found that between 2001 and 2011 the number of Lincolnshire residents who were born outside the UK more than doubled, the non-white population making up 2.4 per cent of the total population in 2011 compared to 1.4 per cent in 2001 (still small when compared with the national non-white population of 14 per cent).[20] In 2012 *The Guardian* drew the following picture from the 2011 Census:

In 2001, the biggest foreign community in Boston comprised 249 Germans. Census figures then showed Boston as having a population of 55,753, with 98.5% indicating they were white British. Ten years on, 10.6% of the town's 64,600-strong population comes from one of the 'new' EU countries such as Poland, Lithuania, Latvia or Romania.[21]

In Boston 75.6 per cent voted Leave.

The exceptional experience of Bostonians does not alter the overall picture: low-immigrant areas voted more strongly for Leave. The scattergram in Figure 1.1 shows this clearly.

Lawton and Ackrill, who reproduce this graph, point out that, nationally, 'of the 270 districts that had a *lower* proportion than average of people born outside the UK in 2011, in 229 (85%) the majority vote was for Leave. Of the 78 districts with a *higher* than average population born outside the UK, only 44% voted Leave [my emphasis].'[22] So there is evidence that high levels of

---

[19] Owen (1995), p. 2; cf. Mounk (2018), p. 165.
[20] Lincolnshire Research Observatory, 'Country of birth, ethnicity and nationality of Lincolnshire residents', www.research-lincs.org.uk/UI/Documents/country-of-birth-ethnicity-and-nationality-of-lincolnshire-residents-census2011-112013.pdf.
[21] *The Guardian*, 11 December 2012, www.theguardian.com/uk/2012/dec/11/census-boston-eastern-european-immigration.
[22] Lawton and Ackrill (2016), critiqued by Eatwell and Goodwin (2018), pp. 165–6.

Immigration 33

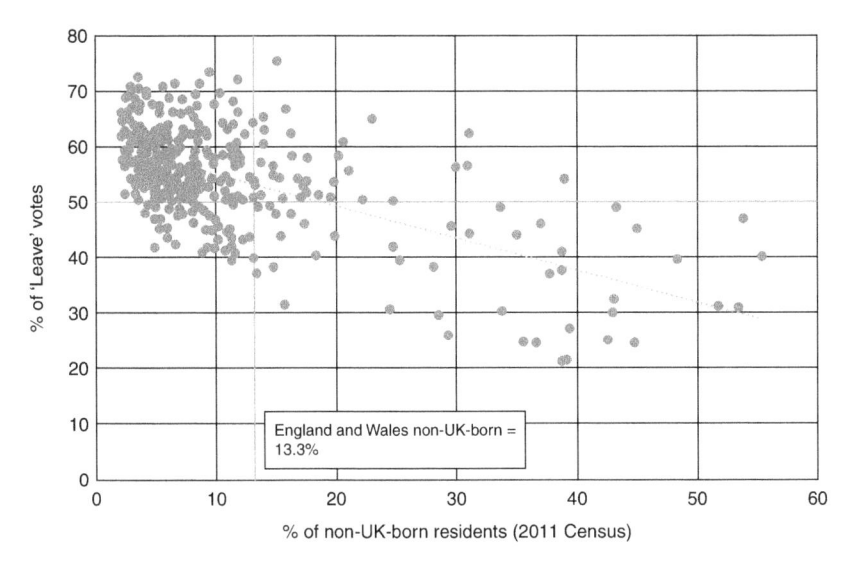

[Scatterplot: % of 'Leave' votes (y-axis, 0–80) vs % of non-UK-born residents (2011 Census) (x-axis, 0–60). Legend: England and Wales non-UK-born = 13.3%]

Figure 1.1 Scattergram for low-immigrant areas voting more strongly for Leave.
Source: Electoral Commission 2016, EU Referendum by Local Authority. Also ONS Crown Copyright, 2012, Table KS204EW: 2011 Census: Country of birth, local authorities in England and Wales. Reproduced by Lawton and Ackrill (2016).
https://theconversation.com/hard-evidence-how-areas-with-low-immigration-voted-mainly-for-brexit-62138

immigration did not necessarily predict Leave. Lawton and Ackrill's (brief) explanation of this skewed pattern is as follows. In areas of relatively low immigration where a relatively high white population *also* suffered significant levels of economic deprivation, voters went for Leave because they held migrants, or foreigners in general, to blame for their suffering. But this is only part of the explanation, as other studies indicate. For instance, a Joseph Rowntree report by Goodwin and Heath (2016) does show correlations between socio-economic deprivation and Leave voting but also emphasises the importance of educational opportunities or lack of them, together with the role of attitudes and values.[23] Further, any simple relationship between deprivation alone and voting Leave is put in doubt by Dorling and Tomlinson, who show clearly that a statistical correlation between deprivation and voting Leave had low probability (the correlation coefficient is given as 0.037, positive but close to zero).[24] In fact, on their evidence, Leave voting was somewhat higher

[23] Goodwin and Heath (2016). [24] Dorling and Tomlinson (2019), p. 306.

34   Identity

in 'Middle England' (deciles 4 to 7 by levels of deprivation) than in the most deprived areas. Dorling and Tomlinson's comment on these findings is important:

> It was not people who were poorer who voted Leave in high numbers, but people who found the propaganda that immigrants created problems believable. They tended to live in areas of low immigration. In areas of high immigration, everyone was more likely to vote Remain.[25]

Without direct experience of immigrants, non-white and non-English-speaking people, those identifying as white British in low immigrant areas were more likely to believe anti-immigrant propaganda. As for the wealthy, the wealthiest group of all tended to vote Remain.[26] However, there were wealthy individuals who were in a position to strongly influence the pro-Brexit vote in all domains of propaganda. The crucial point is that, overall, anti-immigrant propaganda was believable, or made believable, for a significant number of electors, whoever they were.

Blame the EU

The propaganda did not simply switch on anti-immigrant attitudes in credulous people at the moment of the referendum. Can we be sure that such attitudes did not exist before the referendum? More importantly still, how did the EU come to be associated with immigration at all? With regard to the first of these questions, there is clear evidence that something certainly did change at the time of the referendum, as can be seen from Figure 1.2.

The bar chart in Figure 1.2 shows, for the years 1975 and 2015, the relationship between how the people polled viewed immigration and whether they supported leaving the EU. The relationship changed significantly and can be explained by the increase in the number of immigrants coming into the UK from the 1990s on and by the rise in numbers of migrants from the EU after 2004.

With regard to the second question – how the EU came to be associated with immigration into the UK – this key question involves several considerations. In the public mind, prior to 2016, concern about immigration was probably outstripped by concern about the economy following the crisis of 2008. Yet, for a long time in the UK, reaching back at least as far as Enoch Powell, there was a persistent undercurrent of anti-immigrant sentiment. This undercurrent

---

[25] Ibid. p. 306.
[26] See bar chart in Dorling and Tomlinson (2019), p. 299. This chart is reproduced by them from Daniel Gordon Watts. The original is available at https://twitter.com/marwood_lennox/status/925760600755658752?s=03.

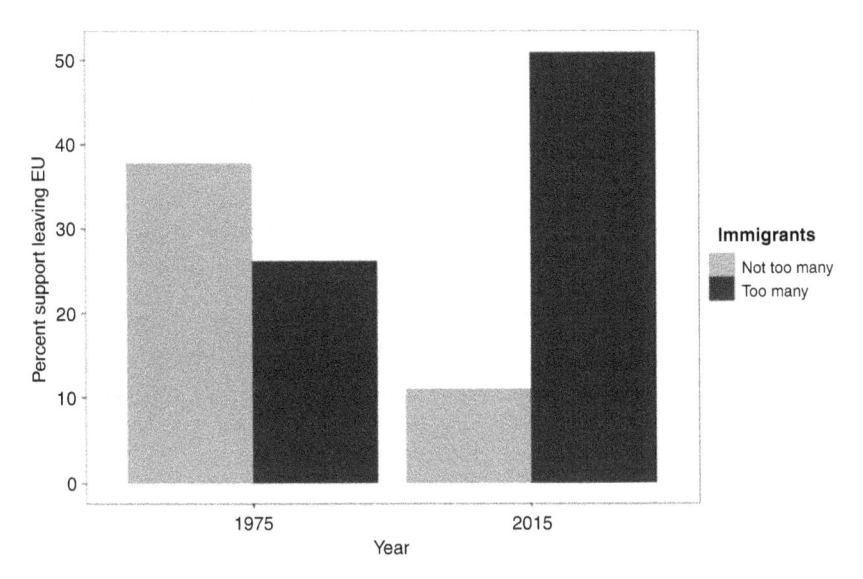

Figure 1.2 Relationship between immigration and Europe in 1975 and 2015.
Source: Evans and Mellon (2019).
https://ukandeu.ac.uk/immigration-and-euroscepticism-the-rising-storm/

had not gone away and was capable of being re-activated at any moment by demagogues.

Such re-activations, however, need a particular political conjuncture. One of the most significant contextual factors in the re-activation of anti-immigrant feelings was the enlargement of the EU, when former Eastern bloc states were admitted and acquired freedom of movement rights under existing EU rights. This context provided the opportunity for pro-Leave propagandists to connect the EU with immigration. As in all propaganda, there was a germ of truth in such a connection. But the pro-Brexit proponents achieved their ends through misrepresentation of what freedom of movement in the EU actually was and still is.

The free movement of persons is a founding principle of the EU and the principle cannot be changed. However, there were and are strict controls on *entry into* both the EU and the related Schengen Area, and anyone originating from outside the Area requires a visa. Despite this, migrants without visas – asylum seekers, refugees, some economic migrants and likely some criminal elements – still manage to enter the Area illegally and travel across its unchecked internal borders. But it is important to note that member states of the EU, including of course the UK in 2016, had the right under EU legislation to 'restrict the freedom of movement and residence of Union citizens and their family members, irrespective of nationality, on grounds of public policy, public security or public health'. The same piece of legislation includes the provision that 'Member States may adopt the necessary measures to refuse, terminate or withdraw any right conferred by this Directive in the case of abuse of rights or fraud, such as marriages of convenience'.[27] The Brexit lobby ignored this legislation and the electorate largely remained ignorant of it.

Under the Brexiters' label 'immigrant', there were actually three categories entailed by the EU framework of free movement. These were fudged by Brexit hardliners. First, there were the long-standing citizens of the EU (the so-named EU-15 countries) who all had the right of free movement within the EU. Second, there were the more recent migrants from the former Eastern bloc countries who gradually acquired free movement rights in the years following their accession to the EU in 2004 and 2007. And third, there were migrants who had illegally entered the EU space one way or another, made their way to the Channel and attempted to enter the UK. All three categories of migrant were conflated under the term 'immigrant' in pro-Brexit discourse, and their entry into the UK was blamed on EU 'freedom of movement'. In addition, Turkey, was represented as if it were already a source of massive immigration into the UK caused by the EU's free movement provisions – though Turkey was not a member of the EU and not likely to be. Such distortion of the facts enabled pro-Brexit propaganda to present immigration as an imminent danger that could only be prevented by the UK leaving the EU. The details of how exactly the pro-Brexit rhetoric built up the threat of an immigrant 'invasion' are examined in Chapter 6.

In 2015 many European countries experienced a refugee crisis, precipitated by large numbers of asylum seekers mostly fleeing the civil war in Syria. When the crisis impacted UK public perception, pro-Brexit campaigners seized another opportunity and proceeded to stir fear of immigrants, blaming the EU as the cause of the increased numbers of 'immigrants'. The reaction to the crisis across the EU was varied, and in the UK also the public mood was changeable. The *Daily Mail*, for instance, contrary to its usual stance on migration of any kind, at first campaigned in favour of child refugees – on 4 September 2015 it had published a distressing photo of a dead Syrian child washed up on a Turkish beach.[28] But a few months later, in the run-up to the referendum, the paper changed its tune. The following May, the *Mail* announced what it called David Cameron's 'major U-turn on refugee children as he opens the door for some living in camps inside Europe'.[29] In the subsequent online forum, contributors

---

[27] EU Directive 2004/38/EC, Chapter VI, Article 27, clause 1. See Guild et al. (2019).
[28] *Daily Mail*, 4 September 2015, www.dailymail.co.uk/news/article-3222148/Six-hours-setting-tragic-journey-claim-life-leave-lifeless-Turkish-beach-little-Aylan-sleeps-photograph-boy-alive.html.
[29] *MailOnline*, 4 May 2016, www.dailymail.co.uk/news/article-3573053/David-Cameron-announces-major-U-turn-refugee-children-opens-door-living-camps-inside-Europe.html.

Blame the EU 37

span the paper's usual line – that these child refugees were probably adults, probably 'economic migrants', that they would be a burden on public services, and that having them enter the country would be contrary to UK citizens' will. Some discussants maintained that such claims were good grounds for supporting UKIP. In all likelihood, the forum constituted a filter bubble. But a key observation, made by Goodman and Narang, was the frequent association of immigration with EU membership.[30]

Was the readers' association between immigration and EU membership a spontaneous reaction on the part of the public, simply arising from enduring hostility to immigrants? Or was it intentionally stirred up by 'believable propaganda'? There is clear evidence that the reaction was not entirely spontaneous, but an intended component of pro-Brexit strategy and a consequence of pro-Brexit propaganda that a lot of people found believable. The evidence comes in an article carried by *The Telegraph* on 19 April in 2016, written by the political campaign consultant and former Conservative Party strategist Sir Lynton Crosby. He wrote:

Currently 41 per cent of the British population would vote Leave. But 52 per cent say that leaving the EU would improve the UK's immigration system. There is therefore a misalignment – this shows that there is at least 11 per cent of the British electorate who are not voting Leave despite believing it will improve the state of immigration in the UK. This demonstrates that for this section of the population, immigration is not important enough or relevant enough an issue at present to bring them around to voting for Leave.

Crosby's conclusion was: 'If the Leave campaign can make the changes to the immigration system or advocate changes that would result from Brexit and so make them more important in voters' decision making, there is up to 11 per cent of the population they can win over.'[31]

Crosby's percentages are in line with part of the statistics for the year 2015 in the bar chart[32] shown in Figure 1.2. According to Evans and Mellon, just over 50 per cent of people 'who believe too many immigrants have been let in would [vote to leave the EU]'. Crosby makes an equivalent statement, with a similar percentage. In the Evans and Mellon chart, the number of people who believed that there were *not* too many immigrants and who would vote to *stay* in the EU was down by more than a third compared with 1975. From Crosby's viewpoint, of course, an even greater swing was desirable, given the April 2016 polls that showed actual voting intentions. He cites a figure of 41 per cent of voters intending to vote to leave – though it is unclear how many of these also thought there were too many immigrants. Taking the figure of 52 per cent who thought there were too many immigrants, he claimed there was a 'misalignment'.

[30] Goodman and Narang (2019). [31] *The Telegraph*, 19 April 2016.
[32] Evans and Mellon (2019).

His argument was in effect that the Leave campaigns needed to persuade anti-immigration voters to see the benefits (to them) of leaving the EU. Although Crosby was not an official advisor to either of the main Leave campaigns, his claims were very influential. This is reflected in the way Leave propaganda, supported by a large part of the media, immediately set about reinforcing an association between immigration levels and EU membership.

In the ten weeks before referendum day 2016, the media stepped up the quantity of its anti-immigrant messages. This phase has all the appearance of being strategically planned by pro-Brexit editors under the prompting of Brexiter politicians and their business backers. Moore and Ramsay, of King's College London, published an analysis of all online newspaper and magazine articles – 14,779 in total – that referred to the forthcoming referendum during the ten weeks of the official campaign (15 April to 23 June).[33] These included national press, digital-only news services, and online news services. Their methods were quantitative and qualitative content analysis. They summarised the way the sympathies of these publication outlets were distributed:

- Eight endorsed Leave: *The Sun*, *Daily Mail*, *Daily Express*, *Sunday Express*, *The Daily Telegraph*, *The Sunday Telegraph*, *The Sunday Times*, and *The Spectator*.
- Eight supported Remain: *The Times*, *The Guardian*, *The Observer*, *Financial Times*, *The Independent*, *The Mail on Sunday*, *Daily Mirror*, and *New Statesman*.
- Buzzfeed, HuffPo UK, Vice UK, *Daily Star* and *Daily Star Sunday* did not formally endorse either side, though the editorial perspective of the first three leaned towards Remain, while the *Daily Star* strongly favoured Leave.
- The BBC, ITV, Channel 4 and Sky were required by law to be neutral.[34]

In the earlier stages of the referendum campaign, the economy was the most frequently mentioned issue, while immigration came second. Articles predicting the damaging economic consequences of leaving the EU were routinely dismissed by the Leave side as 'scaremongering' or 'project fear'. However, immigration-related articles and mentions more than tripled over the course of the campaign. From week three, about ten days after Crosby's *Telegraph* article, there was a marked increase in such coverage, with a further spurt in the last campaign week.[35] On the front pages of the newspapers in Moore and Ramsay's study, immigration-related topics outstripped economy-related ones by ninety-nine to eighty-two.[36] Most front pages on immigration were explicitly linked to the EU. The fact that a few front-page articles about immigration were not explicitly related to the referendum need not detract from their relevance, since readers are likely to interpret their relevance in terms of the day-to-day news context. It was the pro-Leave papers that most often put

---

[33] See also Levy et al. (2016). [34] Moore and Ramsay (2017), pp. 3–4.
[35] Ibid. pp. 28, 36–113. [36] Ibid. pp. 8–9, 40–2.

immigration on their front page (seventy-nine of the ninety-nine front-page immigration-related headlines).

On the qualitative side, Moore and Ramsay show that the coverage of immigration was predominantly negative, migrants being blamed for social and economic problems, especially in the public services. Turks, Albanians, Romanians and Poles came in for special opprobrium. The most active outlets in this were, predictably, the *Daily Express*, the *Daily Mail* and *The Sun*. But there is more to say about how exactly the negative attitudes towards immigrants were stimulated by the language deployed by the media.

In this media language, immigration is blamed on the EU in a framework of fearmongering. The year before the referendum, the *Daily Mail* had linked the November terrorist attacks in Paris with the Syrian refugee crisis, making the claim that the EU's free movement rights made it possible for Islamist extremists to enter the UK. The association of immigration into the UK with the EU is not always explicit. Readers would make such an association on the basis of context, relevance and expectation. Three examples where such implicit association could have occurred are:

- UK's open coastline shambles: 4 missed warnings (*Daily Mail*, 31 May 2016)
- Migrant Crisis in the Channel (*Daily Express*, 30 May 2016)
- Migrants pay just £100 to invade Britain (*Daily Express*, 1 June 2016).[37]

In these headlines, there are prompts for emotional and conceptual reactions that are characteristic of Brexit discourse. Such prompts are the words 'warning', 'crisis' and 'invade', each of which can trigger feelings and thoughts of danger and threat. In particular, 'invade' activates the schematic image CONTAINER and it also depends on prompting mental representations of migration as a violent threat. The meaning of 'invade' is part of the mental frame for 'war', and, more subtly, assumes the image of a metaphorical container whose boundaries can be penetrated from outside. We shall encounter this kind of language many times throughout this book.

It is not just a matter of stirring negative emotions by such means, however. The Brexit movement was facilitated by, and exacerbated, a period of political misinformation, exclusion of information, 'fake news', deliberately misleading language, and downright lies. False or misleading statements were made in the press about the EU, across a diverse range of topics, often packed into a single article. Just two days before the referendum, the *Daily Mail* carried a lengthy article headed 'Daily Mail Comment: If you believe in Britain, vote Leave. Lies, greedy elites and a divided, dying Europe – why we could have a great future outside a broken EU'. After several paragraphs intended to illustrate these claims about the EU, the writer cites a Pew Research Centre poll,

---

[37] Ibid. p. 22.

claiming it demonstrated that the EU was unpopular even with people in its member states. The writer tells readers:

> We needn't look far for the explanation [of the EU's alleged unpopularity]. For not only is the euro destroying livelihoods, but the madness that is the free movement of peoples has brought waves of migrants sweeping across Europe, depressing wages, putting immense strain on housing and public services, undermining our security against criminals and terrorists – and making communities fear for their traditional ways of life.[38]

Readers do not have time to stop and dissect what they are reading; that is why it can affect them unconsciously. And politicians, their propagandists, and the journalists who support them know that. In fact, all orators and demagogues know it, as will be seen again in this book. The long second sentence in the above extract compresses several manipulative assertions about the EU:

> The euro is destroying livelihoods.
> The free movement of peoples has brought waves of migrants.
> The free movement of peoples is madness.
> Migrants are sweeping across Europe.
> Migrants depress wages.
> Migrants put immense strain on housing.
> Migrants put immense strain on public services.
> Migrants undermine our security against criminals and terrorists.
> Migrants make communities fear for their traditional ways of life.

The assertions contain word choices that press both emotive and conceptual buttons. The most revealing example is the wording used in the allusion to the EU's freedom of movement rights – 'the free movement of peoples has brought waves of migrants'. It is a significant distortion that is easy to overlook but none the less capable of reinforcing ingrained misconceptions. The EU legislation actually speaks of the free movement of 'persons', not of 'peoples' *inside* the EU. There is an obvious difference in meaning between *persons* and *peoples*. In using the word *peoples*, the *Mail* was implying that whole alien populations were on the move. It also misleadingly conveyed the idea that it was the right of free movement *inside* the EU that was the cause of 'waves of migrants' from *outside* the EU entering the UK. These distortions were key for the Leave campaigns.

Some of the word choices in this *Daily Mail* article are standard both in anti-immigration discourse and in discourse about the EU. In the expression 'waves of migrants', the meaning structure at work is a conceptual metaphor, one that maps the conceptual frame of *migrant* onto the conceptual frame of *waves* (part of the parent frame *ocean* or *sea* or more generally any

---

[38] *Daily Mail*, 21 June 2016, www.dailymail.co.uk/debate/article-3653385/Lies-greedy-elites-divided-dying-Europe-Britain-great-future-outside-broken-EU.html.

mobile liquid mass): A MOVING GROUP OF INDIVIDUALS IS A MOVING LIQUID. What this transfer does conceptually is turn a large number of individual humans (migrants) into an unindividuated mass that is mobile and hard to resist. There are numerous potential metaphorical entailments. The metaphor packs a lot of associated ideas into one or two words, and spawns other related vocabulary across talk and text of all kinds about migration – words like 'flow', 'flood', 'influx', 'surge', for example, as well as 'sweeping across', which is said of water in the sense of traversing large areas of ground surface. Yet another entailment of this metaphor comes from the fact that water as a moving mass exerts physical force – reflected in discourse in the word 'pressure'. As Chapters 6 and 7 demonstrate, the rhetorical representation of immigrants as a destructive invasive mass has a long and influential history in British political discourse after World War II.[39]

The 'wave' metaphor is only one in a set of similar words used to represent incoming migrants in the populist press. Many of these words are 'associated with natural disasters, epidemics, or incipient catastrophe'[40] – a device that also avoids referring to individual human beings. Large numbers of people may also be referred to by means of words denoting animals on the move – 'flocking', 'swarming', 'stampeding', and 'over-running' an area of ground. Immigration often appears alongside expressions that include the meaning 'out of control', as in 'soaring numbers of immigrants' or 'spiralling immigration'. The idea of a continuing process is often combined with the idea of pain and suffering: 'unsustainable', 'intolerable', 'relentless'. Such word combinations are used not to refer to the suffering of refugee migrants, but to the supposed suffering of the British population. Violence, too, is associated with the migrant, largely through military terms such as 'storming', 'invading', 'besieging'. National borders 'creak', 'buckle', 'collapse', 'implode'. There is a conceptual coherence among all these vocabulary items. I am not suggesting that journalists put these ideas together explicitly, but the way popular discourse can work is by the repeated activation of conceptual schemas that hang together around a core narrative that prompts alarm and anxiety in response to perceived danger.

The coupling of the EU with unwanted migrants is an integral part of identitarian ideology – the base on which Brexitspeak rested. At the centre of Brexitism is a national self, a 'we', with an exceptional history, which, when it loses its self-assurance, requires an alien 'other' to shore itself up. Any account of the UK's departure from the EU must include the UK's historic relationship with empire and loss of empire. The perceived threat of an immigration 'invasion',

---

[39] Several scholars have commented on metaphors for migrants, e.g. Hart (2011b, 2013), Musolff (2012), Taylor (2020, 2021).
[40] Moore and Ramsay (2017), p. 78.

combined with the perceived threat of an expanding EU, provided what was needed. A not dissimilar pattern of thought is found in the nationalist identitarianism that has emerged both in Europe and in America. The most powerful part of the pro-Brexit campaign was the way in which its rhetoric repeatedly represented migrants as 'entering' a space that is 'ours', while simultaneously representing EU membership as 'being in' an alien space to which 'our' historic self does not belong. Making sense of Brexit certainly needs analysis of its economic, demographic, social and political setting. But there is a missing link in the explanatory chain. We cannot understand the referendum result without examining the propaganda campaigns that produced it. Making propaganda believable is achieved by deploying language designed to turn minds. That is why analysis of the linguistic workings of pro-Brexit demagogues will be an essential part of explaining how Brexit happened. One of their favourite devices is the little word 'we'. The next chapter looks at the question: Who do 'we' think they are?

2 We

All English speakers know what *we* means, at least in the abstract. Its full meaning only emerges in particular acts of communication, though not always unambiguously. One of the uses of the word *we* is to arouse sentiments of collective bonding and it played a key role in the national-populist talk and text that surrounded Brexit. The reason for this was that the question of leaving the EU was deeply intertwined with British national identity – the question of who *we* is. Brexit is in many ways a crisis of identity, a crisis that played itself out on the ground in terms of the Leaver we-group and the Remainer we-group.

So how does the word *we* work? All languages have a small subgroup of words, known as deictics, whose referential meaning can only be decided when used *in situ*, and by taking account of non-linguistic clues. Examples are words like *here* and *there*, *now* and *then*, and of course *we*. In context, the relevant meaning of *we* has to be inferred by the hearer(s). Essentially, using the word *we* concerns which group and group boundaries are being indicated. Ideological uses of *we* involve more mental processing – the calling up of a relevant mental frame. In the case of a national *we*, the frame can be quite detailed. Frequent repetition in particular contexts can build up a specific association between the self and a particular social or political group.

Central to the various meanings of *we*, and central to the theme of this chapter, is what linguists call 'clusivity'. The term refers to the fact that in English *we* is ambiguous. It can have an *inclusionary* meaning: 'I the speaker and you the hearer(s)'. Or it can have an *exclusionary* meaning: 'I and you the hearer(s)' but not some other 'you' and not 'them'. In some languages of the world there are different words to mark this distinction. In English and languages that do not mark the distinction, the intended *we*-group is often unclear – a fact that can be exploited rhetorically.[1] Manipulating the national *we* is one of the key features of Brexitspeak, almost always associated with national identity, competition between political parties and campaign organisations, and their respective mindsets.

---

[1] Brown and Gilman (1960), Petersoo (2007), Pavlidou (2014), Buckledee (2018), Wenzl (2019).

44   We

Monolingual *We*

The complaint that foreign languages were increasingly being spoken on the streets of the UK was heard frequently among UKIP supporters and others in the run-up to the referendum of 2016. At the UKIP spring conference on 28 February 2014, Nigel Farage declared:

In scores of our cities and market towns this country in a short space of time has frankly become unrecognizable [applause] whether it's the [...] whether it's the impact on local schools and hospitals, whether it's the fact that in many parts of England you don't hear English spoken any more. This is not the kind of community we want to leave to our children and grandchildren.[2]

He was telling his audience what they wanted to hear. In a press conference afterwards, he recounted his experience of travelling on a commuter train on which he could hear no English spoken, adding, 'Does that make me feel slightly awkward? Yes it does.' And, asked why he minded people speaking in foreign languages, he replied: 'I don't understand them ... I don't feel very comfortable in that situation and I don't think the majority of British people do.'[3]

Although UKIP did not make language policy a prominent part of their anti-EU campaign, Britain's longstanding monolingualism meant that people could easily be persuaded to focus on the speaking of languages other than English. Most of Farage's supporters would have taken it for granted that it is normal and natural to speak one and only one language, and that in the UK, that language must be English. The people Farage overheard speaking another language may well have been bilingual or multilingual, a perfectly natural state of affairs. It is true, all the same, that in many societies divisions can be fomented by political actors who link language with identity, nationhood and social divisions.

On the day the UK formally left the EU, 31 January 2020, a resident of a block of flats in Norwich reported that posters displaying the text shown in Figure 2.1 had been found attached to the fire doors on all fifteen floors.[4]

This is a rich example of Brexitspeak, one that should not be dismissed as 'extremist', or not representative of mainstream Brexit discourse. In fact, the xenophobic and racist ideas in it are implicit in much if not all of Brexitspeak. This short text states explicitly a string of ideas and attitudes that in more public utterances are only hinted at, so that accusations of racism can be denied. Its explicitness illustrates the way in which far-right culture was beginning to openly assert itself. The poster, we may guess, comes from the milieu of the

---

[2] My transcript based on a YouTube video, www.youtube.com/watch?v=A6JgyJp_QJw.
[3] Transcript by Sparrow (2014).
[4] A photograph was posted anonymously on Twitter/X and reposted numerous times. See also BBC News, 1 February 2020: www.bbc.co.uk/news/uk-england-norfolk-51341735.

> **Happy Brexit Day**
>
> As we finally have our great country back we feel there is one rule to that needs to be made clear to Winchester Tower residents.
>
> We do not tolerate people speaking other languages than English in the flats.
> We are now our own country again and the the Queens English is the spoken tongue here.
> If you do want to speak whatever is the mother tongue of the country you came from then we suggest you return to that place and return your flat to the council so they can let British people live here and we can return to what was normality before you infected this once great island.
>
> It's a simple choice obey the rule of the majority or leave.
>
> You won't have long till our government will implement rules that will put British first. So, best evolve or leave.
> God Save the Queen, her government and all true patriots.

Figure 2.1 Nationalist monolingualism post-Brexit.
Source: Photograph posted anonymously on Twitter/X and reposted numerous times. Author's verbatim transcription.

marginalised, the economically deprived and the unqualified – people who were likely to believe national-populist propaganda promoting exit from the EU. It is angry, frustrated and it seeks a 'voice', within a narrow community.[5]

The linguistic details of the notice are worth a closer look. The text imitates the style of official notices written in standard formal English, presumably to give legitimacy to an extreme form of xenophobic nationalism. Apparently the

---

[5] Goodwin and Heath (2016), Eatwell and Goodwin (2018), Schmid (2020), Sobolewska and Ford (2020).

tower block residents were not fooled, since the next day saw demonstrations against whoever posted the notice. Unsurprisingly, the poster writer deploys the word *we*. Clear contextual cues mean it can only be understood as exclusive of 'you', the intended addressees. The underlying racism is not expressed in so many words but is unmistakeably implied via the powerful metaphor present in the one word 'infected'. The infectious disease metaphor works well ideologically because it is conceptually linked with the 'body politic' metaphor, A STATE IS A HUMAN BODY. If states are bodies, they can become 'infected' – by 'parasites' is a potential metaphorical extension. In the same vein, a 2010 election poster of the Hungarian far-right party Jobbik featured an insect trapped in a 'no entry' sign.[6] Political bodies have boundaries that are best kept closed, according to the discourse of the right and the extreme right.[7] By way of the phrase 'evolve or leave' the poster indirectly conveys another racist (indeed Nazi) idea – that the intended addressees are subhuman. Overall, the text of the poster blends racist xenophobia with national-populist monolingualism. As Markus Rheindorf and Ruth Wodak have shown, the suppression of 'foreign' languages has frequently been implemented by national-populist governments.[8]

In 2001, a report by the Labour Party's Community Cohesion Review Team stated the need for a list of national values that included 'a universal acceptance of the English language' and 'expectations' regarding the use of English, with increased government support.[9] The following year, the Foreign Policy Centre[10] published a set of essays with the title *Reclaiming Britishness*. The Labour Home Secretary of the time, David Blunkett, contributed to it an essay, 'What does citizenship mean today?', which was also published separately by *The Guardian*.[11] Unwittingly perhaps, Blunkett's presentation of the problem of immigration fed the monolingual strand in identitarian discourse, including that of UKIP and Conservative Party Brexiters in the 2010s. One passage runs:

Speaking English enables parents to converse with their children in English, as well as in their historic mother tongue, at home and to participate in wider modern culture. It helps overcome the schizophrenia which bedevils generational relationships.

Mild though Blunkett's words were by comparison with Farage's words quoted earlier, and certainly by comparison with the Norwich poster, they were nonetheless on the same continuum.

The implied claim that schizophrenia is caused by multilingualism is scientifically baseless.[12] In fact multilingual people function perfectly in societies

---

[6] Wodak (2015), p. 75. [7] Musolff (2010), pp. 137–8. Cf. Blackledge (2002).
[8] Wodak (2015), pp. 88–94, Rheindorf and Wodak (2020). [9] Cited in Sebba (2017), p. 269.
[10] The Foreign Policy Centre is a generally pro-EU think tank founded in 1998 by Robin Cook, Labour Foreign Secretary.
[11] Blunkett (2002). [12] Pavlenko (2006), Bhatia (2011), Seeman (2016).

across the world and such societies are common and normal. But Blunkett's remark shows how entrenched are false ideas about the superiority of being monolingual. The truth is that such pronouncements are ideological. Promoting national language monolingualism has serious social and political implications. In 1930s Germany, the Nazis regarded bilinguals as inferior and dangerous. The underlying assumption is that if people have two languages they have different identities and allegiances.

Around the turn of the twentieth century, language diversity linked to migration became a political issue across Europe. In the years before the UK's Brexit referendum, calls for monolingual policy were common among right-wing and far-right leaders in several other countries. 'In Rotterdam spreken we Nederlands' ('In Rotterdam we speak Dutch') was a campaign poster of the People's Party for Freedom and Democracy in 2014.[13] Marine Le Pen, leader of the Front national in France, declared: 'Je ne parle pas anglais, moi. Je suis française.'[14] In Germany, the conservative CSU (Christlich-Soziale Union) made proposals in 2014 to require all migrants to speak German both within the family and in public. This line was followed by other conservative politicians, generally with the claim to be furthering social integration. Official language requirements were enforced in some countries as legal obstacles to migration. In the UK, similar ideas had been voiced on the left, as we have seen. But ten years on, they were the property of the right and the national-populist far right.

In 2011, about a year after Farage had become party leader and made UKIP look more politically challenging, David Cameron gave a speech on immigration that contained the following:

Real communities are bound by common experiences ... forged by friendship and conversation ... knitted together by all the rituals of the neighbourhood [...]. That's why, when there have been significant numbers of new people arriving in neighbourhoods ... perhaps not able to speak the same language as those living there ... on occasions not really wanting or even willing to integrate ... that has created a kind of discomfort and disjointedness in some neighbourhoods.[15]

Cameron casually evokes the supposedly divisive effect of speaking a language other than English, combined with a certain degree of xenophobic scaremongering. The prompting of fears of divisiveness were in all probability driven by the need for his party to compete with UKIP.

In 2011 – a time when UKIP was picking up support – a UK national census included, for the first time, a question about language and language proficiency. This may have reflected growing national-populist interest in the speaking of

---

[13] http://heindehaas.blogspot.com/2014/03/in-rotterdam-we-speak-dutch.html.
[14] *Le Monde* 22 April 2015. www.lemonde.fr/politique/article/2015/04/22/marine-le-pen-a-new-york-en-francais-dans-le-texte_4620265_823448.html.
[15] www.theguardian.com/politics/2011/apr/14/david-cameron-immigration-speech-full-text.

English, an issue often brought up in the popular press. The Census found that 92 per cent of the responding individuals spoke English as their 'main language'. Of the relatively small subset (8 per cent) of individual residents of the UK whose 'main language' was not English, 79.3 per cent reported speaking English 'well' or 'very well'. The Census also looked at households as units, and it found the following:

> In 2011, all usual residents in 91 per cent of households (21.3 million) spoke English as a main language. In a further four per cent (868,000) of households at least one adult spoke English as a main language and in one per cent (182,000) of households no adults but at least one child spoke English as a main language. In the remaining four per cent (1.0 million) of households there were no residents who had English as a main language.
> People who did not report English as a main language may be fluent English speakers and were able to report their English language proficiency as 'good' or 'very good'.[16]

These data suggest a high level of language cohesion in the UK. However, the media reports on the Census fixated on the finding of 4 per cent of households where no resident had English as a 'main language', and proceeded to misinterpret (or misrepresent) what that phrase indicated.[17] *The Guardian* (20 December 2012) had to correct its initial reporting of the Census figures as showing that in England and Wales there were 'around a million households that speak no English'. Such mistakes rest on unquestioned assumptions about identity, national languages, and the human language faculty itself:

> [...] the expression 'does not speak English as a main language' has been understood to mean 'cannot speak English at all'. This suggests that for those who made this interpretation, the notion barely exists that a person could speak English satisfactorily alongside another language which is their main language. In other words, the possibility of fluency in two or more languages is effectively dismissed.[18]

For some minds, not speaking English as one's main language is tantamount to not being really British. The assumption that the British nation state is, or ought to be monolingual seems to be pervasive and to subsist alongside inaccurate assumptions about bilingualism and multilingualism, as the Blunkett examples had implied ten years earlier. The press reports of the 2011 Census, and the public comments of some politicians, presented the speaking of one or more languages in addition to English in a solely negative light.

Thus, the *Daily Express*, for example, writes darkly:

> [...] if you only remember one statistic make it this: **more than four million migrants** [bold in original] do not speak English as their main language. The impact of this finding, which comes from newly released details in the 2011 Census, is profound.[19]

---

[16] *2011 Census*, section 10 'Household language'. [17] Wright and Brooks (2019), pp. 57–9.
[18] Sebba (2017), p. 266.
[19] *Express*, 1 February 2013, cited by Wright and Brooks (2019), p. 68.

Readers are left to make sense of this ('*why* should I remember this? *why* profound?'), by drawing on background knowledge using the usual principle of contextual relevance. Such background knowledge will in all probability come from public utterances taken to be authoritative regarding supposed disadvantages, or even dangers, of not speaking English as your 'main' language. The background premise is that it is wrong not to have English as your 'main' language, and even that speaking other languages in addition is wrong. A hardening of anglocentric monolingualism has been reported for the years around the Brexit referendum.[20] In some instances, the implication that British people ought to have only English as their first language is clear, as in the *Daily Mail*:

Astonishingly, one in nine English schools now has a majority of pupils who do not speak English as a first language. The official figures lay bare the **enormous strain** [bold in original] mass migration has placed on our schools.[21]

The *Mail* did not consider whether such pupils may be completely competent in English. Yet fears that children with English as an additional language will succeed at the expense of native English-speaking children are also articulated in the press:

Pupils who speak English as a second language are **outperforming native speakers in core GCSE subjects** as white British students fall behind 10 other ethnic groups, new research showed. **White British pupils are lagging behind** because other ethnic groups are receiving more help from their families [bold in original].[22]

This assertion, and other examples examined in this section, either state openly or presume that being British means speaking English only. It is tantamount to saying: a person who is not exclusively anglophone is not one of *us*.

Cameron: British *We*

On 23 January 2013, David Cameron, then in coalition with the Liberal Democrats, gave a landmark speech at the London headquarters of Bloomberg L.P., a financial and media company based in Manhattan. Politically he was under pressure from inside his party as well as from outside it. His right-wing MPs, notably the ERG (European Research Group), were pushing an extreme Eurosceptic line, and UKIP was increasingly attractive to the electorate, including traditionally Conservative voters. Cameron, who supported the UK remaining in the EU, sought to ward off these forces by raising the possibility of a referendum on EU membership. A close look at the

---

[20] Cain (2018).
[21] Wright and Brooks (2019), p. 73, commenting on *Daily Mail*, 22 February 2014.
[22] Wright and Brooks (2019), p. 74, citing *The Daily Telegraph*, 4 April 2016.

text of the Bloomberg speech shows that he was also seeking to buy them off rhetorically – that is by adopting their national identitarian narrative.[23] At the centre of the speech was the question 'who are we?' As things turned out, the Bloomberg speech did not still the Eurosceptic voices, but reinforced the discourse of Brexit national populism.

Using *we* in an inclusive sense, as Cameron did, necessarily entails an out-group, though it is not always tactically useful to focus on or name such a group. Here, however, it is plain from the context that the *other* is the EU: it is referred to in the third person, as *it* or as *they*.[24] Associated with *we* and *they* are mental representations containing the imagined attributes of the in-group and the out-group. Such linguistically triggered representations of the in-group and out-group are important not only for the ongoing speech event in the immediate assembly but also for those who will read it in reported form in the media. Cameron lays out explicitly the purported attributes of the British national *we*, using traditional myths.[25] Since a large number of the population already have these national *we* frames in their long-term memories, hearing Cameron's catalogue of characteristics would reinforce such frames and consolidate their association with *we* in political contexts. The fact that Cameron was doing this would not have been relevant had there not been generalised uncertainty about what the national identity was, an uncertainty that was already exploited by the national-populist right.

The Bloomberg speech made many truth claims, some quite overt, others less so, about the attributes of the *we*-group. There was little if any substance to the claims. Yet they would appear coherent and plausible to *we*-group hearers:

I know that the United Kingdom is sometimes seen as an argumentative and rather strong-minded member of the family of European nations. And it's true that *our* geography has shaped *our* psychology. *We* have the character of an island nation – independent, forthright, passionate in defence of *our* sovereignty. *We* can no more change this British sensibility than *we* can drain the English Channel. And because of this sensibility, *we* come to the European Union with a frame of mind that is more practical than emotional. For *us* the European Union is a means to an end – prosperity, stability, the anchor of freedom and democracy both within Europe and beyond her shores – not an end in itself. *We* insistently ask: How? Why? To what end? [my emphasis]

What claims exactly were Cameron's words making about the UK? According to him, the United Kingdom, treated as if it were a single person, is 'argumentative and rather strong-minded' in the perception of other European nations,

---

[23] The Bloomberg speech was drafted by Edward Llewellyn, the Downing Street Chief of Staff, with contributions from other aides. The text of the speech is available at www.gov.uk/government/speeches/eu-speech-at-bloomberg. See also www.youtube.com/watch?v=ApcgQDKqXmE.
[24] Cf. Todd (2015).   [25] Anderson (2006), Ashcroft and Bevir (2021).

apparently intending these attributes as virtues and exclusively British. Other Europeans might have said stubborn and unreasonable. In the same sentence he implicitly asserts that the UK is 'a member of the family of European nations', not mentioning the EU itself but only a collection of 'nations'. A lot of ideological claims can be packed into such sentences.

Further, Cameron produces the claim – that 'our psychology' is caused by living on an island, 'our geography'. The supposed effect of this supposed cause is that 'we have the character of an island nation'.[26] Cameron builds up the idea that what is really a political decision (whether or not to be a fully participating member of the EU) is a wholly natural and unavoidable consequence of living on an island. It is the insularity of the Eurosceptic pro-Brexit mindset that Cameron is pandering to, dressing it up as scientific fact. But he is also of course conjuring up an entrenched British myth, with all its Churchillian echoes. Another reason the 'island' idea worked for Brexit supporters is that its use activates the cognitive CONTAINER schema. It is effective because its structure derives from the physical experience of bounded spaces that cut off their contents from their surroundings. Boundaries and the distinction between inside and outside are central to the Eurosceptic nationalist mindset. As for the supposed attributes of British island-dwellers, Cameron trots out the notion that 'we' are somehow uniquely endowed with independent-mindedness, forthrightness and a passion for defending 'our' sovereignty. The culminating item in the list of exceptional attributes is the supposed practicality of the British – spelled out by Cameron's entirely instrumental view of Europe as 'a means to an end – not an end in itself'. In context, this amounts to a refusal to cooperate with the European project, and in particular with any idea of the pooling of sovereignty.

The Bloomberg speech was somewhat conflicted. While Cameron wanted to Remain in the EU on some terms, in order to neutralise the Eurosceptics he had to foreground national identity and national sovereignty. So he had to lay claim to being in some sense 'European'. He did so by directly and indirectly asserting Britain's historical, but long past status as a 'great power' in Europe, not omitting to simultaneously evoke Britain's role as an imperial global power:

But all this doesn't make *us* somehow un-European. The fact is that *ours* is not just an island story – it is also a continental story. For all *our* connections with the rest of the world – of which *we* are rightly proud – *we* have always been a European power – and *we* always will be.

There follows a selective summary of Britain's historical role in Europe:

From Caesar's legions to the Napoleonic Wars. From the Reformation, the Enlightenment and the Industrial Revolution to the defeat of Nazism. *We* have helped

---

[26] Cf. Wodak (2016).

to write European history, and Europe has helped write *ours*. Over the years, Britain has made her own, unique contribution to Europe. *We* have provided a haven to those fleeing tyranny and persecution. And in Europe's darkest hour, we helped keep the flame of liberty alight. Across the continent, in silent cemeteries, lie the hundreds of thousands of British servicemen who gave their lives for Europe's freedom. In more recent decades, *we* have played *our* part in tearing down the Iron Curtain and championing the entry into the EU of those countries that lost so many years to Communism.

The exclusionary use of the pronouns is important here – they distance 'us' from Europe. Not only that, but they omit an important part of the historical facts about the EU – that in the aftermath of World War II, the purpose of the forerunners of the EU was to leave behind Europe's war-torn past.

The frequent activation of the CONTAINER schema to evoke inclusion and exclusion, boundedness and difference does not mean that reversal and denial of that schema are not also deployed. It was used, for instance, to underpin a claim that was to become a staple of Brexit discourse – that is the claim to global outward-looking openness. Cameron says of British history:

[...] contained in this history is the crucial point about Britain, *our* national character, *our* attitude to Europe. Britain is characterised not just by its independence but, above all, by its openness. *We* have always been a country that reaches out. That turns its face to the world. That leads the charge in the fight for free trade and against protectionism.

Thus 'openness' is made into an attribute of the British *we*. In practice, however, the hardline Brexit view excluded the EU, making Britain's global openness another kind of ideological container. There is a fundamental cognitive dissonance in Brexit discourse that was to manifest itself in its post-Brexit legacy.

After the long section about the supposed British 'character', which insistently uses the exclusionary *we*, there is a slight shift in the use of *we* towards an inclusive interpretation. Why is this? Cameron starts off his new section making a demand directed at the EU. Addressing his invited audience, which included representatives from EU member states, as well as Conservative MEP Daniel Hannan, one of the founders of the Vote Leave campaign organisation:

So I want to speak to you today with urgency and frankness about the European Union and how it must change [...].

This constitutes what linguistic discourse analysts call a 'face-threatening act'. In verbal exchanges, speakers frequently mitigate their utterance to 'save the face of' the other person. In this instance, Cameron uses, among other devices, an inclusive *we*. In its context this has to be understood as referring not only to the UK but to all members of the EU. The switch to inclusive *we* is partial. Sometimes it is inclusive, sometimes it refers exclusively to the UK, sometimes it is ambiguous:

There are always voices saying 'don't ask the difficult questions'. But it's essential for Europe – and for Britain – that *we* do because there are 3 major challenges confronting *us* today.
First, the problems in the Eurozone are driving fundamental change in Europe. Second, there is a crisis of European competitiveness. And third, there is a gap between the EU and its citizens [...] And which represents a lack of democratic accountability and consent that is – yes – felt particularly acutely in Britain. If *we* don't address these challenges, the danger is that Europe will fail and the British people will drift towards the exit.
I do not want that to happen. I want the European Union to be a success. And I want a relationship between Britain and the EU that keeps *us* in it.
That is why I am here today: To acknowledge the nature of the challenges *we* face. To set out how I believe the European Union should respond to them. And to explain what I want to achieve for Britain and its place within the European Union.
Let me start with the nature of the challenges *we* face.

The inclusive understanding is signalled indirectly via surrounding context. It is particularly clear when he uses the form *we all/us all*, as he does a little later in his outlining of the changes he wants. In the passage quoted above, the context suggests a *we* that includes Britain and the EU, though there is some possible ambiguity, since the *we* and the *us* here follow 'and for Britain'. When he moves on to say 'if *we* don't address these challenges', the ambiguity is still present – committed Eurosceptics might prefer the exclusive reading that refers only to Britain, while his pro-EU hearers might interpret the *we* as including the EU. It could also be referring to members of the audience. The linguistic context of Cameron's next use of *we* ('keep *us* in') can only be understood as exclusively referring to Britain. However, the following two occurrences of *we* ('... challenges *we* face') have the potential to be understood as inclusive of both parties.

Once Cameron has laid out his 'challenges' or criticisms of the EU, followed by an equally face-threatening 'vision' for it, he moves on to what they 'mean for Britain'. There is a new rhetorical turn at this point in the speech, one which enacts the most risk-laden political speech act for Cameron and for the country. Cameron's strategy, at least at this juncture, was to demand extreme fundamental changes to the European Treaty, which he apparently believed he could obtain, and then put this 'new settlement' to the British electorate in a referendum. Apparently in the belief that it would quieten his domestic critics, he made a statement about a referendum that was more like a threat than an announcement.

He prepares the way oratorically by rehearsing key themes advanced by his backbench Eurosceptics. His rhetorical list includes the 'public disillusionment with the EU', not knowing 'what the point of it all is', wanting simply the 'common market', disliking the European Court of Human Rights, and 'heading for a level of political integration that is far outside Britain's comfort zone'. The implicit claim is that these complaints come from 'the British people', a phrase repeated again and again in Brexit discourse. The list continues, making 'the (British) people' the actors in a string of sentences:

> *They* see Treaty after Treaty changing the balance between Member States and the EU. And note *they* were never given a say. *They*'ve had referendums promised – but not delivered. *They* see what has happened to the Euro. And *they* note that many of our political and business leaders urged Britain to join at the time. And *they* haven't noticed many expressions of contrition. And *they* look at the steps the Eurozone is taking and wonder what deeper integration for the Eurozone will mean for a country which is not going to join the Euro.

From this supposed evidence, Cameron drew a supposed conclusion, presumably believing that his words would help silence his political opponents: 'The result is that democratic consent for the EU in Britain is now wafer thin.' This kind of statement, however, was more likely to encourage Brexiters inside and outside the Conservative Party, and to ensure that such issues became live in the public media. In fact, neither the EU nor a referendum had been in the forefront of public debate in the preceding years. It was not the case that the general public, 'the British people', had come together to formulate the specific criticisms of the EU that Cameron develops in this speech.[27] Nonetheless, the speech put into circulation the perception that Cameron had called for a referendum in response to demand by the 'British people' as a whole.

Farage: British *We*

Two months after Cameron's Bloomberg oration, Farage gave the leader's speech at UKIP's spring conference speech (23 March 2013).[28] A look at Farage's speeches of this period demonstrates the extent to which Cameron had come into line. It is not that Cameron was influencing Farage. Rather, it was the reverse: Farage and UKIP had already been exerting political pressure on Cameron's discourse. Although there are verbal similarities in this respect, the rhetorical functions of *we* were slightly different in the two speeches. The differences have to do with the different types of speech context and the different party situations of the two leaders. Nonetheless, as far as political conceptions and policies are concerned, it is easy to see the convergences.

---

[27] In January 2013, the Economist/IPSOS Mori Issues Index showed the top three issues of concern in the UK were the economy (52 per cent), unemployment (29 per cent), race relations/immigration (22 per cent). The EU did not figure. www.ipsos.com/ipsos-mori/en-uk/economistipsos-mori-january-2013-issues-index.

[28] Cf. Crines and Heppell (2017).

But we should keep in mind that both leaders were engaged in staking claims to ownership of the ideological ground.

While Cameron's Bloomberg event was planned as a high-profile national and international event, with a varied audience both present and virtual, Farage's gathering was a party conference attended by the party faithful. But it was also intended to be heard by the three mainstream British parties and above all by the Conservative Party, as Farage makes abundantly clear. His use of *we* is crucial. Almost all of its occurrences have to be understood as referring to the addressed audience in the hall, as well as to absent members of UKIP. There are few occurrences of a national *we* in this particular Farage speech. When they do occur, they are often ambiguous between a national reference and a party reference. There is throughout a *we–they* antithesis, where *they* is overtly linked to what Farage calls the 'Lib Lab Con' mainstream, the allegedly corrupt, 'careerist', socially and culturally biased liberal-minded 'elite'. This pattern seems to reflect the circumstantial goals of a somewhat marginalised but expanding populist party. There is another notable characteristic, one that is often central in populist verbal performance. All political orators want to interact with their audiences in a way that generates applause and signals of approval. This type of interaction works with 'clap traps' – linguistic features such as contrasts, groups of three and the use of *we*, integrated with paralinguistic features such as rhythmic desk-slapping, hand and arm gestures, voice volume and pitch contour.[29]

In this March 2013 speech, for example, Farage opens with 'Let's hear the Eastleigh roar!', with its colloquial inclusive *we* (in 'let's'). This was an allusion to UKIP outstripping the Conservative vote in the Eastleigh by-election of the preceding year. The *us* in 'let's', referring to the UKIP audience is repeated in sentences that claim political distinctiveness, especially in connection with UKIP's anti-immigration stance and nationalism. Farage claims '*we* are the party that are putting forward positive alternative policies that would make this country a better and prouder place'. In the following, there is a strategic sliding between UKIP *we* and national *we*:

And *our* message is simple. *We* are not against anybody. *We* wish people of all of those former communist countries the very best. But it cannot make sense for *us* to open *our* doors to massive oversupply in the unskilled labour market in this country at a time when *we* have a million young people out of work. That doesn't make sense [applause].

In this extract 'our message' would naturally be understood by hearers as being a UKIP *we*. The second *we* ('we are not against ...') and the third ('we wish ...') are conceivably ambiguous between a party-member *we* and a national *we* – which would suit UKIP's claims. But the 'us' in 'it cannot

---

[29] Atkinson (1984), Heritage and Greatbach (1986), Bull (2003, 2006).

make sense for us' has to be processed, in the context, as indexing the national collective *we*. Among other similar instances of referential blurring between the party *we* and the national *we*, the instances in the following passage were the most politically resonant:

we've made the argument for years, and now it's a mainstream argument, that *we* want an amicable divorce from the political European Union and its replacement with a genuine free trade agreement, which is what *we* thought *we*'d signed up for in the first place.[30]

As the sentence proceeds, it moves from a clear UKIP *we* to a *we* that could index either UKIP or the nation or both. Cameron, in his 2013 Bloomberg speech, was not asking for a 'divorce', but he was making the same point about signing up solely to a free trade arrangement.

By the time of UKIP's autumn conference (19 September 2013), with the May 2014 European Parliament elections coming into view, Farage was promoting the party with increased vigour. His pronouncements about national identity became louder. This was part of a thread of discourse that Cameron's Bloomberg speech had reinforced. At the same time Eurosceptics were emboldened to step up the volume.[31] One was the MP Bill Cash, leader of the opponents of the Maastricht Treaty (the so-called 'Maastricht rebels'). Another was Gordon Henderson, an admirer of Farage who had threatened to defect to UKIP. They echoed Cameron's national myth-making, but they were turning it against him in his stance on the EU.

UKIP had become a threatening force for the Conservatives. But emergent political parties have to establish an identity by rhetorically constructing one within the current political structure. They can do this by establishing an inclusive *we* differentiated from a *they*, that is, the rival parties.[32] When the UKIP conference came along, on 19 September 2013, Farage was still riding high on the by-election gains at Eastleigh in February 2013, as well as some increases at the South Shields by-election of May 2013, both of which had followed gains in the Rotherham and Middlesbrough by-elections at the end of the preceding year. Farage started his leader's speech in the same way as his spring conference – with a rousing inclusive *we*: 'Well, here *we* are.'[33] The remainder of the speech is put together in the same way as the March speech and other speeches. It does not consist of clearly signalled sections and topics, nor does it include patterns of argument. Rather, it consists of bursts of

---

[30] Extracts from Farage's 2013 spring conference speech: my transcripts from Farage (2013a), www.youtube.com/watch?v=bAR0bOdY1mU.
[31] As noted by Cap (2019), pp. 70–2. [32] Cf. Pelinka (2018), pp. 624–5.
[33] For a transcript of Farage's 19 September 2013 speech at the UKIP autumn conference, see Farage (2013b), UKPOL Political Speech Archive, www.ukpol.co.uk/nigel-farage-2013-speech-to-ukip-conference/

interaction with the audience, rapid concept and emotion triggers, generally in the form of slogans. There are three related fixations – the identity of UKIP, the national identity of the UK, and immigration. While numerous policy issues are mentioned, most effort appears to go into fusing anti-immigration sentiment and anti-EU sentiment, both of which involve appeal to a collective national *we* identity. As Hawkins and colleagues observe: 'Unlike traditional ideologies or issue positions that are consciously developed and communicated in a few words, populist ideas tend to be latent and diffuse within a given text.'[34]

This is the technique by means of which Farage picks up on the British history thread that had been a prominent element of Cameron's Bloomberg speech. When he turns to the question of British historical identity, his first move is to engage his hearers in a claim about UKIP's identity:

So who are *we*? Who is the typical UKIP voter? I'll tell you something about the typical UKIP voter – the typical UKIP voter doesn't exist. When I look at the audiences in those theatres there is a range of British society from all parts of the spectrum.

He goes on to answer his own question with a list of attributes. There are positive personality traits attributed to party adherents, such as being 'free' and 'open' in debating topics such as immigration. And there are negative traits ascribed to the various others who are despised, such as alleged evasiveness and dishonesty. The notion of 'openness', also used by Cameron in his speech, is now grafted on to the national *we*. Farage summons up a British identity portrayed by opposition to ('outside of') the EU and rooted in a mythologised past. There are several lexical similarities to Cameron's speech:

We will always act in the interests of Britain. Especially on immigration, employment, energy supply and fisheries. [...] That's *us*. Optimistic. Open to the world. The opposite of insular. Out there trading [...] Not hemmed in by the European Union – but open to the Commonwealth. [...] *Our* real friends in the Commonwealth. Because the fact is *we* just don't belong in the European Union. Britain is different. *Our* geography puts *us* apart. *Our* history puts *us* apart. *Our* institutions produced by that history put *us* apart. *We* think differently. *We* behave differently.

In this extract, the *we* initially refers to UKIP, but it then merges with a national *we* in 'that's *us*'. And the *we/us* is associated contextually with the CONTAINER schema. The latter is triggered insistently, in a claim that focuses on Britain's supposedly exceptional 'openness'. This supposed national character trait is opposed to the EU by evoking notions of EU constraints upon, and limitation of, the UK: '[*we*] are hemmed in by the European Union'. The collective emotion among those present may be connected with patriotic affect as well as the immediate group affect. In the following section of the speech, several topics are interwoven as before.

[34] Hawkins et al. (2019), p. 3.

In common with other Eurosceptics and Brexiters, Farage insists on the superiority of British Common Law and contraposes it, in oversimplified terms, to the civil law systems derived from the Roman legal code. Freedom of speech, too, is presented as exceptionally English:

> The roots go back seven, eight, nine hundred years with the Common Law. Civil rights. Habeas corpus. The presumption of innocence. The right to a trial by jury. On the continent – confession is the mother of all evidence.

Farage then inserts a vivid narration of the case of Andrew Symeou, a British national who was falsely accused and extradited in 2009 to Greece, where he was seriously mistreated while awaiting trial. He had been detained under the European Arrest Warrant (EAW). Notwithstanding the drift of Farage's speech, it was the Greek court that acquitted Symeou and after widespread criticism, the application of the EAW has undergone numerous revisions. In 2014 Farage publicly clashed over the case with deputy prime minister Clegg, who rebutted his claims.[35] But Farage's aim in his speech is to contrast the EU with 'us'. His clear implication is that the British are uniquely concerned about freedom, free speech and justice:

> The European Arrest Warrant is an abomination to those of *us* who care about freedom and justice. And in some sense it was ever thus. The idea of free speech was a reality in England when Europe was run by princes with tyrannical powers. Throughout Europe, England was known as the land of liberty. Here you had the possibility of dissent. Of free thinking. Independent minds and actions. That's *us*. UKIP belongs in the mainstream of British political life throughout the centuries.

This second repetition of 'that's *us*' can be interpreted by hearers in two ways: as referring to UKIP members, or as an inclusive national *we*. Or perhaps both at the same time. It is another example of Farage's merging of the party *we* and national *we*. The initial mental response may be to identify '*us*' with UKIP, as that reference has been primed by the preceding uses, but as the sentence unfolds the referent 'England' is prompted. The mind is processing rapidly and beneath conscious reflection, and that is why such cognitive mergers are likely to be effective in such an audience.

Though different in its details, Farage's speech sustains Cameron's historical narrative of national identity. Farage simply prompts well-known and simplistic historical frames, verbally entwining these with disparaging attacks on continental tradition, again in relation to law. He warns:

> Their [the Europeans'] refusal to listen to the people will lead to the very extreme nationalisms the project [the EU] was supposed to stop.

---

[35] The *Independent* online, 27 March 2014. www.independent.co.uk/voices/comment/nick-clegg-farage-has-modern-justice-and-my-position-on-andrew-symeou-all-wrong-9219343.html.

Farage: British *We* 59

In fact, it was UKIP's obsessive invocation of 'the people' that was fundamentally bound up with nationalism. Furthermore, he claims:

We are the true Europeans. *We* want to live and work and breathe and trade in a Europe of democratic nations.

These words contain, by implication, the nonsensical but rhetorically effective idea that continental Europeans are not 'true Europeans'. There is a half-hidden hint that European nations are not democratic. Unsurprisingly, this is immediately followed by a diatribe against laws, directives and regulations that 'come from Brussels' – not mentioning that democratically elected representatives of the UK participated in formulating those provisions. This is followed by more historical narrative, centred yet again around the legal system:

We have given up *our* concept of civil rights. Magna Carta, 800th anniversary the year after next, at the general election. Habeas corpus. Rights of inheritance. And not just for the aristocracy, as time went by. *Our* civil rights grew and kept pace with the times and expanded through the Common Law into the modern world – Europe has supplanted it with their Human Rights charter.[36] [...] How did they do that to *us*?

The national *we* is in large part defined in populist discourse by *opposition to* – not merely by *difference from*, as in Cameron's speech – some alien other, pointed to by the pronoun 'they'. Thus *our* civil rights are opposed to *their* Human Rights charter, without evidence or argument.

There are interesting similarities between Cameron's Bloomberg *we* and the way *we* is used by Farage, allowing for the differences in setting and purpose. Cameron's Bloomberg speech was not delivered at a party conference, and his *we* primarily focuses on the nation and the EU. Like the leaders of other parties and organisations, he used a UKIP *we* to rouse solidarity. Although the Conservative Party already had a nationalist streak that could be activated to varying degrees, Farage's UKIP and nationalist *we* seems to be rhetorically more explicit and focused. In Farage's and UKIP's discourse generally, there is an overtly ethnocentric *we* – indeed a racist *we*, particularly in the context of immigration. This same use does not appear in Conservative discourse. The main point to make is that Cameron's speech, allowing for differences in setting, did come much closer to UKIP's national-populist discourse. In some minds it would have legitimised and normalised it.

The meaning of *we* in a real political situation depends not only on the local context but on the historical conjuncture, domestic and international. How a political actor uses *we* has to reflect the way prevailing political forces are

---

[36] It's not clear whether Farage is targeting the 1953 European Convention on Human Rights adopted by the Council of Europe or the EU's Charter of Fundamental Rights of the European Union of 2000.

aligned, what the contesting discourses are, what their past evolution has been. Whatever political group the *we* pronoun points to, and whoever the individual speaker, it has the potential to generate the sentiment of solidarity. The Norwich poster was a product of the rise of national-populist discourse. It used a nationalist *we*, but in that instance failed to impress the local inhabitants who read it. One of its main targets was people who spoke languages other than English. The English prejudice against 'foreign' languages was already as deep-seated as the prejudice against 'foreigners'. Aggressive forms of national monolingualism were closely bound up with the ubiquitous national *we* that had been injected into public discourse by national populists. In particular, the circulation of a nationalist *we* came about through its combative use by UKIP and extreme pro-Brexit factions inside the Conservative Party. David Cameron's misguided attempt to outflank them merely ratcheted up the anti-EU rhetoric. This meant that he had in effect come into line with the extremists in his own party as well as in Farage's. But this shift, intended or not, had wider implications. The national *we* in Brexit discourse went along with a characteristic collection of vocabulary items and their associated ideas about national identity. The most significant of these words and phrases in national-populist discourse is *the people*. The next chapter probes its origins and the ways in which it was deployed in Brexitspeak.

3 The People

'We the people still think that we are a great country', said Nigel Farage at the launch of his new Brexit Party (12 April 2019).[1] The close connection between Brexit and national populism could not be clearer. The aim of the present chapter is to examine the idea of 'the people', and how it has embedded itself in political discourse over the course of centuries. This is a long stretch of history that is not just English or British but European. Since the concern in this book is the language of Brexit ideology in the second decade of the twenty-first century, the focus is on certain key words in the speech and writing of pro-Brexit demagogues. The meaning of the phrase *the people* is rooted in its British historical context. Its other equivalents in other European languages are also part and parcel of national histories – think of *das Volk* and *le peuple*. Much has been written about *the people* by historians and political scientists.[2] And it is not the phrase alone that is important but also the company that it keeps. The collocates that stand out are: *sovereign people* and *sovereignty of the people*, *the common people*, *ordinary people*. The phrase *the will of the people* was the Brexiters' most powerful mantra. These words and phrases, long embedded in European political thought, do not stand still. Their precise meanings change over time, from context to context. These meanings are what the philosopher W. B. Gallie called 'essentially contested concepts'.[3] Whether or not the words and their associated concepts are *essentially* contestable, they are certainly contested. And they were certainly manipulated by national-populist Brexiters in producing and promoting their ideology.

---

[1] Video, www.theguardian.com/politics/video/2019/apr/12/no-more-mr-nice-guy-nigel-farage-launches-brexit-party-video.
[2] E.g. Canovan (1981, 1999, 2005), Mudde (2004, 2007), Albertazzi and McDonnell (2008), Pelinka (2013), Mudde and Kaltwasser (2014, 2017), Müller (2016), Weale (2018), Urbinati (2019).
[3] Gallie (1964).

The People, Ancient and Modern

Even though our concern is primarily with political discourse in modern English, ideas about Greek and Roman political institutions cannot be ignored, because they have been more or less continuous, and continuously modified up to the present day. Plato's *Republic* (*Polīteíā*) was translated into Latin in Italy in the fifteenth century, possibly having been translated in some form into Arabic centuries earlier, but not directly from the Greek into English until the eighteenth century. Aristotle's works, possibly including *The Politics* (*Politiká*), were extensively translated into Arabic in the eighth to the tenth centuries, and thence into Latin in the twelfth and thirteenth centuries, with translations into western European languages. In the European Renaissance and early modern period there was a major phase of translation and retranslation into the vernacular languages of Europe, with the new printing technology disseminating them on a Europe-wide scale. The point is that the ideas contained in these texts were actively circulated and discussed among Latin-speaking scholars, laying a lexical and conceptual foundation which has continued to be used in attempts by political communities to think about political institutions and processes.

The various fluctuating meanings of *the people* that can be observed in English and other modern languages are not just accidental or stipulated by some divine dictionary maker. They arise from the development of concepts that have been part of political developments over historical time. There were certain periods and contexts in which 'the people' was a concept that served significant political purposes – for example, the contexts of fifth-century BCE Athens and, more impactfully, the Roman Republic and Empire. As is well known, the Athenian *demos*, which ruled collectively for a time, excluded women, slaves and foreigners. The Greek discourse gave us a word and a concept on which millennia of intellectual discourse, popular discourse and physical political struggle have drawn, sometimes directly but more usually indirectly, by way of translation and interpretation, and by way of summary and selection.

In Athens, the Greek term *demos* was used both to refer to the polity as a whole and to inhabitants who were seen as socially less exalted, depending on context, though in *The Politics*, Aristotle explicitly states that the *demos* is constituted by the poor. The two possible meanings were important for the Roman term *populus*. The *populus* could be used to refer to the entire political community, or only to the lower-status section of the population. One meaning is holistic and vague (the meaning in *senatus populusque romanus*), a meaning that could, depending on its context of use, and its user, refer to all social levels of the population. This is a political meaning that legitimises the reach of the state and government. The other meaning refers to the plebeian level of the population, excluding the patricians, and is sociological rather than political, since it concerns status and hierarchy. As was the case for the Athenian *demos*, the Roman *populus* consisted only of the adult male population who were not slaves or foreigners. The Athenian *demos* was also generally distinguished from the *ochlos* – usually translated into English by the word *mob*, which has its own culture- and context-specific meanings. In ancient Greek thinking, the *demos*, when led astray by a demagogue, could easily be turned from democracy to ochlocracy (frequently translated as 'rule by the mob'), a term first introduced by Polybius (c.200–c.118 BCE) in his work *The Histories*. A similar fear that democracy could be perverted in this way haunted the political theorists of the seventeenth and eighteenth centuries. It is not unreasonable to see the same kind of pattern in the tendency of modern democracies to be undermined by a populist.

In the Roman state, there existed a different, though overlapping, set of words that were to remain influential in the European tradition. These included *populus*, *patricii* (patricians), *plebs* (plebeians) and *vulgus*. The *plebs* (a singular mass noun) was a recognised 'order' of the Roman state, very diverse in itself, but distinct from the patrician order, and historians sometimes refer to the *plebs* with the roughly equivalent English word *commoners*. There were periodic conflicts between the two orders, but the senate and the patricians were adept at satisfying and appeasing the plebeians (bread and circuses). Roman plebeians eventually gained the right to stand for political office, and from early in the Republic they also had their own Plebeian Council, which held plebiscites on its own policy proposals. The term *vulgus* was not understood in relation to a legal or constitutional frame, but was used to refer to low-status individuals, and often implied a low level of education, culture, rationality and self-control. It carried a negative moral evaluation as well. Whereas *patricians* and *plebs* were used to refer to social sectors perceived as relatively determinate and stable, the meaning of *vulgus* involved a conceptual frame that included the idea of instability, as well as being potentially dangerous, physically, socially and politically. Like Greek *ochlos*, *vulgus* is translatable as *mob*. Because of these interconnected meaning elements, *vulgus* was one of those words that could by its very use trigger a fear response. It was the *mobile vulgus*, the fickle (literally 'movable') mob, and this was indeed the expression from which the English word *mob* and its attendant concepts were derived in the late seventeenth century. Even before that, the concept of the threatening untrustworthy mob, as seen by the upper orders, was active in English and metaphorically represented as the beast with many heads (from a much-cited phrase from Horace, *belua multorum capitum*).

The classical Greek and Roman framework for thinking about political regimes and constitutions had a lasting effect on European thought. In today's political discourse many discussions and arguments cluster around vocabulary derived from the Greek *demos* – *democracy, demagogy* (*demagoguery*). The Roman analogue of *demos*, namely *populus*, has survived into modern languages in various forms within various conceptual frames. The politically significant English derivatives include *populace*, (*the*) *people*, and *populism*. The Roman term *vulgus* has not survived, except in the words 'vulgar' and 'vulgarity'. But the Greek word *ochlos*, and more especially Polybius's term *ochlocracy*, have survived among Western thinkers of the modern period. Two other Greek political terms remain important elements of political discourse and discourse about politics. One is the term *oligarchy* (and *oligarch*), that is rule by a group of a few powerful and wealth-seeking individuals. The other is *xenoi*, meaning, as in the English word *xenophobia*, 'foreigners', 'strange people' and people who were not citizens. The word *xenoi* could also mean, depending on context, 'wanderers' or 'refugees'.

Polybius had a cyclical theory of constitutional types and constitutional change, a theory broadly built on the classifications of Plato and Aristotle. According to Polybius, the evidence of Greek and Roman history demonstrated that in the primitive state of nature the 'herd' would be led by a strong leader, for which his term is 'despot'.[4] But once social life had developed, he argued, various forms of political order, good and bad, emerged. The first was *kingship*, which was likely to degenerate into *tyranny*. When resistance emerged, 'and as soon as the people got leaders',[5] tyranny would be replaced by *aristocracy*. These leaders would at first act responsibly, according to Polybius, but later would become morally and financially corrupt, causing aristocracy to degenerate into *oligarchy*. When the populace come to resist the injustices of oligarchs, *democracy* emerges. In turn, democracy degenerates into *ochlocracy*. Polybius further says that the aristocrats who replace kings like to represent themselves as royalty, the oligarchs like to pose as aristocracy, and the leaders of ochlocracy initially adopt the guise of democrats. At this point, according to Polybius, the cycle may begin again, leading again to powerful single leaders.

What is most relevant to us is the way Polybius characterises the decline of democracy into ochlocracy. One translation goes thus: '[democracy] by its violence and contempt of law becomes sheer mob-rule'.[6] The meaning of the original word has various senses – another translation translates it as 'license' in the sense of abuse of freedom or disregard of law and decency.[7] The original word was *hubris* (ὕβρις), which was associated with dangerous overconfidence or arrogance, as in the anglicisation 'hubris'. There are some rather familiar-sounding characteristics of declining democracy noted by Polybius. One is 'paranomia' (παρανομία), translatable as 'lawlessness', or more

---

[4] I refer to two English translations of Polybius: *The Histories* ([1889] 2020), translated by E. S. Shuckburgh, and *The Histories* ([1922] 2010), translated by W. R. Paton.
[5] Polybius ([1889] 2020).   [6] Polybius ([1898] 2020) VI (4).   [7] Polybius ([1922] 2010).

relevantly 'contempt for the law and for norms'. Others include a weakening sense of equality and freedom, alongside the presence of individuals, especially the rich, regarding themselves as superior to other citizens, and 'enticing and corrupting the common people in every possible way'.[8] Given the complexity of today's societies, one would not expect Polybius's account to correspond neatly to phases of political change, but his regime typology and his ideas on the symptoms of regime change strike a chord. In today's world, oligarchs undermine democracy, by way of political donations, by lobbying, and by manipulation of the media.[9] In parallel, populists rouse the populace and undermine representative democracy, putting it on the path to one-man rule. Overweening hubris characterises the exploitation of seemingly democratic processes in gaining and maintaining power. Examples are not just strong-man leaders such as Hungary's Viktor Orbán, but even the post-Brexit Conservative governments of the UK. These are also examples, in varying degrees, of paranomia – the disregard for, and the subversion of the law and the judiciary. As for the degeneration of democracy into ochlocracy, such a process can be perceived in the propaganda of the Brexit leaders.[10] Demagogic actors have been backed by wealthy oligarchs, both groups opposing representative democracy. Their rhetoric has incited 'the people', irrational, misinformed and in some cases under-educated, to turn against 'experts', 'the establishment', 'the elite' and 'immigrants'.

I have attempted to tease out some of the conceptual patterns involved in the meanings of these words because they have not gone away. Like all words, their core meaning potential is subject to modification through time. But these Greek and Latin words have provided a means whereby humans in Europe were able to think about, argue about, and apply in practice a set of social and political concepts that changes sometimes slowly, sometimes suddenly, at historic moments.

The Renaissance period and early modern Europe saw the intensification of discourse among scholars and some of the nobility about 'the people', specifically in relation to the emergence of democracy. The revolutionary episodes of the eighteenth, nineteenth and twentieth centuries saw further discursive developments of conceptual frames linked with the phrase 'the people' and its various analogues in the other languages of Europe. Particularly important is the shift from the concept of a constructed civic people, inherited from the Roman concept of *populus*, to the Romantic movement's notion of 'the people', expressed in the German word *Volk* and its adjective *völkisch*.[11] In explicit political discourse and in tacit background understandings, Europeans of the modern period were left with two frames, where concepts and feelings

---

[8] Polybius ([1889] 2020). [9] Geoghegan (2020). [10] Cf. Padilla Gálvez (2017).
[11] Thom (1995), and for a critical discussion Canovan (2005), pp. 49–51.

combined. On the one hand, there is the civic frame, organised around the legacy of the Roman idea of a law-based *populus*, that is centred on the city, and historically built through political will. On the other hand, there is the Romantic conceptual frame (in which feeling predominates), focusing on the soil, birthplace, belief in distant origins and the organic growth of the *Volk*. These different frames become relevant when considering what the populists mean by *the people*.

The meaning of the word *people* in the modern period has constantly changed. Its various senses and associations at different periods have been built up out of historical experiences as well as political theorising. From the political point of view, the crucial question is: to whom exactly does 'the people' refer for some particular group of speakers? The struggles of political discourse have in large part centred on the struggle to decide on, and impose, a preferred referent. Does it refer to the entire population, does it include manual labourers, does it exclude the upper echelons of a social hierarchy? In this sense, the historic debates and conflicts, from classical times to the present, have changed the meaning of the word, and are still doing so. Also, all words have typical collocates: words that are syntactically connected to other particular words, with varying degrees of probability. Certain collocates of 'the people' trip off the tongue for many English speakers and have relatively high frequency in various kinds of political discourse.

The People and Sovereignty

The meaning of the phrase *the sovereign people* cannot be considered without also looking at its abstract noun, *sovereignty*, and the collocates that have arisen and persisted in anglophone political discourse. The latter include such cases as: sovereign king (queen)/sovereignty of the king (queen), sovereign nation/sovereignty of the nation, sovereign parliament/sovereignty of parliament, and sovereign people/sovereignty of the people/popular sovereignty. These phrases appear frequently in the political lexicon of English, and they have a feel of natural predictability for speakers. All of these notions have become lexically embedded in English after periods of intense political contestation, but the cases we concentrate on in the present section are those of *sovereign people/ sovereignty of the people/popular sovereignty*, because this expression was one that was taken over in Brexitspeak.

The concept of popular sovereignty as the source of political authority has a long history in European languages: from the European Renaissance to the Enlightenment and beyond, it was developed as a 'doctrine' in the work of scholars such as Buchanan, Bodin, Suárez, Hobbes, Locke and Jean-Jacques Rousseau, as well as the thinkers who led the American Revolution and founded the United States of America. It is important to emphasise that *popular sovereignty* as a 'source' or 'ground' for the wielding of power is a theoretical idea. This is how political philosophers and theorists write about it. Some may call it an 'imaginary', a 'discourse' or even a 'myth'. *Popular sovereignty* is a legitimising principle, which, conveyed in text and talk, gives legitimacy to political authority. It has never been an actual instantiation of the direct wielding of power by 'the people'. Politics in European history has often been about making institutional arrangements that approximate to some conceptual model of popular sovereignty, in which 'the people' has a greater or lesser degree of practical involvement – the most familiar model in modern western Europe being that of representative democracy. But people of these democracies today remain haunted by attempts to actualise the sovereignty of the *Volk*, or *narod*, or *rénmín*, that have resulted in dictatorship and violence. Populism can be thought of as another attempt to exploit the meaning potential of *the people* and *sovereignty*: the central idea is to take back control from the elites and return it to the sovereign people. 'Take back control' was one of the most successful Brexit slogans because it evoked this conceptual frame as well as the idea of 'taking back control' from the EU.

The concept of *popular sovereignty* is bound up with social contract theory in the history of political ideas. Thomas Hobbes is the best-known exponent of the relation between a population and some all-powerful sovereign or assembly. According to Hobbes's theory, or vision, individuals collectively do a deal with a sovereign in which they give up their freedom in return for security, peace and prosperity. In this theory, the people consent to the sovereign's rule voluntarily, but have a right to withdraw if the absolute sovereign fails to deliver the benefits. That is the core of the argument. This right aside, Hobbes says that the sovereign cannot be removed. Freedom of speech, the law, and other functions of 'the commonwealth' – these remain under the control of the sovereign. It is this aspect that predominates. Hobbes is insistent that somehow the many are made the one:

A Multitude of men, are made One Person, when they are by one man, or one Person, Represented [. . .]. For it is the unity of the Representer, not the unity of the Represented, that maketh the Person One.[12]

There could hardly be a clearer statement of the metaphor A STATE IS A PERSON. The famous frontispiece to *Leviathan* sums it up (Figure 3.1).

But there is no graphic representation here of a contract, free choice, or free exit from it. Instead there is the nightmarish figure of an absolute sovereign who literally embodies the state, that is 'commonwealth', created by 'the will of every subject'. The sovereign's subjects are entirely contained in the leviathan

---

[12] Hobbes ([1651] 2012), Chapter XVI. Of Persons, Authors, and Things Personated.

68   The People

Figure 3.1 Frontispiece to *Leviathan*.
Source: Wikimedia Commons.
https://commons.wikimedia.org/wiki/File:Leviathan_by_Thomas_Hobbes.jpg

body politic.[13] Furthermore, all these subjects are looking inwards, so have no visible faces. Whatever Hobbes said about free contractual choice and the right to rebel, for modern readers this looks like a portent of totalitarian autocracy.

The question of who was to be sovereign – the people, or a monarch, or parliament – surfaced at moments of revolutionary crisis. Increasing talk of both parliamentary sovereignty and popular sovereignty went along with talk about, in effect, national identity. At the time of the so-called Glorious Revolution of 1688, monarchical sovereignty, the religious identity of Britain, and the legitimacy of popular supporters of the royal contenders, were closely linked. The French Revolution of 1789 is an even more obvious example within French political conflicts and culture.

In international law, 'a sovereign people' has a special sense that is part of the legal concept of the *sovereign state*, which emerged from the pan-European negotiations that led to the Peace of Westphalia (1648) and to the modern

[13] Cf. Banks (2009).

international system enshrined in UN statutes. Among the agreed principles were the inviolability of national borders and the right to non-intervention. At the most abstract level the conceptual schema of CONTAINER comes into play, with its inherent boundedness. It is reflected in the meaning of the phrase 'Westphalian sovereignty'. In this context, we may ask which sense of *people* is active in the phrase 'a sovereign people'. It is likely that its originators had the word and notion of the Roman *populus* in mind.

Historically, the concept of a sovereign parliament was first acted out, though not enacted in law, through victory of the Parliamentarian forces over the sovereign monarch in the English Civil War (1642–51). The principle of parliamentary sovereignty was most definitively introduced into English political discourse through the political settlement that ended the Glorious Revolution (1688–9). This was a largely non-violent uprising that brought about the abdication and exile of the Catholic James II. James's high-handed actions had prompted increasing resistance across Protestant England. Meanwhile in the Protestant Netherlands, there was a growing perception of a security threat if Britain became Catholic and allied itself with Catholic and absolutist France. To replace him, a group of nobles, bishops of the Church of England and other notables invited James II's Protestant Dutch nephew William III of Orange and his consort Mary, who was James's daughter, raised as an Anglican, to become joint sovereigns. It was a transitional parliament, the 'Convention Parliament', that in 1689 transferred to William and Mary the crown of England and Ireland; the Scottish equivalent, the Scottish Convention, transferred to them the crown of Scotland. In parliament, the Bill of Rights of 1689 was drawn up and passed by parliament, enshrining in constitutional law, among a number of democratic rights, the superiority of parliament in the constitution, parliament's primacy over the monarch, parliament's sole right to make all laws, and the independence of the judiciary.

In very general terms, the concept of the sovereignty of parliament (or legislature) involves a framework of governmental institutions over which it has precedence – the separate institutions of the executive and the judiciary. In practice, there is often tension between these institutions in relation to the precise extent of parliamentary sovereignty. In the UK arrangement, Parliament technically consists of the Commons, the Lords (with much reduced powers) and the Crown (with only symbolic powers). There are two important points for our present concerns. The first is that the discourse about parliamentary sovereignty implicitly excludes *the people*. Constitutionally it is understood, though not generally stated explicitly, that 'the people' does not or do not have sovereignty in any direct sense of controlling policy decisions. Rather, 'the people' is or are theoretically 'represented' in Parliament (*de facto*, the House of Commons) through elected MPs. The second point is that, as commentators and politicians themselves frequently note, the executive government (the 'cabinet' of ministers), which sits in Parliament and 'whips' the voting of its MPs, holds considerable sway over parliament.[14]

Since voting in the House of Commons is a 'first-past-the-post' system, one vote can in theory enable 'sovereign parliament' to do what it constitutionally has done since 1688: make and unmake laws on anything at all. In practice, under present arrangements, all bills are reviewed in the House of Lords, but any blocking decisions can be resisted by governments on the grounds that the Lords do not have the right. The members of this second chamber are partly hereditary and partly appointed, so arguments against their right of review can be mounted across the political spectrum. In fact, their powers have been much reduced by successive governments, though not replaced with an elected second chamber whose checking and balancing could have the legitimacy to affect outcomes of the legislative process. In the UK constitutional framework, a government still has powers enabling it to bypass the supposedly sovereign parliament. The other checks and balances of a democracy, the judiciary and the courts, can be challenged by right-leaning, populist politicians, as Boris Johnson did after coming to power in 2019. These weak points in the UK democratic structures famously led a Conservative lawyer and cabinet minister, Quintin Hogg, to describe the UK's governmental structure as an 'elective dictatorship'.[15]

Overriding of the sovereignty of parliament can be done constitutionally by an 'Order in Council', an instrument for exercising what are known as 'prerogative powers'. It is a manoeuvre that has been used only rarely and in limited circumstances. But there were two episodes that came close to it in the aftermath of the 2016 referendum. The first was an attempt by the government of Theresa May to use prerogative powers ('royal prerogative') to bypass parliament in order to initiate the process of withdrawing from the EU that is laid out in Article 50.[16] The second was an attempt by the government of Boris Johnson in the summer of 2019 to 'prorogue', that is suspend, the UK legislature, in a devious and deniable fashion which involved also seeking to undermine the authority of the judiciary.

The weak points in the UK democratic structure and processes are easily penetrated by populist attitudes and ideology. The legitimacy of parliament itself can easily be challenged in populist rhetoric, wherever that rhetoric is coming from, inside or outside of government – for parliament does not by its design represent *the people* directly. An executive with autocratic tendencies that deploys elements of populist language and tactics, like the Johnson government, may feel it acceptable to circumvent parliament. An overtly populist

---

[14] E.g. Grayling (2018), pp. 132–8.
[15] In the BBC Dimbleby Lecture of 1976, reproduced in Hogg (1976).
[16] Article 50 of the Treaty of Lisbon, signed in 2007.

The People and Sovereignty 71

party such as UKIP or the Brexit Party is likely to challenge the sovereignty, indeed the legitimacy, of parliament, along two main lines of argument. One is to present both executive and legislature as composed of 'establishment' and 'elite' members, not 'the people' itself or themselves. The other is to challenge representative democracy itself as not representing directly 'the voice of the people'.[17] After the referendum, a government whose members obviously belonged to the UK's social and educational elite presented itself none the less as servants of 'the people'.

On 5 December 2016, the *Lincolnshire Reporter* – Lincolnshire was among the highest Leave-voting areas in the UK – announced on its front page: 'Nigel Farage in Sleaford: "I believe in sovereignty of people, not MPs"'. The High Court ('enemies of the people', according to the *Daily Mail* headline of 4 November 2016) had ruled that a vote of Parliament was necessary before Article 50 could be invoked by Prime Minister Theresa May. According to the *Lincolnshire Reporter*, Farage 'said that he strongly believed that the Supreme Court should overturn the decision of the High Court, and dismissed the idea that a parliamentary vote was needed to trigger Article 50'.[18]

The debate over Article 50 and the role of parliament versus 'the people' continued for three more years. At the heart of it was whether 'democracy' meant the direct or the representative form of democracy. Equivocation over the term *democracy* is useful for populists across the continent of Europe, and is central to Brexit populism. For example, on 6 December 2018, after a vote by MPs found the Theresa May government in contempt of parliament for failing to publish the full legal advice on her EU deal, the pro-Brexit online magazine *sp!ked* headlined with 'They are all in contempt of the people'. Again, on 28 March 2019, after a minority group of MPs voted to revoke Article 50, *sp!ked* headlined: 'Parliament vs. the people', and its columnist declared, mouthing the familiar populist antitheses:

> more than a quarter of the people in this supposedly democratic chamber stood in symbolic opposition to the largest democratic act in UK history. They defied the people. They pitted themselves, arrogantly, against the public; against the very source of their political legitimacy. If this doesn't capture the gaping chasm between the political elites and the people, the huge democratic deficit of the 21st century, then I don't know what does.

The fundamental ideological opposition of representative democracy and direct democracy is implicit, not stated. To call the 2016 referendum 'the largest democratic act in UK history' only makes sense in the ideological frame that favours direct democracy – from any other standpoint it is a gross

---

[17] See also Wodak (2017).
[18] https://lincolnshirereporter.co.uk/2016/12/nigel-farage-in-sleaford-i-believe-in-sovereignty-of-people-not-mps/.

misrepresentation of the voting figures. There exists now an ideological quasi-polarisation that has come full circle from revolutionary Marxist left to meet itself on the common ground of the libertarian populist right. At both ends of the spectrum the 'elites' in parliament are seen as antithetical to 'the people' outside it. It is 'the people' not parliament that is, or should be, 'sovereign'. This is clear in the utterances of hard Brexiters. Claire Fox, for example, who over her career had swung from one end of the spectrum to the other, and who had recently joined the Brexit Party, said on BBC radio in 2019:

> [...] our own sovereignty at home, has been compromised, when parliament has decided to as it were sideline or ignore the real seat of power and that's the voters and [...] the historic turn has been that Nigel Farage happened to set up a party that gave voice to that popular democratic sovereignty that was expressed around the referendum which had been squeezed out by our own parliament.[19]

In parliament, a few weeks later, a group of MPs held aloft placards reading 'Silenced', in response to Johnson's announcement of the prorogation of parliament. *Sp!ked* responded with the headline 'the silencing of the people' and asserted that the MPs' action was an 'anti-Brexit, anti-democratic' move by the MPs to stall the government's finalisation of the Brexit process. According to *sp!ked*, these MPs were 'silencing the public voice, the very source of their democratic authority', and causing a constitutional crisis.[20]

Indeed, the UK was in a crisis about leaving the EU and in a crisis about democracy itself, a conjuncture of two crises. The point to focus on here is this surfacing of two visions of 'democracy'. Interestingly, *sp!ked* evoked the English Civil War as the last time direct democracy had openly confronted representative democracy (in the form it was then emerging). The point here is that Brexit was a historic democratic crisis, embedded in English political discourse; this was not, of course, ever brought to the surface and debated. The underlying questions were: who is to be sovereign, 'the people' or parliament, and how is the apparent opposition to be resolved?

At the same time, pro-Brexit populists argued that the EU had undermined the British principle of the sovereignty of parliament. This was because the UK accepts the supremacy of EU law in certain very specific areas freely conceded by the UK as a legally sovereign state and recognised by UK courts. Yet it seems that a government influenced by populist discourse may challenge the supposedly sovereign parliament. We refocus now on two adjectives that keep company with *the people* – expressions that were to become key to British populism and Brexitism, namely *common* and *ordinary*.

---

[19] *World at One*, 8 August 2019, interview of Claire Fox and Anna Soubry by Johnny Diamond. My transcript; omissions in square brackets.
[20] O'Neill (2019b), 'The silencing of the people'. See also, among other *sp!ked* articles, Hume (2018), O'Neill (2019a).

The Common People

The ideas triggered at various times and in various contexts by the phrase *the common people* play an important part in British politics. The adjective *common* is highly polysemous – it elicits a network of concepts that look diverse at first sight but are interconnected conceptually. The brain activates particular concepts in the network depending on which other words the word *common* is combined with and in which grammatical configurations. In socio-political contexts, the meaning of *common* may be ambiguous in problematic ways. If certain entities (including people) are frequently encountered, they are *common*; or things may be shared, as in *common* ownership; and if an object is plentiful or if everyone owns it, it is of low value.

These are not mere linguistic curiosities but have implications for political ideas and ideologies, because the way they are understood and used in the culture is embedded in continuously transmitted, contested and modified discourse. Some of the notions triggered by *the common people* have long histories but can still be activated in today's English. The term *the common people* developed its meaning in medieval Europe involving a mental frame according to which society had three vertical divisions: clergy, nobles and commoners (i.e. the common people). This model collapsed during the Reformation period, with the religious wars, the invention of printing, and intellectual exchanges across Europe. The position of, and legitimation for, *the common people* concept changed. In the ferment of ideas that developed, the notion of the dangerous *vulgus* (or the Greek equivalent *ochlos*) acquired importance, in addition to the word *populus*.

Digging a little deeper for the roots of ideas about *the people* in Europe and the British Isles, we can go back further at this point – to Hobbes's predecessor, the Scotsman George Buchanan (1506–82). Buchanan was a truly European intellectual who studied and taught in the major European universities. A multiplier of ideas and information, he resisted absolute monarchy and influenced contemporary debate around popular sovereignty and democracy – disseminating ideas that were to be politically influential a hundred years after his death. In his *De Jure Regni apud Scotos*, published in 1579, written in the form of a Socratic dialogue, Buchanan argues for popular sovereignty with his interlocutor Thomas Maitland:

B. Which of the two is most powerful. The People or the Law? *M.* I think, the whole People. *B.* Why do you think so? *M.* Because the People is as it were the Parent of the Law, certainly the Author thereof, they being able to make or abrogate it as they please. *B.* Seeing then the Law is more powerful than the King, and the People more powerful than the Law, we must see before which we may call the King to answer in Judgement.[21]

---

[21] Buchanan ([1680] 1689), p. 59.

That Buchanan stands in favour of the superior legitimising authority of 'the people' is abundantly clear throughout the dialogue. He was at one in this with younger contemporary scholars Jean Bodin and Francisco Suárez. But who, one wonders, was meant by 'the people' (*populus*)? This is where we see the conceptual frame for the monstrous 'many headed' mob (*vulgus, ochlos*) entering the dynamic play of ideas that was beginning to unfurl.

In the extract cited above, Buchanan has been explaining that 'he would have it in the People's Power, who gave him [a king] the Authority over themselves, to prescribe to him [the king] a Model of his Government, and that the King may make use of that Justice, which the People gave him over themselves'. He thinks that the king should not exercise this transferred authority by force but 'by a Common Council with the King, that should be generally established, which may generally tend to the good of all'. But his interlocutor protests in classic fashion. Buchanan's reply is also classic, but in the historical context a significant one. It centres on democracy and the concept of 'the people':

M. You will then grant this Liberty to the People? *B.* Even to the People indeed, unless perhaps you be of another mind. *M.* Nothing seems less equitable. *B.* Why so?

Maitland's explanation:

M. You know that saying, a Beast with many Heads. You know, I suppose, how great the temerity and inconstancy of a People (*populus*) is.

Buchanan's response:

B. I did never imagine that that matter ought to be granted to the judgement of the whole People in general [*universus populus*], but that near to our Custom, a select number out of all Estates may convene with the King in Council. And then how soon an overture[22] by them is made, that it be deferred to the Peoples judgment.[23]

This particular passage is relevant to us here because it shows the ongoing tension among the concepts associated with the phrase *the people*. Buchanan's position on the role of 'the people' is radical but confronts the counterargument – that of Plato and many other thinkers down to modern times – that people are not rational actors. Buchanan leaves us with an important, though still unclear, model for representative governance, representatives being 'select(ed)' (by whom?) in unspecified proportions from the three then existing estates (clergy, lords, commoners). His idea, loosely based on the classic Athenian constitution adapted to English traditional structures, seems to be that these representatives (*consulatores*, counsellors) confer with the monarch and formulate a proposal, which is

---

[22] For the translator's 'overture' Buchanan used Greek (προβούλευμα (*probouleuma*)), a resolution decided by the Athenian Council (the *boule*, βουλή) and forwarded to the Assembly of the demos, who discussed it and voted on it.

[23] Buchanan ([1680] 1689), p. 20. Spelling and capitalisation as in the 1689 reprinting.

then put to 'the People'. The implication seems to be that the unreliable 'beast' (i.e. the *vulgus*) is somehow selected out for the policy discussions 'in council' – but who constitutes 'the people' to whose judgement the council's resolutions are put? In Buchanan's 1579 original, the Latin word *populus* is used most frequently in the Roman civic sense and, rarely, to vaguely indicate the lower orders; the *vulgus* is distinct and always means the dangerous and uneducated crowd.

It is precisely this vagueness that constitutes the power of the verbal formula 'the people', which has remained the focus of the problem of democracy that modern populism brings up. From the point of view of emergent anglophone political discourse, the phrase 'the people', whatever it was taken to mean, was the source of legitimacy and power. It was not totally new in 1579, but any expression of it in print was seen as seditious, and Buchanan's book was condemned by act of Parliament in 1584. Nor was that the end of it. Buchanan was adopted by various radical and dissenting movements during the English Civil War and the next two centuries.[24] His text reflects a background of political discourse that was struggling with key political concepts. One was the exact denotation of *the people* when used to denote the legitimising part of the populace. Another was the issue of what was to be denoted by *the common people*. And a third was the question whether *the common people* was to be included in *the people*. Modern populism in many respects is a refocusing of this ongoing discourse, not only in English of course, but here we are examining the political culture in which British populism emerged and delivered Brexit.

In seventeenth-century England, the medieval political and social order was challenged by force in the English Civil War and in the emergence of anti-monarchical movements equipped with ideas of popular sovereignty. The Levellers, a political movement that met many of the criteria for what today would be called populism, articulated the principle of popular sovereignty and demanded the enfranchising of *all* of England's (male) Commoners.[25] This movement adopted the ideas of the 'Agitators',[26] a radical core within the Parliamentary army, and began a re-evaluation of the social group referred to as 'the common people', namely, all people who were not members of the order of the nobility. After the defeat of Charles I, some regiments and officers of Oliver Cromwell's New Model Army were angered by the Parliament and its dominant faction (the Presbyterians), who had refused to settle back pay and tried to disband the New Model Army. 'Agitators' (agents) were elected from their ranks to represent them. A General Council of the Army was called by senior

---

[24] Erskine (2016), pp. 289–90.   [25] Foxley (2013), p. 207.
[26] Meaning 'agent' at that period. The term was also confused with the military title of 'adjutant', whence 'adjutator' and 'agitator', a group of them being elected as representatives of Cromwell's New Model Army.

officers ('Grandees'), with Cromwell and his son-in-law Henry Ireton foremost among them. In the discussions that ensued, known as the Putney Debates, the Levellers' agents brought forward radical political proposals. These included a new constitution, near-complete male suffrage, and the vesting of sovereignty in the House of Commons, not in the Monarch or Lords. As is indicated in the title of their document, the 'Agreement of the People for a firme and present Peace, upon grounds of common right and freedome', their legitimising premise lay in the consent of some unspecified concept of 'the people' – the boundaries of that group of people were to come under decisive scrutiny during the autumn of 1647, as were other fundamental questions of representation and power. It was the demand for effective extension of *the people* by enfranchising almost all adult males that disturbed Cromwell and Ireton, while the Leveller Thomas Rainsborough authored the celebrated lines:

For really I think that the poorest hee that is in England hath a life to live, as the greatest hee; and therefore truly, Sir, I think itt clear, that every Man that is to live under a Government ought first by his own Consent to put himself under that Government; and I do think that the poorest man in England is not at all bound in a strict sense to that Government that he hath not had a voice to put Himself under.[27]

Such an idealistic scenario was regarded by Grandee Ireton as tantamount to anarchy. He and Cromwell insisted on a property qualification to ensure that voters had an interest 'in this kingdom', since otherwise there would be no grounds for refusing the vote to foreigners; simply being born in England was insufficient qualification to share in power over the country. While Rainsborough asserted that 'the foundation of all law lies in the people',[28] Cromwell's and Ireton's insistence implied a limitation on membership of 'the people'. They also argued that to do without a property or wealth qualification implied abolition of all individual property, including food and clothes, producing disorder and opening the possibility of property-less men behaving irresponsibly – Rainsborough rejected this line as being an accusation of anarchy. Grayling suggests that Ireton feared ochlocracy at a point when stability was at a premium.[29] One may suspect he also feared an uprising of the *ochlos* – that is, the mob, *mobile vulgus*, the many-headed monster. In fact, the Grandees did have reason to fear disorder among the Agitator and Leveller sections and the lower ranks of the army, who began to mutiny. Cromwell and Ireton succeeded in suppressing the mutiny, forcing a declaration of loyalty to the General Council of the Army and permanently silencing the Levellers.

Buchanan's book undermining the right of monarchs and asserting the superior right of 'the people', even to kill tyrannical monarchs, exerted considerable influence. It was in the 1680s, at the moment of the Glorious Revolution,

---

[27] Putney Debates record book 1647, Worcester College, Oxford, MS 65. Original spelling.
[28] Quoted by Grayling (2018), p. 42.   [29] Ibid. p. 47.

that popular sovereignty and the right to remove kings again came to the fore.[30] The translation of Buchanan's book into English in 1680 and 1689 was one of the ways in which English political vocabulary was developed in association with a network of political ideas under continual contention. The Roman word *populus*, with intended reference to a political, legitimising part of the population, is almost always rendered 'the people', but 'the people' is also sometimes used to translate 'vulgus'. The English context usually makes clear enough that it is not the whole civic people in the Roman sense that is meant but the uneducated and irresponsible 'people'. Out of context, there is nonetheless scope for ambivalence between the whole politically acceptable 'people' and the unacceptable remainder. As for the translator's phrase 'the common people', as a substitute for Latin *vulgus*, it looks as though it was coming to be used to refer primarily to the disapproved, uncivilised and uncivil masses. In strategic political discourse the conceptual frame of the *vulgus*, while not conflated with, was capable of overlapping with, that of the *common people*.

The fear, inherited from Plato, Aristotle and Polybius, that democracy would always be undermined by common people in the above sense continued into the eighteenth century, at the same time as Enlightenment thinkers were promoting concepts such as natural equality, natural rights, natural justice and social contract theory. In Britain, the development of a constitutional monarchy, furthered by the Bill of Rights of 1689, moved forward, as did the growing supremacy of parliament over the monarch. The doctrine of the separation of powers, introduced by Locke and developed by Montesquieu, was to provide an influential model for democratic governance. At the centre of the debate was the question of who, in a democratic system, constituted 'the people' – that is who, among the entire populace, might be entitled to vote without danger to social order and stability. Locke, whose main aim was to defend the powers of parliament, stood back from democracy, referring only to the *consent* of 'the people', without seeking to define it. Montesquieu assumed the classical view of democracy in arguing that any such form of governance was generally undermined by people lacking in political 'virtue' and resulted in disorder. His separation of the powers of the legislature, executive and judiciary was meant to provide checks and balances that would prevent the distortion of democracy.

The United States Declaration of Independence of 1776, composed by Thomas Jefferson, and edited by Congress, was not, however, a democracy in the usual modern sense of the term, since those entitled to vote were restricted to men of property – in classical terms, it was a *timocracy*, that is rule by men of worth, meaning men of property. The motivation behind this delimitation of who constituted 'the people' stemmed from the enduring legacy

---

[30] Erskine (2016).

of the classical philosophers. Jefferson's wording did not state that the powers of governments derive directly from 'the people' but (like Locke) that they derive from 'consent of the governed'.[31] Representation of 'the people' lay not in the modern system of parties and elected delegates but lay with enfranchised men of property and wealth. In *Federalist No. 10*, James Madison expressed concerns about factionalism and the possible emergence of a tyrannical majority; he favoured instead a form of representative republicanism. Madison used the term 'democracy' to refer to small-scale, face-to-face assemblies of 'the people', but was still anxious that even in such democracies 'there is nothing to check the inducements to sacrifice the weaker party or an obnoxious individual'. He added: 'democracies have ever been spectacles of turbulence and contention; have ever been found incompatible with personal security or the rights of property, and have in general been as short in their lives as they have been violent in their deaths'.[32]

Subsequently, the founding fathers of the United States followed Montesquieu in establishing a tripartite system of checks and balances – legislative, executive and judicial branches – designed to counter the risks of despotism on the one hand and degeneration into ochlocracy on the other. The Constitution of 1789, and subsequent amendments, provided for the electorate (however defined) to express opinions, which were then intended to be filtered and refined through further institutional mechanisms. These mechanisms have produced a governmental structure consisting of the directly elected House of Representatives, the Senate, and a Supreme Court, the President being elected by an Electoral College. Enfranchisement was gradually extended. The property and wealth qualifications were changed in 1856; black males received the vote in 1870, though southern states blocked their participation until 1965; women were enfranchised in 1920. Whether the US system has been entirely successful is a much-debated question. On the one hand, lack of consensus among three branches can lead to deadlock, and on the other, consensus may emerge through the dominance of a single party. Moreover, exploitation of the democratic structure can enable a populist demagogue to gain power and, as happened in January 2021, to incite 'the common people' to act as a mob – the very danger feared by the founders.

The French Revolution presented a frightening example of the dangers of democracy for those engaged in the struggles to define and establish structures based on individual freedom and rights. Rousseau had set in train the notion of 'the will of the people' and 'the general will'. Whatever he had originally intended it to mean, this notion was capable of multiple interpretations by populist leaders claiming to know or even embody the 'will of the people'. The

---

[31] Grayling (2018), pp. 78–9.
[32] *The Federalist Papers*, Federalist No. 10, pp. 52, 23 November 1787.

Revolution in effect began with the idealistic *Déclaration des droits de l'homme et du citoyen* in 1789. It proceeded with the dismantling of the *ancien régime*, culminating in the guillotining of Louis XVI in 1793. Food riots, the storming of the Bastille and insurrection produced the Committee of Public Safety and the extreme violence of the Reign of Terror under Robespierre. After the execution of Robespierre in 1795, The Directory was set up with a new constitution, a re-declaration of the rights of man and a bicameral legislature. This new structure failed, however, to contain internal divisions and public unrest, eventually leading to its collapse, to the coup of 1799, and to the establishment of Napoleon Bonaparte as head of the Consulate – bringing in a period of absolute quasi-monarchical rule. These phases of the Revolution bore a striking resemblance to Polybius's account of the replacement of monarchy by failed attempts at direct democracy, degeneration into ochlocracy, violence and a return full circle to tyranny.

The English Parliament's terrified reaction to the French Revolution had the effect of slowing down parliamentary reform. Public demonstrations in favour of parliamentary reform were put down by force – a case in point being the Peterloo massacre in Manchester in 1819. Arguments against extending the rights of *the people* could easily be bolstered by the still powerful frame of the violent and irrational *ochlos,* the *mobile vulgus*, the mob. This could also have been the case when even more extensive riots occurred in major cities in the autumn of 1831, after the House of Lords rejected the Second Reform Bill. The mental frames associated with the phrase *the common people* played an important role in the discussions and disputes leading to the Reform Act of 1832. The question was who exactly should be enfranchised. Who should be allowed to vote, or, rather, who was it *safe* to allow to vote, if you were an aristocrat, one of the landed gentry, or, say, a mill owner? The 1832 Act was the first of an ongoing series of parliamentary enactments, known together as 'representation of the people acts'. In other words, these acts defined the category 'the people' in terms of who was permitted to vote for representatives. In practical terms, the 1832 Act reformed constituency boundaries and enfranchised 'male persons' who were small landowners or tenants of specified kinds. Universal male suffrage did not come until 1918, and the vote was not fully extended to women until 1928.

All these debates were about drawing boundaries around different segments of the population, but when a politician spoke of 'the people' he or she was likely to be reflecting a much vaguer concept. During the nineteenth and twentieth centuries, political thinkers and actors applied the phrases *the people* and *the common people* in a variety of ways, some of which were conservative, others more radical. In the case of *the common people*, the association with the *mob* did not disappear, nor did the classical suspicion of democracy. Edmund Burke had contraposed *the common people* to *the people* for the same reasons the Romans distrusted the *vulgus* – the common people did not have sufficient intellectual skill or knowledge but relied on emotions that could be exploited by a demagogue. After the Reform Act it was implicit that Parliament represented the people, that is the people enfranchised by the Reform Act. This was the sense in which reformers like Lord Brougham used the term *the people*. But it was Parliament that is sovereign, not *the people*. The term *the common people*, in the old sense of the Third Estate was no longer relevant and became more and more referentially vague and value loaded.

From *the Common People* to *Ordinary People*

In the second half of the nineteenth century, Marx and the Marxists developed a model of society, based on an economic analysis, that was to have deep and lasting effects. Marx's model, like the Roman and medieval ones, is tripartite: the bourgeoisie, the proletariat and the *Lumpenproletariat*.[33] As is well known, the bourgeoisie were defined as those who owned the means of production and controlled the labour output of others. The proletariat were defined as those owning no means of production other than their physical and mental labour, which yielded surplus value that was exploited by the bourgeoisie. This left those who had no property and who did not, or could not, work – the *Lumpenproletariat*. This was the category of criminals, beggars or prostitutes, who were not politically 'conscious'. There is a resemblance between the notion of *Lumpenproletariat* and that of the Roman term *vulgus*, and the term *common people* could occasionally be used to evoke a similar notion. As for the Marxist use of *the people*, it has its own history, one that takes us to the end of the twentieth century – a history of 'people's republics' in which *the people* was, as in so many instances, a nebulous legitimising concept for an elite claiming to lead, represent or embody its nebulous referent.

In the capitalist West, *the common people* as a fixed phrase was undergoing significant changes in its use, as the processes of industrialisation and the development of mass society proceeded. The phrase changed form and intended meaning. Radical English political discourse retained *the common people* for a certain length of time, not of course in the sense of 'commoners' of earlier times, but in the sense of *working people*. It was important that this part of 'the people' made itself visible in organised crowds, that is, in demonstrations and rallies. This is not to say that the fear of the *demos* (seen as *ochlos* or *vulgus*) had gone away. In the United States, there was no aristocracy, no medieval orders of society, and thus no 'commoners' or in that sense 'common people'. There was, however, a conceptual frame 'the people of America' that

---

[33] The term 'proletariat' was taken from the Roman census system, referring to those whose only wealth was their offspring (*proles*, whence *proletarius*, 'producing offspring').

From *the Common People* to *Ordinary People* 81

was associated with the working man, industrial, commercial and agricultural – as for instance in the somewhat populist Farewell Address of President Andrew Jackson, which repeatedly refers to an idealised *the people* in opposition to financiers and speculators. The People's Party, also called the Populist Party, active in the United States from 1892 to 1909, spoke of 'the plain people'.[34] This was a left-wing agrarian populist movement that was anti-modern and nativist.

By the mid-twentieth century, a revalorising of *the common people* in the United States was actually being politically promoted. Roosevelt's vice president, Henry Wallace, famously spoke of the 'common man' and 'the common people' in 1942, in a speech on the US war effort:

Some have spoken of the 'American Century'. I say that the century on which we are entering – the century which will come into being after this war – can be and must be the century of the common man. Perhaps it will be America's opportunity to – to support the Freedom[s] and Duties by which the common man must live. Everywhere, the common man must learn to build his own industries with his own hands in practical fashion. Everywhere, the common man must learn to increase his productivity so that he and his children can eventually pay to the world community all that they have received [...] Everywhere the common people are on the march.[35]

In his use of the phrase 'the common people', Wallace makes clear that he means the common people of China, India and Russia as well as of America. The phrase 'common man' did not of course survive the social changes of the post-war era. Yet in 1948 Roosevelt's successor, Harry S. Truman, still spoke of 'the common people', declaring that a government was needed 'that will work in the interests of the common people and not in the interests of the men who have all the money'.

In Britain in the 1940s, it was still acceptable to speak of 'the common people' as George Orwell did in his essay 'The Lion and the Unicorn'. But the phrase has not survived well in political discourse. As Margaret Canovan succinctly puts it, 'In Anglophone countries the "common people" have ceased to be a distinct class and have disappeared into "ordinary people"'.[36] It was of course the concept that disappeared, not a certain segment of the population. Without a hierarchy of social orders it no longer made sense, or not completely, nor was it politically or ethically acceptable to most people. Political actors simply stopped using the phrase *the common people*, while *ordinary people* (without definite article) was taken up especially by populists. The change in adjective is integral with a whole changing social, political and discourse structure. The word *common* has multiple senses, but in social contexts its predominant sense is a disparaging one when applied by a speaker considering

---

[34] Canovan (2005), pp. 29, 38, 59.
[35] Henry A. Wallace, 8 May 1942. See Wallace (1942, 1943).   [36] Canovan (2005), p. 38.

themselves socially superior – the idiom 'common as muck' says it all. In the political context, the word *common* in the phrase *the common people* has been replaced by *ordinary*. And in populist discourse it is intended and received as an expression of approbation. It is the same with the singular noun *person*: 'an ordinary person', 'that person is completely ordinary' is acceptable.

Nigel Farage has rarely, if ever, used the phrase *the common people* or *common people*. In contemporary society, he would be perceived as hierarchical, condescending and offensive. Rather, he regularly deploys a small active set of adjectives that together cover an interesting set of meanings: *real, ordinary, decent, normal*. These are not used in the phrase *the people* (which he uses frequently as it stands), or in the phrase *the common people*, but with *people* (i.e. without determiner). Examples from his public utterances are:

[...] this will be a victory for real people, a victory for ordinary people, a victory for decent people.[37]

[...] there is a detachment between Westminster and ordinary folk.[38]

[...] Normal, decent people have been bullied out of the debate.[39]

Such examples show the need for detailed analysis of the populist lexicon. The words *real, ordinary, decent* and *normal* carry rich mental frames stored in memory – a specific memory bank built from repeated encounters with the language of Brexit. Populist rhetoric is typically inexplicit; ideological principles are not commonly spelled out in propositional form. Populists appeal to a supposed authenticity or 'genuineness' possessed by 'the people' – an idea that was present in the nineteenth-century romanticisation of *the people* (and *das Volk*, and *narod* ...) and which today implies the *in*authenticity of the remainder of the population. From Farage's phrase a hearer might draw the inference that people who did not vote for Brexit – all 48 per cent of them – are not real, not ordinary, not decent and not normal. Jan-Werner Müller suggests that Farage could be interpreted as 'questioning their status as proper members of the political community'.[40] Such hearer inferences may be intended, because they are deniable with respect to one part of the audience but affirmable with respect to supporters. Deniable meanings are a distinguishing feature of populist discourse, though they are deployed in all species of political discourse.

---

[37] From his post-referendum celebration speech, video, *The Guardian*, 24 June 2016. www.theguardian.com/politics/video/2016/jun/24/nigel-farage-eu-referendum-this-victory-for-real-people-video.

[38] From his 2019 European election campaign for his new Brexit Party, *The Guardian*, 19 May 2019. www.theguardian.com/politics/2019/may/19/nigel-farage-brexit-party-on-the-road-populism.

[39] From his speech to the UKIP conference, 19 September 2013. Transcript: www.ukpol.co.uk/nigel-farage-2013-speech-to-ukip-conference/.

[40] Müller (2016), pp. 21–2.

The word *ordinary* is probably Nigel Farage's most frequent choice as adjectival collocate for *people*, and it is found in the population at large as a replacement for *common* as a descriptor of a social type. It is found frequently in all varieties of British populist utterances. To call someone 'ordinary' does not imply the same negative valuation as calling someone 'common', though in certain contexts it can do. In modern English, an *ordinary* person is not the same as a *common* person. It is important that word meanings are linked (in the speaker's memory) with other words in networks, the links being based on conceptual connections and also exposure to repetitive discourse input. Thus, *ordinary* is linked with *common(place)*, *plain*, *regular*, and so on, and also with antonyms such as *extraordinary*, *special* and *exceptional*. There is nothing fixed in these relations in the mental lexicon; they are unpredictably tied in with contingent discourse – of which a prime instance is precisely Farage-speak collocations that associate *ordinary* with *decent* and oppose both to *elite*, *expert* and *establishment*. It is not surprising that *ordinary* and *elite* form a conceptual pair. In brief, historically *elite* (originally from Latin *eligere*, 'pick out') has to do with selection, distinctness, distinction and being 'distinguished', while *ordinary* has to do with standing among what is regular, with being 'in order' and not 'out of order'. The normative value, positive or negative, can go either way with such terms depending on the user's intention and surrounding cultural, social and political cues. Taking this a little further, it may also be that populism prefers sameness, and conformity in general.[41] More specifically, it prefers some set of 'British' values and behaviour patterns, and is hostile to those who break with what are regarded as norms. It is conceivable that populism appeals to a personality type that is emotionally uneasy with uncertainty and blurred categories. Such feelings can be contingent on economic conditions or they may be triggered verbally.

Farage's collocation, on numerous occasions, of the words *normal* and *decent* with the word *people* has another function in Brexitspeak. This is to circumscribe the concept of *(the) people* by making it the polar opposite of *elite* and related items such as *establishment*, words denoting categories that come in for particular opprobrium. The opposition itself is set up in people's minds by the contexts in which the terms occur in national-populist propaganda. In the Brexiter worldview, it is not possible for the 'elite' or 'the establishment' to be 'normal', 'decent' or 'real' – it is not, as it were, 'grammatical' in this discourse. This small network of words – *ordinary, real, decent, normal, elite, expert, establishment* – subsists in a conceptual frame that also involves quasi-moral evaluation combined with emotions of hostility and contempt. In use, there is also an implicit self-legitimation by way of a claim to the myth of an authentic, 'real' people, *the* people. The phrase *the common people*, then,

---

[41] Kanai et al. (2011). Cf. Adorno et al. (1950), Stenner (2005).

has dropped out of use and given way to what has been made into a marker of committed Brexitism. The *ordinary people* brought a cluster of words that carried a mindset – a framework of concepts, moralised attitudes, polarised values and strong emotions.

Populist movements and leaders have their various distinctive shapes and colours, but all have in common the claim to represent the voice of the people. And 'the people' is their rallying cry. However, the meaning of 'the people' is far from straightforward. Wherever it occurs, it lies at the confluence of numerous currents of continuous thought, in both space and time. Just as the populist Brexit ideology was in many respects continuous with the contemporary waves of populism and nationalism across Europe, so it was connected to centuries of thinking flowing down through the minds of European thinkers and political leaders. It does not matter that today's Brexit populists do not consciously choose to echo these currents; they and their hearers are formed by them anyway. This is why, in order to grasp the historical context of Brexitspeak, and to understand its historic impact, we need to consider the sources, past and present, of its core ideas. As these ideas have changed, so have the words, and vice versa. In politics, the change comes about through debate, conflict and crisis. With the Brexit crisis there has been a significant change in political discourse and in the consequences for the economy, society and culture that are slowly becoming more apparent.

Though national populism was a European phenomenon (as well as a worldwide one), the British case had its own special characteristics. The concepts of 'the people' and 'the common people' had been contested for centuries. But Brexiters cut themselves off, in imagination at least, and despite protestations to the contrary, from the rest of Europe. Ideas about, and talk about, 'the people' in all shades of its meaning, had to take on red-white-and-blue colours. What was pictured when someone said 'common people' and then 'ordinary people', was thoroughly English. Once Euroscepticism had morphed into Brexitism, when someone said 'the people', what was invoked was a particular set of ideas about the British and their identity. The next chapter continues to pursue the question, 'Who do the British think they are?'

4 The British People

At the core of British populism, there exists a cluster of ideas about national identity that have accumulated and been passed down over several generations. Around the turn of the twenty-first century, these ideas were recovered and re-activated in the UK by right-wing movements and parties. It was all part of a similar process across Europe, from East to West. National-populist ideas and rhetoric were opportunistically borrowed by mainstream parties that opposed 'the ordinary people' to 'the elite' – social-democratic as well as conservative, Labour as well as Conservative. Inevitably, all populist movements also revived their respective national narratives about 'the people', that is the people of their own national culture. In the UK national populism produced the historic disruption of Brexit, in large part because of Britain's unresolved loss of imperial identity. Brexitism became, for a time, its ideology, unformulated but nonetheless coherent in its own way, a spider's web of connected concepts. What were these concepts and where did they come from?

Nation and Empire

The conceptual overlap between *nation* and *the people* has played a significant role in political discourse and in discourse about politics, both among political actors and among scholars of politics. In practice, this means there is a strong ideological overlap between populism and nationalism in various forms. In many instances, one sees a particular concept of 'the people' being constructed for the contemporary moment and being blended with existing concepts of nationhood that have been transmitted already over time, sometimes in combination with the concept of the state. This is exemplified, too, in the case of Brexit and Brexitspeak: ideas of *the people* and *a people* are blended with readily available British nation discourse. It is appropriate therefore to characterise that movement as 'national populism'.

There is room in such blends for conceptual confusion, vagueness and political exploitation. *A people*, in the sense of an ethnic entity, is not necessarily coterminous with nation – except, explicitly or implicitly, in far-right ideologies. In terms of objective fact, the proportions of ethnic and civic elements constituting a nation will vary; the ways in which the same nation is imagined, proposed and propagandised may well not coincide. A feature that *a people* and *nation* have in common as concepts is that they both seem to include, for many speakers, some notion of natural given-ness, with *a people* seeming the more 'natural' entity of the two. Etymologies can be revealing: *nation* comes from the Latin for 'birth', and carries thus notions of origin, place and genetic identity. In certain conceptual frames, in certain political contexts, this naturalness lends itself to a dominance of the ethnic ingredient in the notion of *a nation*, obscuring the fact that nations are constructed, 'built'. Such frames underpin what is generally called nativism.

Every time an English-speaker utters or hears *the British people* a mental frame is activated, in which some basic idea of *nation* is implicit. What is a nation? Benedict Anderson was one of the rare historians and political scientists who took languages seriously, seeing them as intrinsic to the formation of political entities, in particular nation states. He described their emergence from the early modern period through to the twentieth century, not just across Europe but across the Americas and Asia. He attempted to account not just for the *idea* of the nation but for the emotional component of national belonging. His approach is what might be called 'conceptualist', in so far as he seeks to describe the consciousness of different historical epochs. To some degree this was compatible with later work in sociolinguistics, cognitive linguistics and discourse analysis, even though he did not have these tools to hand.

The central, best-known point is that the concept of 'the nation' is a social construct. In their different ways philosophers and sociologists make the same point, and it is now a commonplace. This is not to say that many people and many political actors do not prefer to have *nation* conceptualised as a natural, indefinitely existing, thing. As Grayling says, 'nations are artificial constructs, their boundaries drawn in the blood of past wars'. He notes that no country is mono-cultural, as nations are often imagined to be, but 'home to more than one different but usually coexisting cultures'. It follows that 'cultural heritage is not the same thing as national identity'.[1] Ruth Wodak, building on Anderson, adopts a 'social-constructivist' approach to *nation* that also borrows ideas from cognitive linguistics (image schemas, conceptual metaphor and frames, for instance) combined with description of the ways the emotion of national belonging can be aroused through language use.[2]

Anderson's starting point is the proposition that communities, especially those called 'nations', are 'imagined'. He writes:

In an anthropological spirit ... I propose the following definition of the nation: it is an imagined political community – and imagined as both inherently limited and sovereign.[3]

---

[1] Grayling (2001), pp. 78–9. [2] Wodak (2015), p. 77ff. [3] Anderson (2006), p. 5.

By 'imagined' Anderson means that individuals and local groups can think of themselves as part of a larger group that includes other individuals whom they do not encounter and never will. He argues that larger group awareness became possible historically with the invention of writing, and most powerfully with Gutenberg's movable type technology and print capitalism from the mid-fifteenth century in Europe. This cultural revolution was subsequently reinforced by language standardisation in emergent nations in the early modern period.

'Imagined' is ambiguous. On the one hand, there was the imagining of unseen beings (God, saints, fictional literary characters …) from within one's own group. On the other hand, there was the imagining of past human histories – that is, mythic narratives. Both dimensions are needed. Anderson does indeed allude to the role specifically of narrative in the construction of national identity,[4] but narratives as such are not his central concern. It was the spread and inculcation of national stories that was fostered by the print trade. One of his major concerns is to understand the role of the emotions in the formation of national identity. Anderson's account is significant not only in his 'anthropological' sense, and not only because of his interpretation of the historical development of nations. It is important also because he opened up both the psychological and the linguistic components of the concept of *nation*. There are further questions to ask. Why have nation and nationalism had such a powerful hold on the imagination, to the extent that people will not only die for them, but also kill for them? Why can verbal stimulation of national feelings still work on certain populations? Why did a new nationalism arise towards the end of the twentieth century, with a boost from the populist movements of the twenty-first? And how is it bound up with Brexit?

There exists a shadowy set of beliefs and assumptions that colour the phrase *the British people*. The crucial element of the *Britain* frame is the concept *nation*. And in the imagining of nations, supposed origins, national heroes, selected historical narrative, and idealised national 'character' are essential. The British origin story, combined with race and race theory, enters into national-populist discourse, where it is presented as under external threat. In an interview on TalkRadio on 4 October 2017, Henry Bolton,[5] the newly elected UKIP leader, was asked by the presenter Julia Hartley-Brewer:

HARTLEY-BREWER: […] you have spoken about how British people feel their culture, their traditions, their way of life is in your words being buried and pushed aside by Islam and you feel that it is the weight of immigration. In what way is British culture, and our traditions, being buried by Islam?

---

[4] Anderson (2006), pp. 208–10.
[5] Henry Bolton stepped down amid controversy on 17 February 2018 and started another party, Our Nation, deregistered on 4 November 2019.

88   The British People

BOLTON: Er er it not not overall erm but in certain communities then the indigenous … English Anglo-Saxon … Anglo-Saxon population is is nowhere to be seen on this.

HARTLEY-BREWER: You're talking about ghettos?

BOLTON: er er I wouldn't put it as ghettos. I would put it that we've got entire areas entire areas of towns where there are almost no er it's if you like er y'know Anglo-Saxon … Anglo-Saxon British people. They are they're new arrivals over the last ten twenty years er and are are entirely dominant in that area.[6]

The main detail of interest here is of course the reference to the 'Anglo-Saxon population'. Bolton's hesitations and incoherence are telling. He seems unable to answer the question and saves himself by trotting out the 'Anglo-Saxon' myth. One cannot really say he is making explicit claims about Anglo-Saxon origins, but he has selected the expression and collocates 'Anglo-Saxon' with 'British'. At one point the interviewer says: 'you talk about Anglo-Saxon, I think you mean white Brits'. Bolton does not demur; he lets the statement stand. But he has managed to make a racist point in a round-about way, by having the interviewer make it for him, making it deniable, and without overtly being 'politically incorrect'.

Why Anglo-Saxon? One of the heroes in the Britain myth is Alfred the Great, king of the Anglo-Saxon occupants of England at the end of the ninth century, who was notable for educational and legal reforms. In the national narrative, however, he makes his main appearance fighting Viking invaders. People seem to be less interested in mentioning the Norman inheritance, despite the fabled invasion, the line of Norman kings of England and the lands now belonging to wealthy families descended from Norman conquerors. The British story has had a way of not presenting the Norman French as conquerors of an 'indigenous Anglo-Saxon' population, but somehow imagining them in the national narrative as part of a continuous British stock. The evidence regarding the Anglo-Saxon genetic component in the present-day population points to about 38 per cent for eastern England, and about 30 per cent for the rest of the British Isles including Scotland and Wales.[7] In any event, the Anglo-Saxons were not indigenous but Germanic migrants from mainland Europe. Nor were they always mythical British heroes – in a different narrative, they were the invaders they actually were, and were resisted by another mythical hero, King Arthur.

The insistence on 'Anglo-Saxon' origins has its own history on both sides of the Atlantic. Anglo-Saxonism was a late nineteenth-century and early twentieth-century current of thought which idealised Anglo-Saxon law, Christianity and language.[8] It also explicitly racialised the imagined national community of the British. This coincided with the contemporary notion that the world was divided

---

[6] My transcription; the online public record of the interview is no longer accessible.
[7] Schiffels et al. (2016), Sayer (2017).   [8] Yorke (1999), Vucetic (2011), Da Silva (2021).

into 'races', combining with half-digested Darwinian ideas such as those of Francis Galton, the founder of what he called 'eugenics'. Galton wrote that the English elite were genetically superior and that peoples colonised by the English were of inferior minds.[9] By the 1890s, this supposedly superior racial strain was attached to the 'Anglo-Saxon race' and identified with nations that spoke the English language. Thomas Jefferson used the idea of Anglo-Saxon origins to argue that the English migrants to America should rule themselves independently, just as the Anglo-Saxons had separated themselves from their continental forbears. The Victorians, who were interested in playing up the Germanic ties of the royal family, promoted the idea of Alfred as the founder of the nation.[10] Language was a strong element in this Anglo-Saxonism on two counts. On the one hand, Anglo-Saxon was seen as the foundation of modern English (which historically it is, though with massive input from Norman French). On the other, English was the language of a world empire that was seen as embodying moral as well as political superiority.

Nations are not the only kind of imagined community. After World War II, the idea of an 'Anglosphere' with its geopolitical centres in London and Washington D.C. was dominant. In fact, 'the anglosphere' should include Britain's imperialist legacy of English-speaking subjects spread across the globe. Britain's loss of its colonies, however, and post-war immigration from the Caribbean and India, produced questions of who belongs to the imagined nation and what is its role in the world. The British ruling elites have not revised their imagined national self and given it settled form in foreign policy and trade policy. Nor have they revised the old education system that sustains it. Anglo-Saxonism began as a legitimising national myth in the imperial age, and it is not surprising that its ghost reappears in Brexit discourse. It served the purpose, consciously or not, of filling an identity gap created by the failure of British government and British culture to develop an identity that has a European dimension. Identity formation does not absolutely and inevitably require differentiation of a Self from an Other, but the most visible forms of nationalism do require it, and they thrive on it. The original nineteenth-century Anglo-Saxonism differentiated itself by reference to an Other that was Roman (Romance, Latin), Asiatic (Russian) or Oriental (India, China and also Africa).

In Brexitspeak, the Self is the 'British people' and the Other is the multilingual EU and Islam. This opposition provides the irrational bedrock of extreme forms of Brexit ideology, however much its leaders protest that they love Europe and only hate the EU regulatory order. What this strain of rhetoric does is align the UK with the Anglosphere, leading Brexiters to imagine easy trade deals within this sphere after separation from the EU single market. One explanation for such economically erroneous visions is precisely the underlying Anglo-Saxonism – an

---

[9] Tomlinson (1990), pp. 104–6, Dorling and Tomlinson (2019), pp. 84–6.   [10] Yorke (1999).

ahistorical assumption that the former empire would provide markets as once it had. In 2016 at Manchester Town Hall, Liam Fox, a member of the Conservatives' European Research Group (ERG) and promoter of the Vote Leave campaign, delivered a speech on free trade. Into it were woven ideas of the British people's exceptionality, and even hints of genetic specialisation:

> The global influence Britain enjoys today is largely down to our proud trading history, a history steeped in innovation and endeavour. [...] We were, quite simply, the workshop of the world. A small island perched on the edge of Europe became the world's largest and most powerful trading nation. [...] For the British people, trade is in our DNA.[11]

Similar speeches followed. The next year, 9 March 2017, Fox gave an address to the trade ministers of the Commonwealth, the first ever. Again, Britain was 'a small island perched on the edge of the European continent [which] became a leader of world trade'. The assembled ministers of Britain's former colonies were told that they and Britain had a 'shared history' in which they had experienced the benefits of 'free trade'.[12] In 2019, on 14 January, he gave a speech outlining a programme for a 'global Britain', and on 25 June that year a speech at the Centre for Policy Studies outlining a 'vision' for a specifically UK-US trade deal. This did not at all fit with the plain fact that the UK's closest and largest trading partner was the EU, and was likely to remain so. The 'vision' also carried the implication that the UK was fundamentally different from the whole of mainland Europe as a historical and cultural entity.[13] The Brexit vision was an attempt to project an expired imperial role onto a totally transformed geopolitical and economic reality. Above all, Brexiters dreamt of a trade deal with the successor to the Thirteen Colonies – their ideal Anglosphere partner. They disclaimed impossible imperial fantasies, but still fantasised about a world-dominating role for Britain. In the same way, Boris Johnson proclaimed that the hope of the new post-Brexit world was

> to rediscover some of the dynamism of these bearded Victorians: not to build a new empire, heaven forfend, but to use every ounce of Britain's power, hard and soft, to go back out into the world in a way that we had perhaps forgotten over the past 45 years: to find friends, to open markets, to promote our culture and our values.[14]

The historian Robert Saunders notes that, in the wake of the 2016 referendum, '[t]he use of "trade" as a euphemism for "empire" became a staple of Brexit ideology'. The unpleasant realities of the British Empire were kept out

---

[11] www.gov.uk/government/speeches/liam-foxs-free-trade-speech.
[12] www.gov.uk/government/speeches/commonwealth-trade-ministers-meeting-towards-a-free-trading-future.
[13] www.ukpol.co.uk/liam-fox-2019-speech-on-global-britain/.
[14] Johnson speaking at the Foreign and Commonwealth Office, 15 July 2018. www.telegraph.co.uk/politics/2018/07/15/rest-world-believes-britain-time-did/.
  Cf. Saunders (2019).

of view – at least, until the historical memories of its victims and their victimisers were quickened by the 'Windrush scandal' that broke in 2018. The scandal took its name from the ship *Empire Windrush* that had brought hundreds of Jamaicans to the UK in 1948, in anticipation of the British Nationality Act. Seventy years later large numbers of these people were deported, threatened with deportation or detained, thanks to successive governments failing to provide documentary evidence of their right to remain. Up to 57,000 former Commonwealth migrants could have been affected, 15,000 of whom were from Jamaica.[15] Despite the mistreatment of imperial subjects in the past, and of former imperial subjects in the present, pro-Leave British islanders recycled the myth of imperial greatness. The groundwork for this pattern of thinking went back to the post-World War II period. Cameron picked up the thread. Evoking Churchill's 'island race', he declared in his Bloomberg speech that 'our geography has shaped our psychology'. He took it for granted that there is something called 'the character of an island nation' and a 'British sensibility' that is permanent and separates the UK from the continent of Europe.

The Will of the People

The phrase *the will of the people*, meaning the will of the *British* people, was key to Brexit discourse. It was a kind of linguistic trap that presupposed the existence of a particular unitary people and the existence a unitary will belonging to that people. The media, especially the popular press, took up and spread this key phrase. An article in the *Daily Mail* two days before the referendum told its readers:

> If you believe in the sovereignty of this country, its monarchy, its unwritten constitution and its judicial system; if you believe in the will of the people and don't want to be ruled by faceless bureaucrats; if you are concerned about uncontrolled immigration; if you wish to control the destiny of the UK; if you want a government you can vote for and in turn vote out of office if it breaks its promises; and if you believe in Britain, its culture, history and freedoms, there is only one way to vote. Brexit.[16]

The *if* clauses do a lot of work: they introduce unexplained ideas and attitudes carrying the expectation (including in the moral sense of the word) that readers should 'believe in' them. In the context, the 'if' is not a logical 'if', but seems intended to mean something more like 'given the fact that you believe' or 'because you believe'. So, the *will of the people* appears as one article of faith in the Brexit credo.

The phrase was not unique to overtly populist parties and movements. In March 2017, Theresa May made a statement to Parliament concerning the

---

[15] Gentleman (2017, 2019), Williams (2020), The Migration Observatory (2023).
[16] *Daily Mail*, 21 June 2016.

government's letter to the European Council President notifying him of the UK's withdrawal from the EU:

> European leaders have said many times that we cannot cherry pick and remain members of the single market without accepting the four freedoms that are indivisible. We respect that position. And as accepting these freedoms is incompatible with the democratically expressed will of the British people, we will no longer be members of the single market.[17]

The four freedoms that the PM was struggling with are four principles of the Single Market that even some Leave voters may have wished to retain – movement of goods, persons, services and capital. For reasons seemingly related to immigration fears, and probably to the proclaimed connections between national sovereignty and national control of borders, vocal hard-line Brexiters wanted to be rid of freedom of movement. Overriding the fact that some Leavers may have wanted to retain access to the Single Market – not to mention ignoring the 48 per cent of voters who had voted to remain in it – May simply rehearses the Brexiter message that there is such a thing as a will of the people, democratically expressed in the referendum. She had become fluent in Brexitspeak.

Fifteen months later, probably in an effort to retain her premiership, May sounded even more clearly populist, actually opposing Parliament to the people's will:

> we need to make sure that Parliament can't tie the Government's hands in negotiation [with the EU] and can't overturn the will of the British people.[18]

When Johnson succeeded Theresa May, *the will of the people* continued to be an intrinsic part of the government's rhetoric. In a leadership campaign interview in 2019, Boris Johnson paraphrased 'the will of the people' as 'what people want' – a characteristically populist pitch:

> My commitment is to honour the will of the people and take this country out on October the 31st and to get this thing done. That is what people want.[19]

The Brexit Party propaganda opens, unintentionally no doubt, a philosophical can of worms. Having refused to use the term 'manifesto' to state its policies, it launched its election campaign in November 2019 with a pamphlet bearing the title CONTRACT WITH THE *PEOPLE*. In its opening paragraph, it stated:

> Acting on the biggest popular mandate in British history is crucial to restore faith in our democracy. What sort of democratic society do we live in, if a few Parliamentarians can defy the expressed will of the people?[20]

---

[17] Hansard, 29 March 2017: Column 253.
[18] Reported in the *Daily Express*, 18 June 2018, www.express.co.uk/news/uk/975883/Brexit-news-UK-EU-European-Union-Theresa-May-Brexit-bill-vote-referendum-NHS-funding.
[19] BBC Radio 4, *World at One* interview, 14 July 2019, www.youtube.com/watch?v=oO7h1cX4a74.
[20] www.thebrexitparty.org/wp-content/uploads/2019/11/Contract-With-The-People.pdf.

Thus the pamphlet begins by bringing into play the populist conception of democracy. It is one in which 'the will of the people' takes precedence over Parliament – that is, a direct not a representative democracy. And it is one that is bound up with the pamphlet's title, with its echo of social contract theory.

The pamphlet in effect redefines the term *contract*: 'our Contract with the People is a targeted set of deliverable pledges'. This muddles contracts with pledges. Contracts in the usual legal sense are a specific sort of speech act necessarily involving two parties, but the Brexit Party's 'Contract' is distinctly one-sided. In any case, pledges and contracts are very different kinds of speech act.[21] Contracts are complex speech acts built up on particular social institutions, including legal institution, while pledges and promises do not require such institutional conditions. In the domain of politics, 'pledges' and 'promises' have their own characteristic – you either believe them or you don't, depending largely on your own political inclinations. One of the 'pledges' in the Brexit Party 'Contract' is to 'introduce Citizens' Initiatives to allow people to call referendums', presumably one of the 'fundamental democratic reforms to fix our broken political system and make Parliament serve the People'. This is another example of a commitment to direct democracy, here proposing quite a radical constitutional change. Even though 'contract' does not strictly make sense in the Brexit Party's text, 'contract with the people' does have the advantageous effect of appearing to engage directly with malcontent voters. In talking about a 'contract with the people', the Brexit Party were treading the same path as some of their European counterparts. The Swiss People's Party, at their party congress in 2011, had staged a theatrical 'signing' by over 200 candidates of a 'Contract with the People' (*Vertrag mit dem Volk, Contrat avec le peuple*). It was in fact a party manifesto for forthcoming parliamentary elections. Silvio Berlusconi had done the same thing, signing a *Contratto con gli italiani* in 2001, on a TV show, making policy promises in a bid for election as prime minister. In 2009 a civil court, unsurprisingly, found it had no validity in law.

Rousseau inevitably springs to mind.[22] According to his *Social Contract*, humans can only escape the primitive state of nature by forming a social pact, so they surrender themselves to the common good. They transform themselves into a *moi commun* (collective self). This metaphorical 'public person', as Rousseau calls it, has a will of course, and so there is a general will of all the individuals that the 'public person' embodies. But because he thinks that 'the people' are not enlightened enough to see their true interests, and that it is impossible for them to write their own laws, he argues that an ideal *législateur* (lawgiver) is necessary. This is a figure who has superior intelligence and insight into what the will of the people really is. The problem with this

---

[21] Searle (1995), pp. 63–4.
[22] Cf. Canovan (2005), p. 115, Mudde and Kaltwasser (2017), pp. 16–17, Weale (2018), pp. 22–6.

argument, however, is that participation in free deliberation by citizens is meaningless if it is 'guided' by an all-knowing 'lawgiver'. Someone who 'guides' is a 'leader' – history was to show how all-knowing leaders would turn out. Political scientists and philosophers have pointed out that social contract theory contains the seeds of authoritarianism.

As Jan-Werner Müller notes, populists typically believe that the 'will of the people' is directly known to the leader.[23] They have an idea of representation that is nothing to do with electing deputies. It is the leader who symbolically 'represents', 'speaks for', 'is the voice of' the people. While referendums are often demanded by populist leaders as a democratic instrument, in fact they believe they already know what the people's 'will' is, because they know who the 'real' people are. It follows that the populist 'will of the people' is not discovered through vote counting. It is some sort of conceptual abstraction that is almost mystical. In this respect, populist patterns of thought are in tune with a long line of authoritarian thinking. The abstract idea of the people goes hand in hand with the equally abstract idea of the nation, and with the danger that both these ideas become interpreted in ethnic terms.

Populist actors who make statements about 'the will of the people' are making several kinds of implication. One is that there exists such a thing. A second is that they know what it is, and that the hearer or reader also knows or should know. Consequently, if you do not commit to this supposed 'will', then you are not one of 'the people'. That inference should surely carry a contradiction because 'the people' is not supposed to have exceptions – 'the people' is undivided and homogeneous. In the real world, populations are split and diverse – in the case at hand, split roughly 48 per cent to 52 per cent. But in the populist mental world, the 'real people' cannot be split, for the imaginary *the people* subsists whole and entire, beyond the realities of elections and votes.

The Mandate of the People

In political theory, there are two main types of mandate: free and imperative. A free mandate is a key idea in representative democracy. In this sort of mandate an election legitimises parliamentary representatives to enact policies that they committed to in their or their party's manifesto, while leaving latitude to exercise their own judgement in the deliberation of complex matters. The representatives are assumed to represent the entire nation. In imperative mandates, individuals are elected to enact a specific policy of a people's assembly (maybe local ones, separate from central government). In this theoretical perspective, the assembly may have the power to recall the mandated individuals if they are judged not to be

---

[23] Müller (2003), Müller (2016), pp. 25–30.

carrying out the people's wishes.[24] In the case of highly complex national issues – such as withdrawal from the EU – representative democracy should ensure accurately informed and rational deliberation. In a populist perspective that favours direct democracy, referendums tend to be seen as binding on governments – since they express 'the will of the people'. In many representative democracies, the criteria for holding referendums are defined in constitutions. In some, the elected delegates need to define the terms of a referendum for each occasion.

The distinction between free and imperative mandates has become important in EU governance because of what was widely perceived as a crisis in representative democracies arising from the multiple challenges from populist movements. This crisis was obscured in Brexitspeak uses of the term *democracy*. The European Commission set its face against imperative mandates in a 2009 *Report on the Imperative Mandate and Similar Practices*.[25] The problem of how to respond to the evident demand for increased democracy, without feeding the authoritarian seeds in populism, remains. Populist parties around Europe frequently demand an imperative-mandatory right to recall their representatives, whom they regard, in effect, simply as messengers.

At the time of the Brexit referendum, the constitutional position of the UK was that it had no institutions working with an imperative mandate. If there is need for constitutional democratic reform in this respect, then it would require careful consultation. But Brexiters of all parties and none behaved and talked as if there already was some such institution consisting of 'the people' who legitimately issued mandates. Through a series of manoeuvres, misinformation and inattention, the UK polity ended up with a manipulated referendum.[26] It was as if the UK already had an imperative-mandate constitution, with parliament not actually deliberating on what was a historically complex matter. Indeed, Parliament came increasingly under pressure from a pro-Leave executive, from Brexit lobbies and from the media that supported them, in a way that kept its members from deliberating much at all.

After the referendum, it was just taken for granted by many Leavers that the government had received a mandate to withdraw from the EU. Theresa May, for example, said in her announcement of the June general election of 2017:

We have also delivered on the mandate that we were handed by the referendum result. Britain is leaving the European Union and there can be no turning back.[27]

---

[24] Müller (2016), p. 31.   [25] Tomba (2018).
[26] On this, see Grayling (2016) and Grayling (2017), pp. 189–97.
[27] Theresa May outside 10 Downing Street, 18 April 2017, www.bbc.co.uk/news/uk-politics-39630009.

She was speaking the same populist lines as UKIP was going to use in their election manifesto:

More than 17 million of us voted 'Leave,' giving the government the largest democratic mandate in the history of British politics. There should be no question of turning back, yet the Tories are leaving the door to the EU wide open. UKIP is the only party that will genuinely respect the referendum result.[28]

After Johnson had replaced May, he faced MPs from both sides who were determined to prevent a no-deal Brexit, producing parliamentary deadlock. The pro-Leave *Daily Express* front page insisted that the referendum result constituted a mandate given by 'the will of the people':

How can MPs possibly ignore this HUGE Brexit mandate?
  MPs are busy arguing who is more undemocratic – Boris Johnson or those blocking a no deal Brexit – but there is a huge Leave mandate everybody appears to be ignoring.[29]

The popular press in general placed parliament in opposition to the people. Johnson, too, made clear that he saw parliament as subservient to what he regarded as an imperative mandate. He told the CBI (Confederation of British Industry) conference in November 2019 that

the country is being held back, let's be clear, by politics, and by a parliament that for the last three and a half years has simply failed to discharge its basic promise made umpteen times to honour the mandate of the people and to deliver Brexit.[30]

In essence, this kind of statement sets representative parliamentary democracy against direct democracy and rule by referendum.

What about the Labour Brexiters? Gisela Stuart, chair of Vote Leave, who later quit Labour to support Boris Johnson in the 2019 general election, believed in the existence of 'the mandate':

[I]t may be a good time to remember what this is all about.
  It's about implementing a direct mandate given to the Government and MPs in Parliament by the people they entrusted with the decision of whether we should remain in the European Union or leave. […] The mandate then was and still is to leave the European Union. […] The mandate, delivered in the referendum on a turnout of 72 per cent and with a clear majority of 3.8 per cent, was accepted by the two main political parties in the 2017 general election.[31]

---

[28] UKIP manifesto, General Election 2017, p. 6, https://lexically.net/downloads/elections/2017_election/UKIP_Manifesto_June2017opt.pdf.
[29] *Express*, 6 September 2019, www.express.co.uk/news/uk/1174644/brexit-news-leave-vote-mapped-boris-johnson-eu-referendum-remain-mps-parliament-spt.
[30] 'Prime Minister Boris Johnson's CBI Conference speech', 18 November 2019, www.theguardian.com/politics/2019/nov/18/boris-johnson-to-shelve-planned-cut-in-corporation-tax.
[31] Gisela Stuart on the blog ConservativeHome, 13 November 2018, www.conservativehome.com/platform/2018/11/gisela-stuart-the-referendum-gave-the-political-class-a-chance-to-mend-their-ways-so-far-they-are-flunking-it.html.

The local Councillor Brendan Chilton, who chaired the pro-Brexit campaign group Labour Leave was also committed to the mandate of 'the British people'. Writing just after Labour's defeat in the election, he urges Labour members to support Boris Johnson in 'getting Brexit done':

[Labour] must work with the Conservative Government in a collaborative and constructive fashion to get Brexit done. This means accepting that the Government now has a mandate to proceed with its Withdrawal Agreement and it means accepting that the British people have, for the umpteenth time, voted to leave the EU.[32]

In contradiction to all this, the question of whether a referendum on the EU should be mandatory had been introduced in two private members' bills under the Cameron-Clegg government. The bills failed to progress through both Houses, but a revised version was brought back in 2015, again addressing the question whether the referendum was to be mandatory. A briefing paper stated that

this Bill does not contain any requirement for the UK Government to implement the results of the referendum, nor set a time limit by which a vote to leave the EU should be implemented. Instead, this is a type of referendum known as pre-legislative or consultative, which enables the electorate to voice an opinion which then influences the Government in its policy decisions. [...] The UK does not have constitutional provisions which would require the results of a referendum to be implemented.[33]

As a briefing paper, it does not count as an authoritative government statement. However, an authoritative statement *was* given by the Minister for Europe in the debate on the European Referendum Bill in the House of Commons:

The legislation is about holding a vote; it makes no provision for what follows. The referendum is advisory, as was the case for both the 1975 referendum on Europe and the Scottish independence vote last year.[34]

The legislation did not stipulate that the government must implement the outcome of the referendum; it was understood that the bill passed into law as advisory only. This interpretation was made clear retrospectively in no uncertain terms by the High Court (3 November 2016, [2016] EWHC 2768 (Admin)), especially in its paragraph 106, which states that the 2015 Referendum Act was 'advisory' only:

The Act falls to be interpreted in light of the basic constitutional principles of Parliamentary sovereignty and representative parliamentary democracy which apply

---

[32] BrexitCentral, 'If Labour is to recover from this defeat, it must work with the government to get Brexit done', 13 December 2019, https://brexitcentral.com/if-the-labour-is-to-recover-from-th is-defeat-it-must-work-with-the-government-to-get-brexit-done/.
[33] Uberoi (2015), p. 25, Briefing Paper Number 07212, European Referendum Bill 2015–16.
[34] David Lidington, Hansard, 16 June 2015: Column 231. https://publications.parliament.uk/pa/ cm201516/cmhansrd/cm150616/debtext/150616-0002.htm.

in the United Kingdom, which lead to the conclusion that a referendum on any topic can only be advisory for the law makers in Parliament unless very clear language to the contrary is used in the referendum legislation in question. No such language is used in the 2015 Referendum Act.[35]

This statement constitutes a defence of parliamentary representative democracy against the wave of populist sentiment favouring direct democracy. Despite this, however, constitutional scholars knew, before the referendum vote, that '[w]hatever the legal position, [...] the political reality is that the government will have to respect the result. If the vote is to leave the EU, the Prime Minister will announce that the UK will indeed leave'.[36]

In other words, it would be expedient realpolitik rather than the rule of law that would win out. Following the referendum result, pro-Leave politicians argued, irrespective of what the legal position might be, that statements issued by the government counted as grounds for claiming the referendum was binding. Philip Hammond, Secretary of State for Foreign and Commonwealth Affairs, for example, had said in the House of Commons, during a debate on the Referendum Bill in June 2015, that 'the decision about our membership should be taken by the British people, not by Whitehall bureaucrats, certainly not by Brussels Eurocrats; not even by Government Ministers or parliamentarians in this Chamber'.[37] Hammond was deploying Brexitspeak. The simple phrase 'the British people' and the mention of Whitehall bureaucrats ('experts' or 'elites') would be enough to trigger the whole populist mental frame, along with its concepts, emotions and values. Numerous Brexiters referred to a government leaflet distributed prior to the referendum, which included the sentence: 'This is your decision. The Government will implement what you decide.'[38] This did not have any legal status, but it had a legitimising function for Brexit supporters. Once again, there was an underlying polarisation between constitutional representative institutions of democracy and growing direct-democratic populist sentiment – a polarisation that had not come to the surface in public debate. What did come to the surface, however, was the trend for the populist Brexiters to refuse the legal decisions of the High Court and the Supreme Court regarding the legally binding structures of representative deliberative democracy.

Thresholds for a constitution-changing referendum are required in the constitutions of many countries. Britain's being unwritten, instances are decided as

---

[35] See www.judiciary.uk/wp-content/uploads/2016/11/r-miller-v-secretary-of-state-for-exiting-eu-amended-20161122.pdf.
[36] Renwick (2016), prior to the referendum.   [37] Hansard, 9 June 2015: Column 1056.
[38] HM Government, 'Why the government believes that voting to remain in the European Union is the best decision for the UK', https://assets.publishing.service.gov.uk/government/uploads/system/uploads/attachment_data/file/515068/why-the-government-believes-that-voting-to-remain-in-the-european-union-is-the-best-decision-for-the-uk.pdf.

they arise. Very convenient for interested parties in some circumstances. As the Briefing Paper 07212 carefully explains (pp. 26–7):[39]

> Discussion of the need for some form of threshold usually arises in the context of ensuring the legitimacy and acceptance of the outcome of a referendum. Certain states require constitutional change to be validated by a special majority in a referendum. This incorporates the idea that major constitutional change is something more important than the result of ordinary elections, and therefore should be the outcome of something more than a simple plurality of the votes.

No threshold was included in the legislation for the referendum. There are various political reasons why parliamentary debate around this question did not seriously develop. The usual reason given for Cameron's introducing a referendum bill in the first place is that he did not expect to lose, so he thought it unnecessary to consider a supermajority. Moreover, the strength of the Conservative Eurosceptics was sufficient to prevent a debate on the matter taking place. Whatever the reasons, the populist movements were increasingly prominent in the political arena and saw referendums as 'the voice of the people'.

So Who Was the British People in 2016?

One way of thinking about who 'the British people' were was to equate it with the electorate, the total number of electors. Some commentators argued that the franchise should (on grounds of democratic equity, consistency and practical rationality regarding the future) have included other groups. One group, for example, was sixteen- and seventeen-year-olds. Another was UK citizens having lived abroad for more than fifteen years – they were excluded from the referendum in line with a rule that excludes this group from parliamentary elections. And another was EU citizens living in and paying taxes in the UK – only EU citizens from Malta, Cyprus or the Republic of Ireland were included. There was a particularly strong case for the inclusion of sixteen- and seventeen-year-olds, who had the longest-term stake. However, amendments to the bill were defeated in the Parliament primarily due to the weight of Eurosceptics, who were aware of the likely voting preference of that age group. There had been a recent precedent for the inclusion of sixteen- and seventeen-year-olds in the 2014 Scottish independence referendum, as well as EU citizens living in Scotland. There would also have been a case for including UK citizens who had lived abroad for *more* than fifteen years, given that they remained citizens, and given the importance of the issue at hand. Regarding EU citizens living in the UK, the inclusion only of citizens of Malta, Cyprus and the Republic of Ireland reflected historic relationships and pointed to a nationalist stance rather than

---

[39] There is also a House of Commons Library paper, 'Thresholds in Referendums' at https://commonslibrary.parliament.uk/research-briefings/sn02809/.

principles of equity or even economic advantage. But the principle of no taxation without representation should have sufficed – as it had in the case of the Scottish independence referendum. These are ideal rational arguments, whereas what is called 'political reality' in the UK was already veering towards an irrational, populist and nationalist view of the world.

After the results were in, the tide of populist sentiment, within Parliament and beyond it, inhibited the government from acting in a strictly constitutional manner. The narrow result was treated as if it came under the first-past-the-post system. It was not handled on the basis upon which the House of Commons had actually voted to hold a referendum – that it was to be advisory and made no provision for implementation. Yet the fallacious populist claim that the result embodied 'the will of the British people' prevailed. Viewing the situation in this light, the statistical result points to a significantly undemocratic moment, despite what the populists and populist press maintained.

The referendum outcome figures – 51.89 per cent Leave vote versus 48.11 per cent Remain – have been interpreted or manipulated differently by the two sides. Remainers can argue that the 51.89 per cent who voted Leave represented no more than approximately 37 per cent of the total referendum electorate. Additionally, they can argue that this electorate was restricted beforehand so as to favour the pro-Brexit vote – in other words, gerrymandered. Leavers focus attention repeatedly and solely on the brute results and on the relatively high turnout. The approximately 72 per cent turnout is cited as significant by Leavers, but the percentage is based on the restricted referendum franchise. Leavers also cite the absolute number of those who voted Leave, approximately 17.4 million, out of a total turnout of roughly 33.5 million, saying that this is a very large number of citizens. But Remainers could argue that the difference between Leave votes and Remain votes of roughly 1.3 million gave an insufficiently large majority on which to decide a matter of historic importance for the population of the UK as a whole.

Complex arguments are involved, but that complexity is one of the reasons why, for referendums, a threshold needs to be specified and the electorate needs to be appropriately inclusive. It is also why the Briefing Paper 07212 states that the referendum result was not to be binding. It is possible, however, within the populist frame of thought, to argue that while the referendum was not legally and constitutionally binding, it was still mandatory by 'the will of the people'. Farage himself seems to have accepted that referendums were not currently constitutionally binding, but he wanted the constitution clarified to make them so: 'I take the advisory point and I would now wish to see constitutional change to make referendums binding.'[40] Willy nilly, the 2016 referendum implies constitutional change.

---

[40] Andrew Marr Show, 6 November 2016, BBC One.

The claim that the referendum constituted a mandate of the people remained a discursive construct, a very powerful one, dangerous for parliamentary representative deliberative democracy. As for the question who *the British people* are, we do not of course find an explicit answer anywhere. What we have is a deniable implication – most hearers presume that 'the will of the people' is the will of the *whole* people. And if the will of the people mandated Brexit, the individuals who did not want to mandate Brexit were not members of *the people*. Thus, 48 per cent of those who voted were not members of *the people*. So who were they? To some Brexiters they were the enemy: 'traitors' who included 'the elite', 'the establishment', the judiciary, and any citizen who had voted to remain in the EU.

The English phrase *the British people* is attached to no clear and distinct idea, but it is not meaningless. It is uttered in numerous contested contexts and political milieux. When the members of a group use it among themselves, it is meaningful, because it gets its meaning from a cluster of associated ideas and feelings. In Brexitspeak, *the people*, *the British people*, *the will of the people*, and *the mandate of the people* are part of the populist conception of democracy. The word *democracy* was highly ambiguous in the context of the 2016 referendum campaign, since it could be understood as denoting either some form of direct democracy or some form of representative democracy. This ambiguity made it possible for populist Brexiters of left and right to declare that they 'defended democracy', while in effect opposing its representational form. In the mouths of populist demagogues 'democracy' is a dangerously confusing term.

All political identities are fictions constructed for political purposes, not naturally given as nationalist discourse claims. The various myths about Britain had been built up mainly in Victorian times, and the Conservative party had taken its turn in passing them on. But UKIP deployed them to great effect in the service of national-populist Euroscepticism, making it electorally necessary for Conservatives to reclaim them. The result was a coalition of shared political concepts, a basis on which national identity could be constructed. A shared story of Britishness was the common ground of Conservatives, Brexiters, UKIP, and to some extent Labour. The overall drift was towards a nationalism that was once again rearing its head across Europe.

'The British people' resides in the mind as a conceptual blend. It is the intersection of two conceptual frames, each of which has different elements. The narrative of Britishness and its associated details combines with the notion of 'the people' and the whole mental frame that goes with that. It is clearly the case that even in the simplest varieties of Brexitspeak, the notion of *the people* is an amalgam of concepts built up over centuries, and certainly not only by the British themselves. Many of these concepts, and the emotional triggers they carry, come from classical times, now intertwined with the political thinking of the Enlightenment. What is extracted from this tradition by national populists is 'the people' seen as an abstract personified unit, with a 'will', and the power to directly 'mandate' their choices to government. In Brexitism 'the people' is no longer the demeaned *vulgus* but the esteemed 'ordinary people'. This is the conceptual core of British national populism. This is not the whole story, however, since national identities need also to define themselves by the invention of a foreign Other.

5 Fear of Foreigners

One of the ways in which populist groups and their leaders seek unity is by stoking up hostility against an 'other'. A popular leader with some sort of charisma – a demagogue – is integral to that process. Fear of foreigners, a phobia with regard to people who are different, is not inborn and we need to ask how it can be so easily tapped in human societies. The same is true for what is called racism. It is clear that social and political context is crucial to the arousal of xenophobia, and contexts are a product of a history. In the UK's history, xenophobia and racism ran a line from Empire through two world wars to loss of Empire, followed by the implosion that was Brexit. The 2016 referendum was a major historical turning point for the UK. It should not have come as a total surprise, though figuring out and fully understanding how and why the vote went the way it did will take time. A key element was social and national identity, a phenomenon not confined to Britain and an essential element of the many manifestations of national populism across Europe. The basic features of the campaign discourse poured out by Vote Leave and Leave.EU were already in place. The sources of the campaign's national populism were diverse. But its ethnocentric and racist stream had one of its major sources in the speeches of one particularly powerful demagogue.

Xenophobia, Racism, Ethnocentrism

There is clear evidence that what was happening in the 2000s and in the run-up to the 2016 referendum was the activating of an existing pattern of thought. But there are several concepts involved when anti-foreigner attitudes are analysed.

In 1965 the United Nations adopted the International Convention on the Elimination of All Forms of Racial Discrimination and it came into force in 1969. The document makes clear that it uses the terms ethnocentrism and racism equivalently, and it does not distinguish between *ethnicity* and *race*.[1] But there are distinctions to be made. The word *race* is defined within the fallacious mental framework of biological racism. In that framework 'races'

---

[1] United Nations (1965), McDougall (2021).

are differentiated on the basis of physically observable characteristics – prototypically skin colour and physiognomy – with some 'races' being seen as genetically superior to others. The term *ethnicity* is more ambiguous. It can refer, in an anthropological perspective, to a social group, an *ethnos*, that self-identifies itself in terms of some combination of language, culture and history. Or it can be conceptually conflated with the racist framework. In the latter case *ethnicity* might be being used as a cover for the racist sense, depending on the speaker and the circumstances.

Is fear of foreigners the same thing as racism? What they have in common is that both are coupled with the idea of defending and preserving 'our people', or, as some would put it, 'our race'. Ambalavaner Sivanandan argues that there is another, new kind of xenophobia which

> bears all the marks of the old racism, except that it is not colour-coded. It is a racism that is not just directed at those with darker skins, from the former colonial countries, but at the newer categories of the displaced and dispossessed whites, who are beating at western Europe's doors.[2]

This is an important point, since it provides a new definition for a new set of attitudes that arose with the increase in numbers of refugees and asylum seekers in the 2000s. In the UK, the long-standing currents of racism, targeted at non-white immigrants from its former colonies, were combined with hostility towards white immigrants from the EU. EU citizens had a right to enter the UK, as much as any other EU country, under the free movement provisions of the Maastricht Treaty. They nonetheless were treated with hostility by part of the British population. This racialised fear of foreigners generally was injected into the term *immigrants*, legal and illegal, and directed at the EU itself by Brexiters. Ethnocentrism is the complement to any kind of xenophobia, racialised or not. It involves not only exclusive attention to one's own society and culture but also the assumption that they are in some sense superior to others. The *us* is opposite to, and better than *them*.

The question arises as to what it is that brings people to xenophobic and ethnocentric preoccupations in the first place. There are numerous approaches to this question. One is the theory that ethnocentrism, hostility to out-groups and identity conflicts are naturally selected for in human evolution. There are folk beliefs along these lines also – 'it is only natural' to be wary of outsiders. The scientific and social-scientific consensus, however, does not give this approach credence. A different approach has shown that individuals are not *born* ethnocentric. Ethnocentrism is a relatively stable personality characteristic that is acquired in adolescence – it is a learned behaviour. In modern societies it is not evenly spread across populations and this variation has

---

[2] Sivanandan (2001), p. 2. Cf. Fekete (2001).

explanations in terms of demography and access to education. These factors can influence what kind identity a person may develop within a society. Sobolewska and Ford, for example, argue on the basis of research evidence that ethnocentrism is predominantly found in the identity-conservative social groups. In their account, voters with dominant identity-conservative traits are

white voters with lower levels of formal education who most frequently hold ethnocentric worldviews, making them more strongly attached to in-group identities like national identity and more threatened by out-groups such as migrants and minorities.[3]

Further, there is statistical evidence that '[e]thnocentric voters hold negative views of the EU, seeing it as a threatening out-group which constrains the sovereignty of their national in-groups'. The statistics also indicate a tendency for those scoring highly on measures of ethnocentrism to hold other negative views – for example, on immigration, equal opportunities, the EU, devolution and constitutional reform.[4] 'Identity liberals' come in two kinds. The first is 'conviction liberals', who are mostly university graduates inclined to be pro-immigration, pro-diversity, anti-racist, and international in outlook. The second is 'necessity liberals', those from ethnic minorities who are liberal because of their experiences of hostility from many in the majority population. The two groups are in line with one another above all on issues of diversity and racism. Demographically speaking, white identity conservatives who are early school leavers are of an older generation, since the later expansion of higher education has passed them by. The older generations, and the younger ones who missed out, remain ethnocentric and suspicious of people coming from outside the white national in-group.[5]

Lack of education is not, however, the only explanation of ethnocentrism; after all, there exist highly educated individuals who exhibit ethnocentric traits. Some social and political scientists turn to psychological frameworks. A frequently referenced theory is that of the 'authoritarian personality', a psychological type described by Hannah Arendt as an essential element of totalitarian systems. It was theorised in wider terms by Theodor Adorno and colleagues under the influence of the psychoanalyst Erich Fromm. Both Arendt's and Adorno's approaches reflected their experiences of Nazism, the Holocaust and World War II.[6] The outbreaks of authoritarian political activity in the early twenty-first century, including within the wave of populist governments, means that the explanatory contributions from social psychology remain highly relevant.

Going beyond Arendt and Adorno, more recent experimental enquiries into the authoritarian personality type have been carried out by the psychologist and

---

[3] Sobolewska and Ford (2020), p. 22. [4] Sobolewska and Ford (2020), p. 62.
[5] Sobolewska and Ford (2020), pp. 5–6.
[6] Adorno (1950), Adorno et al. (1950), Arendt (1951).

political scientist Karen Stenner, who builds on the research by the psychologist Bob Altemeyer.[7] It is Stenner's empirical findings that confirm the intuitive impression that the authoritarian personality tends to be associated with ethnocentric outlooks.[8] It should be noted, however, that this need not be the only causal factor, or a sufficient one – there may be ethnocentric people who are not authoritarian. Similarly, there may be authoritarians who are not ethnocentric. Further, authoritarian types may not exhibit either authoritarian or ethnocentric traits all of the time. The expression of such traits requires an activating context. The condition most likely to excite ethnocentric reactions is perceived insecurity around values and norms. Stenner's central argument is that 'normative threats are the critical catalyst for the activation of authoritarian predispositions and their expression in intolerant attitudes and behaviors'.[9]

In other words, when there are latent authoritarian tendencies and intolerant attitudes in a community, they can be activated if people think their way of life is at risk. Stenner's findings suggest that the authoritarian and ethnocentric personality types are more sensitive to perceived threats of this kind, and more likely to be consciously monitoring them. They are also more likely to respond politically. The kinds of community where this is likely to happen are the identity-conservative ones.

We still need to ask how an authoritarian personality manages to dominate a society politically. The Polish-American historian Anne Applebaum regards Stenner's view of the authoritarian personality as highly relevant to the decline of democracy and rise of authoritarian government in eastern Europe in the 2010s, but does not regard it as a full explanation: 'No contemporary authoritarian can succeed without [...] the writers, intellectuals, pamphleteers, bloggers, spin doctors, producers of television programs, and creators of memes who can sell his image to the public.'[10] These are the modern demagogues who, in Western democracies also, convey the propaganda of national populist leaders. The UK's Brexit upheaval is the most glaring example.

Sources of Brexit Xenophobia

How then did the context become ripe for demagogic activation of latent xenophobia and racist attitudes? What were their historical roots?

Reconstruction after World War II took place across Europe in a context of ongoing decolonisation. It inevitably involved social, demographic and economic change. Political actors, not only in Britain, used memories of war to maintain dying imperial fantasies. In Britain, however, these kinds of

---

[7] Altemeyer (1981, 1988, 1996), Stenner (2005), Stenner and Haidt (2018).
[8] Results published in Stenner (2005). Cf. Sobolewska and Ford (2020), pp. 40–1.
[9] Stenner (2005), p. 19.   [10] Applebaum (2020), p. 17.

discourses persisted, maintaining belief in the exceptionality and superiority of the country. For almost all continental European states national identities had to be reconstructed. Britain's course in this respect was confused and remained so. At the official level, the British Nationality Act of 1948 defined what 'being British' was, at least within a legal framework. The Act created the status of 'Citizen of the United Kingdom and Colonies', instead of 'British subject'.[11] Under the Act, all residents of Britain and of the current and continuing territories of the British Empire were to hold common citizenship. This gave them identical rights, including the right to settle and work on the British mainland and to engage in its political system. The authors of the Act set no restrictions or gradations. The Act also avoided any hint of a 'colour bar'. This apparently liberal aspect of the Act may reflect a strategy of maintaining some element of global power by maintaining a paternalist narrative of benevolent Britain.[12] Or maybe the authors just did not expect that non-whites would immigrate to Britain in significant numbers.

The arrival of the *Empire Windrush*, while the 1948 Act was passing through Parliament, was a news event in Britain that was presented positively. For the government, however, it was not welcome. The Minister of Labour declared in Parliament that there would be no encouragement for others to follow suit. The Secretary of State for the Colonies wrote memorandums to the effect that though the landing of the migrants could not be prevented, the government was opposed to it and that the Colonial Office and the Jamaican government would discourage future such migrations. The Privy Council sent a note to the Colonial Office: 'we should not make any special efforts to help these people [...] otherwise it might encourage a further influx'.[13]

However, the 'influx' did continue throughout the 1950s. Economic reconstruction produced abundant employment opportunities for increasing numbers of migrants from the West Indies, India, Pakistan and Commonwealth countries. Migratory chains led to increasing and self-sustaining flows, to permanent settlement, and gradually to community formation. It seems that, as was the case among other governing elites in western Europe, there was a failure to take account of the historical fact that migration generally leads to settlement, and that the liberal British 1948 Act in particular was likely to do the same. It should not have been beyond the bounds of imagination to publicly welcome migrants whom the country actually needed. Schierup notes that in some cultures 'myths of nation-building explicitly celebrate immigration and incorporation of settlers into the national community', while in contrast 'Western European

---

[11] The Canadians had already established their own citizenship in 1946.
[12] Ashcroft and Bevir (2021), pp. 122–3.
[13] Dorling and Tomlinson (2019), p. 206, citing Winder (2004), p. 338.

countries have tended to write immigration out of their histories because it contradicted myths of national homogeneity'.[14]

The British government does indeed seem to have adopted a policy of not encouraging Commonwealth migration.[15] The Trades Union Congress did officially welcome Commonwealth immigrants in 1955 but soon expressed doubts, albeit not publicly.[16] By 1958, race riots in Notting Hill and in Nottingham were evidence of changing discourses on the part of the white community. The race riots were initiated by white, male youths ('Teddy boys') from the same impoverished circumstances as their black neighbours, but there are grounds for thinking that far-right, ideologically racist groups and their leaders encouraged the racist attitudes. One of these leaders was the avowed fascist Oswald Mosley, imprisoned during the war, who re-emerged to found the Union Movement in 1948 and to campaign on an ideologically racist, anti-immigrant, pro-repatriation platform. Another active element of the far right of the 1950s was the White Defence League, started in 1956 by the neo-Nazi Colin Jordan, who had been a member of the League of Empire Loyalists. The latter had been set up in 1954 by current and former members of the Conservative Party, whose twin goals were prevention of the dissolution of the British Empire and prevention of the immigration of black people. This internal tendency was eventually rejected by the Conservative Party, but the links and some of the attitudes may well have persisted into successive generations. Groups expressing such attitudes were certainly still active ten years later, and led to the foundation of the National Front (NF) in 1967.

By the end of the 1950s, the government was beginning to feel itself under pressure from various bodies to introduce immigration restrictions. Economic stagnation began to reduce the need for overseas workers. Within the Conservative Party, the right-wing Monday Club, formed in 1961, opposed non-white immigration and supported South Africa's apartheid system. There was also pressure from the public, and the Commonwealth Immigrants Act of 1962 tightened the 1948 Act's definitions. Immigration controls were placed on certain categories of people from the Commonwealth, thereby ending the automatic right to settle that the 1948 Act had provided. Subsequent Acts (1968, 1971) imposed still tighter restrictions.[17] And in 1981, The British Nationality Act revised the generous 1948 Act entirely. This Act ended, among other things, the automatic right of children born in the UK to Commonwealth immigrants to have citizenship and settle here. This became the legal position, and it severely limited the 1948 Act, though in practice many children of immigrants still acquire British citizenship.

---

[14] Schierup (2006), p. 39. Schierup references Noiriel (1988). [15] Hansen (2000), p. 19.
[16] Ibid. p. 7. [17] Ibid. p. 111.

It is sometimes suggested that it was the rapid increase of immigrants from Commonwealth countries which were not subject to controls till the 1960s that 'generated unease among voters'.[18] Opinion polls for the period are few but indicative. Gallup numbers for 1961 show 69 per cent of respondents approving government measures to control immigration. In 1963 the response was similar: 70 per cent replied positively to the question, 'Do you approve of legislation restricting the rights of coloured people coming into Britain from the Commonwealth?'[19] The pollsters at that time commonly asked about 'coloured' immigrants, so the question was not about immigration as such but skin colour. Opinion polls can of course only indicate gross trends and they do not tell us about the complex interactions influencing the opinions that are sampled. People born into British communities in the 1940s, 1950s and early 1960s were still having it conveyed to them that the white British were the rightful rulers of a global empire consisting of 'natives'.[20] A lot of these attitudes have persisted in the private schools ('public schools') and have been emulated in other schools too, in one form or another.[21]

Populism exploits social divisions in all polities where they appear. In the UK, the divide between identity-liberal and identity-conservative worldviews was already becoming apparent in the decade after the Notting Hill and Nottingham race riots. Many of those born during or just after World War II grew up to challenge the norms, beliefs and politics of the preceding generation. They left school by the mid-1960s having benefited from the 1944 Education Act, the Welfare State provisions, and, across the entire social spectrum, from increasing access to universities. This generational group initiated cultural changes that had high public visibility by the late 1960s. The year 1968 saw the Prague Spring, political protests against the old order on the streets of Paris, and anti-Vietnam War demonstrations across the United States and Europe. That year also witnessed the assassination of the black leader Martin Luther King. This was a strange and challenging world for conservative ethnocentric minds, not just among the working class but also among the middle and upper classes. It was just as alien and disturbing, if not more so, to elite ethnocentric personalities such as Enoch Powell.[22]

Enter Enoch

In addition to the broad context of a rapidly changing world, there was an immediate context that provided opportunities for a populist demagogue. In March 1968, the Commonwealth Immigrants Act received royal assent, further

---

[18] Eatwell and Goodwin (2018), p. 137. [19] Sobolewska and Ford (2020), p. 91.
[20] Cf. Tomlinson (2018, 2019). [21] Dorling and Tomlinson (2019), pp. 70–3, Kuper (2019).
[22] Esteves (2019).

limiting the rights of Commonwealth citizens to migrate to the UK. This Act was a response on the part of the Labour government to the rapid increase in immigrants from Kenya, following the Kenyan government's 1967 introduction of restrictive laws affecting Kenyan Asians. Amendments strengthening the first Race Relations Act of 1965 were also passing through. Powell had already expressed his opposition to the whole notion of race relations legislation, arguing that recognising a minority and protecting it from discrimination would worsen relations between the black and white communities. To his mind this was demonstrated in the lethal 1967 race riots in Detroit, which he connected with the communal violence in India of 1947 following partition, and with the loss of India to the British Empire.[23] More locally there had been a continuous dispute, reported in some detail by the national and international media, over the wearing of turbans by Sikh transport workers. In February of 1968, around 5,000 Sikhs and supporters from around the UK marched in protest though Wolverhampton. Powell responded with a speech in Walsall criticising what he saw as 'communalism'. This speech attracted the attention of white conservative letter writers, whose views Powell claimed to be quoting two months later in his most notorious speech.[24] Powell addressed various other Conservative associations around the country in the early part of that year but did not attract great press interest. But his 'rivers of blood' speech in Birmingham's Midland Hotel on Saturday 20 April changed that (see Figure 5.1). The next day Edward Heath, Leader of the Opposition, sacked him from the shadow cabinet, with the full backing of his shadow cabinet colleagues.[25]

Powell's immediate audience was the Annual General Meeting of the West Midlands Area Conservative Political Centre. His aim was clearly to make both a local and a national impact, not simply to address a small number of like-minded members of the local Conservative Party. The content and the rhetoric were manifestly designed to stimulate attention and to produce an effect on potential multipliers – the national press, radio and TV, the local press, and word-of-mouth transmission. The speech did indeed seize attention and has continued to exert political influence ever since.[26]

Criticism of Powell across the political spectrum, including from within the Conservative Party, was fierce. The Conservative leader, Edward Heath, said the speech was 'racialist' and dismissed Powell from his post as Shadow Defence Secretary. Nevertheless, Powell's activity continued. He broke the taboos, such as they were, on xenophobic and racist expression in public and reinforced,

---

[23] Brooke (2007), p. 671, Schofield (2013), pp. 213–14. [24] Schofield (2013), p. 218.
[25] *The Guardian*, 14 April 2018. www.theguardian.com/world/from-the-archive-blog/2018/apr/14/enoch-powell-dismissed-speech-1968.
[26] See Hillman (2008), Manzoor (2008).

Figure 5.1 'Rivers of blood' speech, 20 April 1968.
Source: BBC Motion Gallery Editorial/BBC News/Getty Images.

sanctioned and extended xenophobic discourse in society at large. Such discourse may have been less acceptable among the political elites than among the broader British population.[27]

For five years, Powell spread his word through the eager channels of the press and public meetings. Days after the Birmingham speech, as the Race Relations Bill was being debated, a thousand dockers marched to demonstrate in favour of Powell, Smithfield meat porters handed in a petition in his support, and other workers held demonstrations in London and in Wolverhampton.[28] In 1972 Powell had another opportunity to raise his public profile around race and immigration. The Heath government was facing a crisis caused by Ugandan Asians taking up their right to residence in Britain, after being expelled from Uganda by Idi Amin. Heath approached the problem in a relatively liberal fashion. Powell's reaction was to attack his own party and government for their policy of recognising the Ugandan Asians' right to settle. He led a campaign of public speeches against the admission of Ugandan immigrants, undercutting the Conservative government and appealing to the racist ethnocentrism of certain sections of the population. The public increasingly regarded the government and the Conservative Party as weak on immigration.[29] Powell's activity created the potential for far-right parties to attract support from ethnocentrically aroused individuals during the 1970s. The Labour government from 1974 to 1979 was relatively liberal on immigration, providing a political target for far-right anti-immigrant and racist rhetoric.

---

[27] Cf. Ford (2019), p. 13; Soblewska and Ford (2020), pp. 95–8. [28] Lindop (2001).
[29] Sobolewska and Ford (2020), pp. 103–7. Cf. Crines et al. (2016).

112   Fear of Foreigners

In the 1979 election, immigration was not a forefront issue, probably because immigration matters were less prominent relative to the issue of economic 'stagflation'. However, statistical evidence shows Powell's effect on Conservative policy and on voters' anti-immigration views lasting throughout the governments of Thatcher and Major.[30] That was not the end of the story, for Powell had brought into action two connected strands of political discourse: the one anti-immigration, the other anti-Europe. It was these strands that were able to be re-activated, decisively, during the Brexit campaign. That was only possible because there existed an underlying discourse continuity. Although Margaret Thatcher had refused to include Powell in her shadow cabinet when she became leader of the Conservatives in 1975, she could not escape the effects of his wider political and ideological impact. In Camilla Schofield's view, 'There is no doubt that Powellism helped to produce Thatcherism, or that Powell contributed both to the New Right's political and economic thinking and to Thatcher's rhetorical style.'[31] In a Granada TV interview in 1978, Thatcher voiced a position on immigration that was probably due to the pressure arising from Powell's transformation of public discourse. Her aim was clearly to increase the attractiveness of her party for the anti-immigrant vote, and her opening statement, in response to the interviewer's first questions, was:

[...] there was a [Home Office] committee which looked at it and said that if we went on as we are then by the end of the century there would be four million people of the new Commonwealth or Pakistan here. Now, that is an awful lot and I think it means that people are really rather afraid that this country might be rather swamped by people with a different culture and, you know, the British character has done so much for democracy, for law and done so much throughout the world that if there is any fear that it might be swamped people are going to react and be rather hostile to those coming in.[32]

This was not the deliberate breaking of verbal norms of a Powell or a Farage; it was the middle-class accent, euphemisms and style of the home counties. But it is the same conceptual and attitudinal universe. The phrase that struck the public – 'people are really rather afraid that this country might be rather swamped by people with a different culture' – contains effective linguistic triggers. Thatcher does not mention race or skin colour, but instead speaks of having a 'culture' that is 'different'. The audience knew what was being referred to. The 'swamped' metaphor caught the journalists' eyes. Underlying this metaphor is the PATH schema, combined with another metaphor that conceptualises a crowd of moving people as a mass of moving

---

[30] Ford (2019), pp. 26–7.   [31] Schofield (2013), p. 330, Porion (2019a).
[32] Margaret Thatcher, TV interview for Granada 'World in Action', 27 January 1978. Margaret Thatcher Foundation website: www.margaretthatcher.org/document/103485.

water – metaphors already well established in anti-immigrant discourse. In the 'rivers of blood' speech, Powell's most frequently evoked image is 'flow'. And Thatcher's use of the same metaphorical source in 'swamped' was no accident. Speaking of immigrants in terms of flows, floods, swampings and connected words is a fear-activating strategy, as is Thatcher's mention of fear and prediction of hostility in the population. Twenty years on, in her memoirs published in 1995, she was still using language similar to Powell's in sympathising with the anti-immigrant attitudes of 'indigenous' householders having to 'watch their neighbourhoods changing and the value of their house falling'.[33] She took it for granted that such attitudes were natural and justifiable.

Thatcher's 1978 interview produced an immediate increase in the Conservative Party's rating for its anti-immigration stance, in all likelihood contributing to Thatcher's election success the following year. Once in office, she went on to replace the 1948 British Nationalities Act with her 1981 British Nationality Act, which defined the right of abode in the UK in terms of birthplace and ancestry. The Act in effect redefined British citizenship on the basis of an ethnocentric conception of national identity: the 1980 Green Paper bore the title 'Who Do We Think We Are?'

Powellism

Even after Powell's exit from front stage, his influence had insidious effects at all levels of British society. Powellism continued up to the time of Brexit and beyond as part ideology and part cult. It is important not to focus only on established mainstream party politics. Far-right nationalist parties were an integral element of the political culture in which Powellism thrived.

Powellism and the NF emerged in parallel. The NF was formed the year before the 'rivers of blood' speech, by Arthur Chesterton, a former member of the British Union of Fascists. Leadership of the NF was taken over by the neo-Nazi John Tyndall in 1972, the year of the Ugandan Asian crisis. The party grew for the rest of the seventies until Tyndall left in 1982 to found the British National Party (BNP), which subsequently eclipsed the NF. The BNP became particularly prominent in the 2000s in the context of increased immigration, primarily from the EU. At the 1974 general election, the NF had acted like a mainstream party, making its own election broadcast and fielding ninety candidates. Though all of them lost their deposits, the party's public profile was raised – benefiting from the heightened prominence of the anti-immigrant and racist discourse to which Powell had contributed. Any electoral support the

---

[33] Thatcher (1995), cited by Sobolewska and Ford (2020), pp. 108–9.

NF had gained was lost at the 1979 election, when Margaret Thatcher promised changes in nationality criteria and delivered them two years later.

Powell did have personal contacts with the NF, but he declined, or evaded, moves to make him into the charismatic leader that the movement needed. In 1977, there were rumours in the press and in government circles that Powell had accepted the NF leadership. The rumours were quashed by Powell. In fact, Powell was ideologically distant from the NF on most points, except his opposition to immigration. He was not a fascist corporatist but a Conservative free-marketeer and nationalist. He also maintained that he was not a racist – in the narrow sense, so it seems, of biological racism. This sense excludes the wider meaning that denotes witting and unwitting attitudes as well as institutional racism. He might well have been equivocating, and he never actually criticised the term 'racism'.[34] The important point is that Powell had established an extreme anti-immigration discourse that was capable of being exploited by the NF and other parties. His social and political status were used for legitimation, and in some groups and networks, he had, willy-nilly, a unifying and activating function – he functioned and still does as an 'icon'. In 2018, the NF commemorated Powell's 1968 Birmingham speech.

The 1981 Brixton riot – a violent confrontation between black youths and the police – looked to some like Powell's worst prophecies fulfilled. It also looked like a vindication of the new British Nationality Act which, it was claimed, would reduce the likelihood of such unrest by reducing immigrant numbers. The Scarman Report, published at the end of the year, focused on the serious social, economic and political disadvantages suffered by the non-white communities, and criticised the discriminatory use by the police of stop-and-search powers and its 'Operation Swamp 81'. When the report was debated in the House of Commons, Powell intervened as an Ulster Unionist MP, deploying a framework of conceptions and values entirely different from Scarman's. In an astonishingly arrogant academic manner, he seized on Scarman's use of the term 'accident' (as opposed to 'essence') and most revealingly the terms 'alien' and 'alienation'. Scarman was reported by *The Times* (15 April 1981) as saying that 'It was the relationship between the police and all the youth of the area, not just the blacks ... Certainly black is merely an accident'.[35] Though the intended meaning is clear, Powell decides he has to lecture the House on the Aristotelian sense of 'accident', then proceeds to assert that Scarman is incorrect. The core of Powell's argument was that Scarman was incorrect in saying that being 'black' was 'merely an accident'. In other words, he, Powell, believes that being 'black' is of the essence and is thus the cause of the riot. He rejects the report's statement that the cause of the riot is the alienation of the

---

[34] Powell (1977), p. 5, Schofield (2013), p. 311, Porion (2019b), p. 153.
[35] Quoted from Powell's speech, Hansard 10 December 1981, Commons Sitting.

'black community' (a phrase he dislikes because it reminds him of 'communal disturbances' in colonial India). And he disparages the report's assumption that this alienation is caused by economic, occupational and environmental disadvantage. Instead, he asserts his own explanation of the alienation:

> There is another possible explanation of the alienation. It is that the community, being of that size and composition and in those circumstances, is alien: alienation can be a manifestation of being alien. It can be the self-perception and the being perceived by others as different and distinct; and, in the case of a black community – [. . .] – it is a difference which is instantly and mutually visible and which produces mutual coherence or repulsion.[36]

For Powell, being alien is an *essential* feature of being different, which seems to mean for him both perceiving oneself to be different and being perceived to be different by others. It is evident, though not fully explicit, that for him being different means being visibly different and specifically of a different skin colour. Furthermore, he appears to be saying that an automatic response to 'visible difference' is either 'mutual recognition' (within one community) or 'repulsion' (between members of different communities). 'Repulsion' is a staggeringly strong expression for what is the perception of skin colour.

In the 1980s, anti-immigrant and racist discourse did not significantly diminish. As in Brixton, in certain areas hostile discourse and violent clashes were common. And this was so in the younger generation as well as the older generation. It was a time when the NF would enter school premises to beat up pupils.[37] In Manchester in 1986, in Burnage High School, where racial violence was rife, an Asian boy was stabbed by a white pupil. The police initially dismissed the incident as not 'a racist murder', but four years later an inquiry under Ian MacDonald QC found that while the event was complex, it reflected the racist structure of society.[38] In real terms, that means of course that hostile racist discourse structured the event. That racist discourse structure was reflected in the responses to a letter to *The Independent* that ventured to explain the measures many teachers had begun to take to counter the apparent assumption among young white people 'that they have any social, moral or political right to harass or attack their non-white fellow citizen'. A torrent of protesting letters to the original correspondent included one that had the following Powellist rejoinder: 'Non-white people in this country are not our fellow

---

[36] Hansard 10 December 1981, Commons Sitting. https://api.parliament.uk/historic-hansard/commons/1981/dec/10/scarman-report.
  The omission in brackets is a parenthesis concerning the phrase 'ethnic minority', provoking the Jewish Labour MP Alex Lyon to ask if Powell uses the word 'alien' in relation to the Jewish community.
[37] Danny Dorling, personal testimony in Dorling and Tomlinson (2019), p. 212.
[38] Macdonald et al. (1989), alternatively known as the *Burnage Report*.

citizens. They are aliens temporarily living here until the English people come to their senses'.[39]

Nearly a decade later, the figure of Powell and his rhetoric influenced a racist murder. At a bus stop in South East London in 1993, Stephen Lawrence was stabbed to death by a gang of young white men, two of whom were convicted of murder, but not till 2012. For four years, courts dismissed the case on the grounds that the evidence was unreliable. Questions were raised about police attitudes. In February 1997, the *Daily Mail* – surprisingly, given its record on race and immigration – started a front-page campaign on behalf of the Lawrence family. And a few months later, the new Labour Home Secretary, Jack Straw, launched a judicial inquiry into the police handling of the killing, chaired by Sir William Macpherson. There was no trial of the suspects until 2011. Police surveillance evidence of a conversation at the flat of one of the accused was of crucial importance for the inquiry. A transcript of the videotape was included in the Macpherson Report, published in February 1999.[40] Two youths, labelled A and B, are talking about Powell:

B: 'ya remember that Enoch Powell – that geezer he knew straight away he went over to Africa and all that right – [...] he, he knew it was a slum, he knew it was a shit hole and he came back here saying they're uncivilised and all that and then they started coming over here and he knew, he knew straight away he was saying no I don't want them here no fucking niggers they'll ruin the gaff and he was right they fucking have ruined it [...]
A: I wanna write him a letter Enoch Powell mate you are the greatest, you are the don of dons get back into parliament mate.

This obscene racist conversation speaks for itself. It is the sort of talk among young males that has the job of generating solidarity in socially and economically deprived groups – precisely the groups most susceptible to racist rhetoric.

There is no way to show that Powell's public utterances are the direct cause, or that without them these individuals would not have held such attitudes and talked such language. But there can be little doubt that they reference Powell as a source and a justification. The police transcript also indicates how elite discourses can activate overt racist discourse. This effect is not confined to alienated working class youth. In other social milieux, explicit public racism was becoming socially unacceptable, but it was replaced by a new form of racist talk, as Martin Shaw has emphasised. This was a covert racism performed by means of verbalisations that could be denied as racist, and which operated by means of hints, innuendo, in-group catchwords, and other kinds of dog whistle.[41]

---

[39] Dorling and Tomlinson (2019), p. 211, Tomlinson (1988).
[40] Macpherson (1999a, 1999b), *The Stephen Lawrence Inquiry*, Appendix 10, Sequence 11, 3, December 1994, 23:25:28 to 23:28:00. Cf. Chilton (2004), Chapter 7.
[41] Shaw (2022), pp. 25–30.

The murder of Stephen Lawrence was committed in a context in which extreme racialised nationalism was rising. In the 1990s, neo-Nazi white supremacist groups (the group known as 'White Wolves' and the international 'Combat 18', for example) advocated terrorist attacks against non-whites, Jews and others perceived as racially alien. The number of individuals killed in racially motivated attacks remains significant. The Institute of Race Relations, which monitors deaths with a known or suspected racial motivation, has reported that, in the twenty years after the killing of Stephen Lawrence, there were at least 105 such deaths in the UK.[42] It would be unjustifiable to link Powell himself directly to the neo-Nazi racists. Nonetheless, Powell*ism* contributed to and helped sustain racist-nationalist ideology in British society.

The internet revolution, and the development of social media, brought the propagation of political ideologies, irrational beliefs, and cults into an entirely new dimension. It is the most insidious form that propaganda can take. The cultic character of Powellism reveals itself in full view on online platforms. Monika Kopytowska has examined two examples, both on YouTube.[43] In one case, a young, conspicuously white woman reads Powell's speech, with pauses and glances at the camera after 'rivers of blood' and such phrases.[44] This kind of re-performance and re-contextualisation demonstrates how Powell's verbal attacks on the non-white communities of his day are powerfully recycled into the world of a much younger generation.

The other video (see Figure 5.2) was posted on 'Xurious', a neo-Nazi website. It consists of a static image of Powell's face wearing an expression of grim foreboding. On a black strip positioned across his eyes we read what he foresees: RIVERS OF BLOOD. In the fiery background is a shadowy female figure resembling a classical statue – suggesting the white European civilisation that far-right ideologues claim to defend. The soundtrack is a recording of Powell giving his notorious speech over a background track – a heavy marching drumbeat overlaid by a four-note riff, creating an overall effect of looming danger. This is an example of 'fashwave', a popular-music genre cultivated by far-right and neo-Nazi networks.[45]

The community of responders to this platform picked up on the religious undertones, and echoed them back in comments such as the following, in one case using the pervasive invasion metaphor:

- Enoch was right on foreign immigration invasion. A man who foreseen [sic] the future displacement of our people. but [sic] the tide is turning and the great awakening of our people is happening. God speed this transformation[.]

---

[42] Institute of Race Relations, 'Racial violence statistics'. https://irr.org.uk/research/statistics/racial-violence/.
[43] Kopytowska (2022).
[44] 'Dancing Dove: Enoch Powell's Rivers of Blood Speech', www.bitchute.com/video/1A4xuxkuxJpc/.
[45] Hann (2016), Larsen (2022).

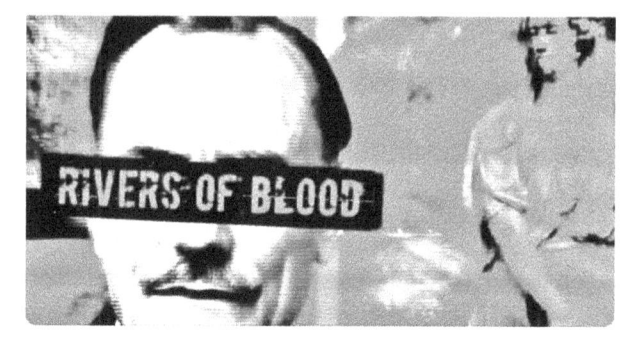

Figure 5.2 Neo-Nazi Powellism.
Source: YouTube, 'Xurious – Rivers Of Blood', reposted after account closure, now available at: www.youtube.com/watch?v=Es2pPwbCR34

- Rivers of blood are inevitable at this point. I just pray we win. Otherwise the world is doomed[.]
- A prophet is not welcome in his own country.[46]

Powell's forename, Enoch, may play a part in these vaguely biblical allusions – the biblical Enoch is viewed by some as a prophet. The 'displacement of our people' is biblical in style and in far-right communities evokes their idea of a 'great replacement' of Europeans. The 'great awakening' is a phrase used historically in religious revivalist movements in the United States and is currently used by the Christian right. Powell talked like a prophet, is regarded by his devotees as a prophet, and was not entirely welcome in his own country.

The Path to Brexit

The murder of the MP Jo Cox in 2016, one week before the referendum, was not racist in itself. However, it was certainly a product of a far-right mindset that was not only racist but saw anti-racist and multicultural activists as traitors and collaborators with an enemy. Cox was a newly elected Labour MP, on her way to a constituency surgery, when she was shot and stabbed by an individual shouting 'Britain First!' (though witnesses vary on the exact words). 'Britain First' is the name of a fascist group, formed in 2011 by former members of the BNP. The police later found that the killer, Thomas Mair, lived in a house crammed with neo-Nazi print material and memorabilia. What Mair shouted as he struck was in keeping with the slogans of the Leave campaign, which could have acted as a catalyst for the action of this obsessive-compulsive loner. If he was connected with the Britain First group, it is worth noting that Britain First

---

[46] Cited in Chilton and Kopytowska (2022), p. 245.

strongly supported UKIP (which denied any association). Some researchers argue that Britain First may have boosted the Leave.EU campaign with social media material that reached many more users than UKIP itself.[47] Causal connections in socio-political contexts are difficult to prove. But the likelihood of a connection between Brexit propaganda and increased racist offences was borne out in the judgement of the Metropolitan Police Commissioner three months after the referendum. At a London mayoral hearing, commenting on statistics that showed that there were more than 2,300 race-related offences in the thirty-eight days after the referendum, compared to 1,400 in the same period before the referendum, the Commissioner said:

> We couldn't say it was absolutely down to Brexit, although there was obviously a spike after it. Some of them [race-hate offences] were attributed to it because of what was said at the time. We could attribute that, and eastern Europeans were particularly targeted within the race-hate crime [category]. So there certainly was a spike related to it.[48]

Powellism may not have been a factor in the murder of Jo Cox, but the linkage between far-right ideologies, Powell and Brexit is closer than might be imagined. It is not confined to alienated working class individuals. It was a group of senior Conservative politicians and the sophists behind them – the advisors and ideologues – who produced the celebratory volume *Enoch at 100*, edited by Lord Howard of Rising, in 2012.[49] Such groupings intersect with other right-wing politicians – factions, lobbies, and political clubs such as the Swinton Circle, the Monday Club and the European Research Group (ERG). The Monday Club's relations with the far right go back at least to the 1970s, when its executive became concerned that the NF was taking over Club branches.[50] One of the most influential Conservative admirers of Powell at the time of the referendum was Daniel Hannan, a prime mover of Vote Leave. Those for whom Powell's utterances functioned as a source and inspiration were highly diverse in their social, cultural and political origins. There were important differences in their views, but there was also much common ground. At the opposite end of the socio-economic spectrum to the murderers of Stephen Lawrence and Jo Cox, there are open admirers of Powell among the UK's social and educational elite. Here are three examples.

The first is the philosopher of Conservatism, Sir Roger Scruton. In a 2006 article titled 'Should he have spoken?', Scruton writes of Powell that he was the silenced victim of liberalism. Like Powell, his attitude towards immigrants is

---

[47] Shaw (2022), pp. 14, 128.
[48] Sir Bernard Hogan-Howe, reported by Matthew Weaver in *The Guardian*, 28 September 2016, www.theguardian.com/society/2016/sep/28/hate-crime-horrible-spike-brexit-vote-metropolitan-police.
[49] The contributors included Iain Duncan Smith, Frank Field, Simon Heffer, Andrew Roberts, Margaret Mountford and Roger Scruton. Heffer is the author of a biography of Powell.
[50] Schofield (2013), pp. 310–11.

wholly negative. Like Powell, he obscures contestable facts with innuendo and irony, counterposes migrants to 'indigenous citizens', and takes for granted that readers take the same underlying stance:

> [Immigrants] come as the heads of families, and even if the family might comprise four wives and twenty children, it arrives to a red carpet of legal privileges, eagerly unrolled by publicly funded lawyers, and to a welcome trough of welfare benefits that few indigenous citizens can claim, however much they have contributed to the common fund.[51]

There are two points in his article worth dwelling on. First, he wishes to defend Powell's 'vision' (a word much repeated) of traditional Englishness. This is something Scruton is very sympathetic with, for he laments the failure of the British to replace the Empire with a new English and British nationalism. Second, he defends the notion of the 'noble' political lie, which he conflates with political myth. Citing Plato, he distinguishes between the philosopher's search for truth and the politician's devices of rhetoric. In the latter case, he distinguishes between the 'noble lie' and the 'ignoble lie', and gives a description of 'the noble lie':

> among the rhetorical devices of politicians, it is still possible to distinguish the noble lies from their ignoble negations. The noble lie is the untruth that conveys a truth, the myth that maps reality.

For Scruton, what Plato said about the 'noble lie' was an attempt to 'describe the role of myth in human thinking'. And myth, in Scruton's view, is a more profound kind of truth. He tells us that myths are 'attempts to capture difficult truths in symbols' and that they 'arm us against realities that are otherwise too fateful or disturbing to bear contemplation'. What has this to do with Powell? Scruton further tells us that Powell's 'vision of England might be seen as a noble lie', which he equates with an 'ideal image [...] shaped by myth'. His main point is that ideal myth and noble lies are being undermined by liberal-minded people and their liberal Enlightenment 'creed' which drives them to tell 'ignoble lies'. These people, according to Scruton, simply do not acknowledge

> the fundamental truth, which is that indigenous communities have legitimate expectations which take precedence over the demands of strangers.

It is not only a matter of immigrant outsiders settling in the UK, but the wider 'foreignisation' of Europe by Islamisation. This was a fear that Powell had not encountered in his own day. Nonetheless, Scruton was acting as a vehicle of Powellism throughout his own communication networks, every bit as much as

---

[51] Scruton (2006); see Portes (2019) for comment. Originally published in *New Criterion*, Scruton's article was also issued by the white supremacist website, *American Renaissance*.

the racist murderers of Stephen Lawrence were in theirs. He was a perpetuator of Powellism for high culture, for Conservative politicians, and for populist ideologues. And he assisted its continuation into the next generations.

The second example of posh English Powellism is Douglas Murray, who was educated at Eton and Oxford. Murray is in tune with Powell's perspective of half a century earlier, as well as with Scruton's. Though he regards Powell's outspoken rhetoric as politically incautious, he thinks that Powell's predictions were 'understated' when compared with the multi-ethnic and cultural situation of the twenty-first century.[52] In fact, he uses the same kind of metaphors as Powell. His book *The Strange Death of Europe* warns that Europe is now 'committing suicide' by permitting the mass migration of non-European peoples. The 'flow' of migrants across the Mediterranean has become a 'flood' sweeping across Europe's borders and threatening its civilisation and culture. There is under way, Murray asserts, 'the replacement of large parts of the European populations by other people'. And in Britain, 'London has become a foreign country'.[53]

This species of Powellite discourse, surfacing in numerous outlets under Murray's name, provided support and authority to UKIP's own propaganda. He perpetuates the Powellist vision via multiple networks. These include links with the far-right identitarian movements across present-day Europe and the US, and with right-wing populist leaders and politicians, including among others Victor Orbán and Steve Bannon. Murray himself rejects the label 'far right'. His anti-immigration and nationalist language overlaps with that of Generation Identity, particularly with its notion of 'the Great Replacement'. This idea derived from the far-right identitarian French writer, Renaud Camus, who declared himself as being in the ideological line of descent from Enoch Powell. Murray's contacts include members of Pegida, the German populist anti-refugee movement that made a significant political impact in 2014. He also writes in praise of Tommy Robinson (Stephen Christopher Yaxley-Lennon) for his role as an initiator and leader of the English Defence League (EDL).[54] Robinson is an important communications node in the politically active anti-immigrant and anti-EU web of far-right organisations.[55] Murray is also a part of this web and plays a significant role in propagating and legitimising extreme ethnocentric ideas.

The third example is Raheem Kassam, whose activity is spread through extensive and inter-connected far-right channels. He was another supporter of Pegida,[56] became a 'special advisor' to Farage and was briefly a candidate for UKIP's leadership in 2016. Born into a practising Shia family in London, he abjured his Islam faith, and began his political activism in the Conservative

---

[52] Murray (2017), pp. 16–17. [53] Murray (2013). [54] Murray (2017), pp. 238–9.
[55] Busher (2018). [56] Kassam (2016a, 2016b).

Party, contributing to its think tanks and to other right-wing policy organisations. He was hired by Steve Bannon to set up the London branch of *Breitbart News*. Kassam disseminates his nationalist ideology on blogging sites, as well as in traditional campaigning. His book *Enoch Was Right*, first launched digitally, demonstrates the transformation of Powellism into a quasi-religious cult. The wording of the title was associated with the Conservative MP John Townend after a racist speech in 2001, and with a Conservative parliamentary candidate, Nigel Hastilow, who was deselected for using it in 2007. By Kassam's time, the phrase was a buzzword on the right and a part of rightist popular culture displayed on badges and t-shirts.

The book lays out Powell's 'rivers of blood' text at the outset, and the reader is urged to become familiar with it before proceeding to Kassam's seven-chapter commentary on successive sections – as if the text were holy writ and the chapters an exegesis. The commentary mainly consists of insistent defences of Powell against his many critics from 1968 on – repeated reassertions of the view that national societies are naturally and normally homogeneous with respect to ethnicity, culture and language. The likely inference by readers that this requires *racial* homogeneity is not voiced, and it is even denied. Throughout, there is a thread of reverse racism – that is, the claim that it is those who espouse national cultural homogeneity who are the ones truly victimised, victimised by a type of 'racism' perpetrated by non-white people and white liberal people. Powell himself is represented as a victimised revealer of 'the truth', and Kassam repeatedly lays claim to this 'truth'.

In line with his association with UKIP, Kassam attaches Powell's supposed truth-telling in the 'rivers of blood' speech to Powell's anti-EU (European Economic Community – EEC) stance. For Kassam, there is a direct line from that speech to Brexit:

In truth it was a speech that would pave the way for a slow burning revolution in British politics, eventually leading to the nation voting to leave the European Union in 2016.[57]

Thus, Powell paved the way for Brexit. Whether one agrees with Kassam's value judgements or not, it is fair to say that Powell sowed the seeds of Eurosceptic national populism. What (marginally) carried the day at the referendum was a fanatical blend of Englishness, British exclusionary sovereignty, ethnocentrism and racism. All of that was packaged and sold to the electorate with a guarantee that the 'influx' of immigrants would thus be held back from Britain's shores.

Powell's ethnocentric and racialised worldview was logically linked with an intense Euroscepticism, which he expressed decades before the 2016 referendum. It followed from his nationalist ethnocentric view of the world that

---

[57] Kassam (2018).

The Path to Brexit

Britishness was not and could not be a part of a multilingual, multicultural economic and political entity. The counterpart to foreigners entering Britain was Britain entering the EU, or EEC as it then was.

Under both Labour and Conservative governments Powell continued to receive publicity primarily for his anti-immigrant stance, whether his political sights were trained on Labour or his own party. However, the reason he gave for voting for Labour at the 1974 general election was that Heath had signed the treaty for accession to the EEC without a popular mandate. Powell had already voted against Britain's joining the EEC in 1969 and had spoken against that in the following years. On 23 February 1974, at a public meeting in Birmingham's Bull Ring Centre, he declared:

This is the first and last election at which the British people can be sure of [will be given] the opportunity to decide whether their country is to remain a democratic nation, governed by the will of its own electorate expressed in its own Parliament, or whether it will become one province in a new European super-state under institutions which know nothing of the political rights and liberties that we have so long taken for granted.[58]

This populist wording – the talk of a super-state, of a province, of ancient rights, liberties and so forth – was to become very familiar forty years on. Like the Brexiters, he made sweeping claims about loss of control. And he accused the Heath government of deceiving Parliament. According to Powell, the bill to proceed to negotiations with the EEC 'turned out to be a comprehensive renunciation by the House of Commons of its control over the laws of the land, the taxes of the people, and the policies of the executive'. He spoke of Britain being 'hijacked into the E.E.C.'. What was to be the foundation of Brexit thinking – the linkage of nationality, historical identity, the British people and British sovereignty – played the central role in his rhetoric:

Heath does not want the British people to decide at the ballot-box the most momentous transformation in their history [...] The question is: can they now be prevented from taking back into their own hands the decision about their identity and their form of government which truly was theirs all along.

At the same meeting, Powell saw it as his duty to urge his audience to vote Labour. Five days later he did so himself, in all likelihood increasing Labour's vote.[59] In another general election in October the same year, held because of a hung Parliament, Powell stood as, and was returned as, an Ulster Unionist MP. What Powell had wanted was a popular referendum on EEC membership, which he plainly assumed the people would reject. The Wilson government that

---

[58] Powell (1974). This is the version hand-corrected by Powell. The version in Collings (1991) is in square brackets.
[59] Ford (2019), p. 24.

124 Fear of Foreigners

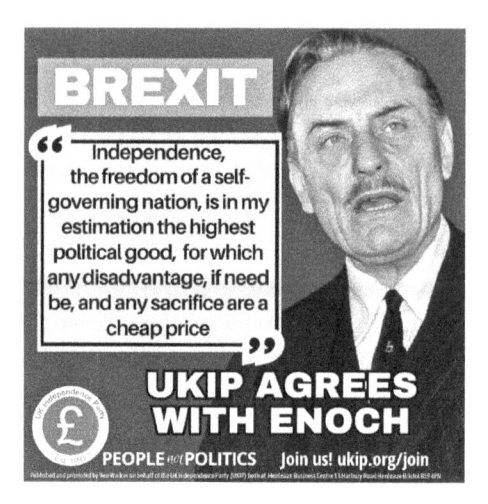

> Figure 5.3 UKIP Powellism.
> *Source*: UKIP via Twitter/X.
> https://twitter.com/UKIP/status/1694605464976457905

was elected shortly after Powell spoke did indeed hold a referendum on new British membership terms in 1975. Powell campaigned for a 'no' vote. The referendum result confirmed the treaty of accession to the EEC with the decisive majority of 67 per cent.

Four decades later Powell's image reappeared in the campaign for Brexit. One example is the UKIP ad in Figure 5.3. Unsurprisingly, social media was mobilised to spread a series of posts that combined nationalist Europhobia with implicitly racist xenophobia.

The quotation on the poster comes from a speech given in Stockport in 1973.[60] At that time Powell was demanding a referendum on whether the United Kingdom should remain a member of the European Communities. His speeches poured forth many of the claims and arguments that were to become stock Brexiter war cries in 2016. The Twitter/X ad in Figure 5.3 and similar UKIP ads were downloadable only by UKIP members, who were urged to spread the word by way of flyers and posters. Enoch Powell evidently gave ultimate sanction to UKIP's blend of overt nationalism and dog whistled racism.

Xenophobia and ethnocentrism were already embedded in British society, but Powell fired this up and his charisma kept it alive through time and across social strata. And the anti-immigration and anti-Europe trade unions and political

---

[60] At the Stockport Luncheon Club, 8 June 1973. See Powell (1973).

tendencies on the Labour side should not be forgotten. Powell's devotees have persisted as an expanding network of secondary demagogues, who are not professional politicians but wield their own kind of influence and power. The elite and the non-elite anti-immigration networks interact. They operate through varied channels – gangs, crowds, social movements, pressure groups, fringe parties, and now the all-pervasive internet. By the time of the 2016 referendum, the propaganda of Vote Leave and Leave.EU deployed the instruments of digital data analysis, personal profiling, and messages tailored to those profiles. Powell's influence continued right through to Conservative figures who were prime movers in the Leave campaigns of 2016. Indeed, Powell laid the foundations of the pro-Brexit discourse that swayed the electorate at the referendum and that was ideologically perpetuated by the post-referendum governments.

6 Fear of Foreigners Mobilised

Brexitspeak did not just appear out of the blue. It came out of a culturally continuous way of talking and thinking about national identity – the identity of the inhabitants of the British islands. At the same time, it rested on complementary mental representations of, and emotional reactions to, perceived foreigners. Ethnocentrism, xenophobia, nationalism and outright racism among certain sections of the population – these attitudes of mind were endemic in the UK's cultural and political discourses. Such attitudes had constituted a continuous tradition at least since the formation of the British state and its development as a colonial and imperial power. It was a relatively easy rhetorical task to activate and intensify this latent and not-so-latent tradition in the service of Brexit propaganda. British Euroscepticism, out of which the Brexit movement developed, appeared in the twentieth century on the British right. After the introduction of freedom of movement between the EU's member states, the financial crisis of 2007–8, and the European debt crisis of 2009, the context was ripe for the emergence of the United Kingdom Independence Party. A rising tide of demagoguery followed, boosting the political pressure to hold a referendum on the UK's EU membership. By the time of the vote, the electorate was flooded with falsehood and irrationality.

The Rise of UKIP

The decade from the turn of the millennium – roughly the late 1990s to the 2010s – saw significant changes in the rise of far-right ethnocentric social and political movements in the UK. The British National Party (BNP) was given an internal boost by its new leader, Nick Griffin, and its membership grew rapidly in the 2000s. It became the most successful ever British far-right party, though by 2014 it was being overtaken by the English Defence League (EDL). Under Griffin, the BNP started to keep quiet about its previous biological racism, adopting the argument that the party was not racist but was simply responding to anti-*white* racism. Instead of race, its leaders talked of cultural incompatibilities. It remained vocal on its policy of excluding non-white migrants, but it spoke now of voluntary repatriation rather than its earlier compulsory deportation policy.

After the 'twin towers' terrorist attacks of 11 September 2001, the BNP's prime target changed to Muslim migrants. It maintained hostile discourse against the EU.[1] Although there was significant ideological overlap among the adherents of the BNP, EDL and UKIP, both the BNP and EDL were outshone by UKIP after the 2010 general election. The BNP virtually disappeared after the 2014 European election, when Griffin lost his seat as an MEP (having won it in 2009). After the 2015 general election it was no longer functional. The BNP's decline left a niche in the electoral landscape that could be filled by UKIP, which had been rapidly increasing its electoral visibility and respectability.[2] The EDL, having developed links with BNP breakaway elements, failed to make inroads into electoral politics, and lost any respectability it may have had. Its membership fell away and the party was overshadowed by UKIP after 2011, following the conviction of EDL supporters for plotting to bomb mosques, violent disorder at rallies, and reports of some supporters' links with terrorists. UKIP was also attracting members who were interested in anti-EU activism.[3] It also received support from Tommy Robinson, then EDL leader, who urged his own members to vote tactically for UKIP in the May 2013 local elections – support that UKIP was careful to disassociate itself from.[4] The point here is the continuity, cohesion and idiosyncratic character of the British right-wing tradition with its focus on immigration, non-white citizens and dislike of European integration. This was ready to be awakened and mobilised: it was UKIP, with its populist appeal and demagogic capabilities, that proved to be the mobiliser.

UKIP's organisational origin was the Anti-Federalist League (AFL),[5] started by the academic historian Alan Sked in 1991. One of the early members was Nigel Farage. The AFL's purpose was to oppose the Maastricht Treaty, which significantly increased the powers of the European Commission. All three mainstream political parties were committed to ratification of the treaty, and it eventually came into force in 1993. Sked and his associates, however, maintained that voters had not had the chance to vote for or against Maastricht, and their AFL was aimed at rectifying what was seen as a democratic deficit. Sked was also a founding member of the anti-integration think tank known as the Bruges Group that had been started in 1989. Though officially a cross-party grouping, it was primarily linked with major Conservative Party figures. Sked left the Bruges Group in 1991.

The AFL had been set up as a political party and fielded a number of candidates in the 1992 general election, losing all its deposits. Sked stood

---

[1] Goodwin (2011). [2] Ford and Goodwin (2014a, 2014b).
[3] Winlow et al. (2017), Busher (2018). [4] MacDonald (2013). [5] Merrick (2017).

twice in by-elections the following year, at Newbury and at Christchurch – he came fourth in both. The subsequent developments are testimony to the growing role of anti-immigrationism at the grassroots level. In September 1993, Sked, Farage and others decided that the AFL should be renamed and have the structure of a populist party, with the intention of contesting the 1994 European Parliament elections.[6] It should be noted that Sked himself opposed the growing ethnocentrist and racist elements of the organisation. The internal presence of the extreme right, and division on policy towards potential UKIP seats in the European Parliament, led to Sked's resignation from the party in 1997, following the general election. Sked's political views were in general centre-left, and he went on to publicly criticise UKIP for its far-right extremism as well as for what he regarded as its incompetence.

At this juncture, Farage's faction within UKIP became dominant, Farage himself becoming leader in 2006. Under his leadership, from 2006 to 2009, the party focused on anti-immigration and anti-EU sentiment. UKIP's growing success was partly due to a certain middle-class and middle-aged respectability, but mainly to its ability to combine this with its appeal to white working-class voters. Furthermore, under Farage, UKIP managed to blend together its ideological opposition to any integration of the UK with the EU on the one hand, with, on the other hand, the native British xenophobia that had its own separate origins. Its xenophobia was much more overt and outspoken than other parties, apart from the BNP and other far-right groups. Farage stepped down in 2009 to contest a seat at the 2010 general election, and after failing to be elected, he regained leadership of his party. In this position he remained from November 2010 until the referendum, when he stepped down again, resigning from UKIP two years later. In 2018 he co-founded the Brexit Party, with the financial trader Catherine Blaiklock, who had also previously been active in UKIP.

Farage's UKIP leadership from 2010 to 2016 was important not just for the increased political prominence of his party but also because of his particularly effective rhetorical activity. His demagoguery was able to attract media and public attention and to increase UKIP's share of election results. An important milestone was the Eastleigh by-election of February 2013. The Liberal Democrats retained the seat, but with a much-reduced majority (32.1 per cent of the vote, a downswing of 14.4 per cent), while UKIP came second (27.8 per cent, an upswing of 24.2 per cent). The Conservative candidate came third with 25.4 per cent, a drop of 13.9 per cent. UKIP – and its ideological position on the EU – had a month earlier been one of the key political drivers of Cameron's Bloomberg speech. Eastleigh remained a significant poll for Farage, who was working to build UKIP's political

---

[6] Farage (2011), p. 78.

identity against the mainstream. At the time, UKIP blamed the Conservatives – who had already begun to talk about new immigration measures and whose candidate was explicitly anti-EU – for splitting the vote. Nonetheless, the relationship between UKIP and the Conservatives has been described as 'symbiotic'.[7]

It was not only local factors that helped Farage at this juncture. It was five years since the global financial crisis, the eurozone debt crisis had burst in 2009, austerity policies had been implemented across Europe, and the UK's measures had begun to bite. Added to this, the parliamentary expenses scandal had fuelled popular discrediting of politicians. After Cameron's announcement of a referendum on EU membership, the Conservatives were preoccupied with internal disagreements about renegotiations with the EU and about the timing of a possible referendum. Alarmingly for Eurosceptics, the EU's 'transitional restrictions' on the admission of new member states were due to come to their legal end in January 2014. Already in August 2013, just before the UKIP annual conference, this prompted unfounded headlines in the press, and in the mouths of some politicians, especially UKIP ones – 'tidal waves' of immigrants were going to 'swamp' the job market. All these events and issues constituted a political opportunity for a populist leader to come up stage front.

Under Farage, UKIP took on key characteristics of the growing wave of national populist parties across Europe, mobilising the not-so-latent xenophobia of sections of the UK's identity-conservative populace. The party tapped into the persistent influence of Enoch Powell, going back to Powell's role in the 'no' campaign of 1975. Passed on to millennials, Powellism remained present in the right-wing nationalist culture. Powell himself had spoken in support of Sked at the Newbury by-election in 1993. Farage, despite his occasional tactical disavowals, exploited this continuous political-cultural thread. In his personal story, *Flying Free*, he tells us how from his schooldays Powell had been a symbolic figure for him. He describes him as 'a singularly great man: principled, with a formidable mind, the courage of his convictions and enduring independence of spirit'. He tells his readers this while recounting how he met Powell in person when he was helping Sked in his campaign at the Newbury by-election. The 'great man' was visiting to speak at an event on behalf of Sked's AFL.[8] The common ground is clear. Simon Heffer, Powell's biographer, notes: 'There is [...] a clear ideological continuity between Powell's and UKIP's discourses on Europe.'[9]

From the mid-1990s, there were undeniable increases in existing post-war migration trends from the Commonwealth and additional major population shifts across Europe. Migrant arrivals, encouraged by New Labour reforms,

---

[7] Bale (2018).   [8] Farage (2011), p. 74.
[9] Simon Heffer, cited by Cowley (2017). See also Tournier-Sol (2019), p. 165.

increased from around 300,000 a year in the mid-1990s to 500,000 by 2002 and remained more or less at that level.[10] In 2004, the process of enlargement of the EU yielded the simultaneous accession of ten new countries, seven of which were former Soviet bloc states. The citizens of some, such as Poland, Lithuania and Hungary, had longstanding motivations to migrate to the UK. The Labour government did not impose restrictions on this movement – unlike some EU countries, which did impose temporary limits. Because this position constituted a commitment to the EU, it was viewed with considerable hostility by various political groupings, and this made for a ready blending of anti-EU and anti-migrant sentiment with the existing ethnocentric and xenophobic discourses.

These demographic shifts are regarded by some political scientists as a second post-war 'wave' of immigration, and the statistics are clear. However, this second surge was different from the first. It was not a consequence of the decline of an empire but of two new historic developments: the unexpected collapse of the USSR and the gradual emergence of an integrated Europe. The new migrants were not all non-white people from Africa, Asia and the Caribbean, but white Europeans from eastern and central European countries. The New Labour governments and their supporters from the growing identity-liberal sections of the population viewed the increased immigration as economically beneficial, and respected norms not accepted by the remaining identity-conservative sections. And New Labour did not anticipate the populist surge, nor could they match its anti-migrant rhetoric, which had rooted itself in discourse since 'rivers of blood'.

An Ipsos MORI poll for 1997–2018 charts the percentage share of respondents naming migration as one of the UK's most important problems.[11] There is a steep rise from about 2 per cent of people expressing concern in 1997 to about 30 per cent in 2002. There is a further rise to about 36 per cent in 2006–7, coinciding with migration from the countries that had recently acceded to the EU. Then there is a decline to around 23 per cent by the end of the Labour government and the first year of the Cameron-Clegg coalition. At this point, following Cameron's unfulfilled election promise of unprecedentedly large cuts to immigration, there is a steep rise in discontent to almost 50 per cent in 2015–16. These statistical peaks occurred in tandem with the increase in migrant arrivals over the period. It was a period that also coincided with the decade when the BNP was increasingly active and when the AFL was turning itself into the more xenophobic and more active UKIP.

One could say that both the opinion poll indicators and the rise of the anti-immigrant parties 'reflect' the increased immigration, or a supposedly natural anxiety prompted by it. However, the increased public focus on immigration was to be found mainly among voters who were already anti-migrant. This can

---

[10] Sobolewska and Ford (2020), p. 143.   [11] Ibid. p. 144.

reasonably be seen as evidence that what was happening was not an overall surge in xenophobia but the activation of pre-existing hostility to migrants in a specific group – primarily identity-conservative individuals. How was that hostility activated? The answer is that it was done by focusing mental attention on immigration, and targeting the most susceptible. What happened throughout the country was the turning up of the rhetorical volume, notably by UKIP and the pro-Leave actors, on a wavelength that combined xenophobia and Euroscepticism. Recognising a rhetorical link in the causal chain helps explain the socio-political process as a whole.

Anti-migrant Propaganda

At the beginning of the referendum campaign, it was uncertain whether economic issues would carry the day against the immigration issues. Certainly, Cameron and Remain campaigners seemed to think that was the case. There was plenty of reliable information in the public domain about the potentially negative effects of a Leave vote on the economy, including on jobs, wages and public services. One document that should have held some authority was a letter signed by a group of economists, both academic and non-academic, published in *The Times* on 12 May 2016. The letter made it plain that the evidence indicated that leaving the EU would inflict significant long-term economic damage.[12] The Governor of the Bank of England, Mark Carney, stated at a news conference on the same day, 'A vote to leave the EU could have material economic effects – on the exchange rate, on demand and on the economy's supply potential – that could affect the appropriate setting of monetary policy.'[13] He was immediately accused by pro-Brexit politicians of acting unconstitutionally; anti-Brexit politicians referred to his remarks as important evidence of the economic risks in leaving the EU. Carney defended himself on the grounds that he was acting responsibly in drawing attention to economic facts. Ipsos MORI conducted a poll of members of the Royal Economic Society and the Society of Business Economists. The results were that '88% thought it most likely that real GDP would be negatively impacted in the next 5 years, if the UK left the EU and the single market'.[14]

This professional consensus carried little weight. A bunch of academics and other experts easily countered by the Leave side. Experts belonged to the 'establishment', according to Brexit demagogues. Most of the press treated factual evidence as no more than opinion. The Brexit demagogues did not care about facts – they knew that manipulating minds and emotions was far more

[12] Wren-Lewis (2018), pp. 167–70.
[13] *The Guardian*, 12 May 2016, www.theguardian.com/business/2016/may/12/bank-of-england-keeps-interest-rates-on-hold-as-brexit-fears-bite.
[14] Ipsos MORI, 28 May 2016, www.ipsos.com/en-uk/economists-views-brexit.

effective. Faced with the economic facts, the trick they used was to accuse the other side of emotional manipulation, claiming by implication that it was they, the Leavers, who possessed the true facts. Thus Boris Johnson accused the pro-Remain campaigners, Britain Stronger in Europe, of scaremongering when they warned of the negative economic effects of leaving the EU. Such warnings were labelled 'project fear'. The label resonated and spread easily. The pro-Leave campaign managed to neutralise rational economic concerns, turn voters' attention onto immigration, and promote their own 'project fear' – the fear of foreigners. By 23 June 2016, the opinion polls were indicating that public opinion against immigration had overtaken the economy as a motive for voting.[15]

Conservative politicians were already well practised in mobilising the fear of foreigners. The xenophobic strand went back over the preceding twenty-five years – and further back still, as we have seen. The tendency developed further during the period when the Conservatives were in opposition. The Blair government saw significant changes in society and politics. Labour had a pluralist and socially liberal policy stance, with no ideological aversion to immigration. This policy perspective was inimical to most Conservatives and the right-wing, identity-conservative nationalist movements of the country. The extreme Eurosceptic and anti-immigration European Research Group (ERG), which had established itself in 1993, put more and more pressure on the Conservative leadership. The Eurosceptic bloc as a whole was inflamed by the EU's Citizens' Rights Directive of 2004, which consolidated freedom of movement across national boundaries internal to the EU. Immigration from EU countries, adding to the existing rise in immigration generally, provided the populist right with more opportunities to exploit. The overall increase was comparable to that of the 1950s, and much of the British population was ill-prepared for such a demographic change.[16] The right-wing populist press stoked anti-immigrant reactions. Thus, from the beginning of the millennium, the way was made ready for the emergence of Brexitism.

There were some significant milestones while the Conservatives were out of power and looking for electoral leverage. William Hague, leader of the Conservative Party from 1997 to 2001 and later Cameron's Foreign Secretary, spoke in populist mode of a liberal elite not recognising the people's needs. At his party's spring conference, during the run-up to the 2001 general election, Hague gave a speech that contained the populist themes that became so familiar fifteen years later.[17] According to Hague, it was time to 'bring back [...] the decent,

---

[15] Ipsos MORI, www.ipsos.com/en-uk/immigration-one-biggest-issues-wavering-eu-referendum-voters.

[16] Bale (2017).

[17] 'William Hague – 2001 Speech to Conservative Spring Forum', Political Speech Archive, UKPOL.CO.UK, www.ukpol.co.uk/william-hague-2001-speech-to-conservative-spring-forum/.

plain speaking common sense of [this country's] people'. Brussels was giving instructions to the British Chancellor, and Parliament's powers were being 'parcelled out in every direction'. Labour listened only to 'self-appointed experts'. False asylum seekers were crossing Europe to get into Britain. But what perhaps had most rhetorical impact was the idea that the EU, the Labour government and liberal social values were foreignising Britain: 'Let me take you on a journey to a foreign land ...' – a land where the Euro was displacing the pound, rules were imposed by the EU, serious criminals were being released early, and more. The speech was primarily aimed at the imagined consequences of Labour's social and economic policies. But Hague was shamelessly pressing anti-immigrant buttons. And there would have been some in the audience who would have picked up on unmistakeable echoes of Powell:

For reasons which they [the British population] could not comprehend, and in pursuance of a decision by default, on which they were never consulted, they found themselves made strangers in their own country.

This election, he went on to proclaim, is 'your last chance to vote for a Britain that still controls its own destiny'.

The connecting of the EU with increasing immigration rates, a device that would be crucial to the Brexiters' campaign, was already implicit in Hague's language. It was, like that of the Brexiters, allusive and designed to stimulate feelings of alienation, resentment, anger, and even panic ('your last chance'). Soon after Hague's speech, the Conservative John Townend came out with a more outspoken statement promoting hostility to foreigners – to the extent that Hague had to publicly distance himself.[18] In a speech on immigration, Townend was reported as citing Powell's Birmingham oration, saying, 'homogenous Anglo-Saxon society has been seriously undermined by the massive immigration – particularly Commonwealth immigration – that has taken place since the war'.

Four years later, in the 2005 general election, the Conservative campaign posters took a dog whistle approach. In one of these (see Figure 6.1) the wording presupposes that there were people – by implication in the Labour Party – saying that limits on immigration *were* racist. Simultaneously the words denied that this was the case. The question at the bottom was even more insidious: 'Are you thinking what we're thinking?' It was intended to prompt, without being up-front about it, thoughts and feelings about immigrants in general, not only 'limits' on immigration. During the campaign, this rhetorical question frequently occurred alone, inviting readers to supply an answer in line with other slogans, posters and statements that 'we' had produced. It was by the same token seeking to get readers to identify with 'us'. It is a prime example of propaganda by insinuation.

---

[18] Cf. Ingram (2001).

134   Fear of Foreigners Mobilised

Figure 6.1 'Are you thinking what we're thinking?'
Source: Jeff Morgan 16/Alamy Stock Photo.

   David Cameron, in coalition with the Liberal Democrats from 2010 to 2015 and with a Conservative majority after the 2015 general election, struggled to appease his hard right. And UKIP were matching and outmatching the Conservatives in term of nationalism, social conservativism, and appeals to 'the people' and to British sovereignty. There was ideological common ground between the ERG and UKIP in terms of dislike for liberal-representative democracy, as opposed to some form of direct popular democracy with a conservative-authoritarian leadership. The rhetoric targeting 'experts' and 'elites' soon came to be deployed by Conservatives and UKIP alike. Their deepest commonality was entrenched British xenophobia. This undercurrent was by this time indirectly expressed in terms of the notions and emotions associated with the word *immigrant*.
   Cameron's moves involved, initially, attacking Brussels and talking up any clashes with, and complaints about the EU. Then during his election campaign in 2010 Cameron announced an election 'pledge' (on *The Andrew Marr Show*) to radically reduce annual net immigration to below 100,000. Once he was in office, this policy at first produced a noticeable reduction of immigrants from *outside* the EU. But it was subsequently frustrated by large increases from *inside* the EU, especially of southern and eastern European workers, who were suffering from economic austerity policies and the eurozone crisis. Under the EU free movement regulations, the arrival of these people did not constitute

Anti-migrant Propaganda 135

Figure 6.2 A 'go home' van.
Source: Home Office. Reproduced here from Mary Reid (2013).
www.libdemvoice.org/wp-content/uploads/2013/09/Go-Home-Poster-Van.png

'immigration'. Nonetheless, the way right-wing politicians and newspapers talked and wrote about the arrivals fuelled British xenophobia. The conditions were being created for Brexiter demagogues to take advantage of the conceptual association of the EU with immigrant 'influx'. In fact, though government ministers and others blamed the EU's freedom of movement laws, immigration from *outside* the EU also began to rise again.[19]

The anti-immigration trend entered a more aggressive phase with the 'hostile environment' policy introduced by the Home Secretary Theresa May in 2012. This involved a propaganda campaign executed by various means, including notices in newspapers, shops and the religious buildings used by ethnic minorities.[20] It was the harshest anti-migrant measure deployed ever in the UK and further boosted British xenophobia – as a United Nations Human Rights Council report stated.[21] In the August, the Home Office organised a poster bearing the message 'In the UK Illegally? Go home or face arrest', which was displayed on vans and trucks touring immigrant areas of London, along with a picture of handcuffs (see Figure 6.2).

The policy's aim was to deport ('deport first appeal later') immigrants who did not have legal authorisation, including EU citizens who were homeless.

---

[19] *The Guardian*, 26 February 2015.
[20] The operation was code-named 'Operation Vaken' by the Home Office. The word 'vaken' is Swedish for 'awake' and is cognate with the German verb *erwachen*, which occurs in a poem by the Nazi writer Dietrich Eckart: 'Deutschland erwache!' This was used by the Sturmabteilung and by Hitler at Nuremburg rallies (Hattenstone 2018).
[21] Bulman (2019).

Landlords, charities, banks, the NHS and other agencies were required to carry out ID checks. In the following year, 2013, the Home Office commercial agent Capita began to target large numbers of Caribbean born people of the 'Windrush generation', who had lived legally in the UK for decades, erroneously telling them they had no legal right to remain. While the literal terms of the legislation affected only illegal immigrants, it naturally had the effect of being read as aimed at all immigrants, legal or not. Theresa May's anti-immigration stance was to persist well beyond the referendum.

In 2013, with a general election on the horizon, all this anti-immigrant discourse was, we may assume, part of Cameron's attempt to head off mounting pressure from the ERG and UKIP. He apparently believed that the referendum they were demanding would not be won by the pro-Leave side. Yet in an effort to keep his right wing happy he adopted the language of Brexit in his 2013 Bloomberg speech. What he had not bargained for was that his making nationalist and anti-immigration noises would be exploited by Eurosceptic and ethnocentric parliamentarians and activists. At Bloomberg, he had announced his intention to hold a referendum on EU membership, should he win the general election of 2015. When he did win, with a clear majority, he duly set a date, 23 June 2016, for the promised referendum. The influence of the ERG's neoliberal nationalist ideology in government was thereby strengthened, and in the ensuing referendum campaign the manipulation of British anti-immigration sentiment became a key element in sufficiently swaying the voters. It was propitious for the Brexiters that the post-2004 'wave' now included a large number of eastern and central European migrants. It became easy to fuse anti-immigration sentiment with Euroscepticism. It was obvious – government could not impose curbs on migrants from EU countries while the UK was still an EU member, so we had to get out.

Invasion

The populist right talked as if people had a natural negative reaction to increased immigration. The evidence is, however, that xenophobia was intentionally intensified by the propaganda apparatus of the Leave campaigns. It was clear to analysts that the Remain versus Leave arguments corresponded to focusing on the economy versus focusing on immigration. In April 2016, a YouGov poll showed the voting intentions of Remain and Leave were extremely close, with Remain running at 41 per cent and Leave at 42 per cent. As was seen in Chapter 1, such polling statistics had not escaped the notice of Leave's campaign advisor Lynton Crosby, and it was his view that the Leave campaign should focus on the immigration issue in order to get more voters to vote for leaving the EU. The Remain campaign, by contrast, had good reason to focus voters' attention on the well-founded arguments that leaving the EU would have deleterious economic consequences for the UK. Simon Wren-Lewis cites evidence from

YouGov showing that when people were asked to imagine how they would vote if Brexit were to make them just £100 worse off per year, this changed the result by 12 percentage points, and by 18 points in the case of undecided voters.[22] While the question filters out all the many factors involved in real voting, this poll showed how focusing on financial interest in a concrete manner might shift voters significantly towards Remain. So the Leaver demagogues had good reason to shift voters' attention onto the supposed dangers of immigration.

The obvious move was to obscure the evidence that Brexit would damage the economy, and to claim instead that it was immigrants who were, already, damaging the British economy. Brexiters and the right-wing press had ready to hand the mantra that migrants were stealing British jobs. The *Daily Mail* ran a series of scare headlines, including the following:

EU migrants working in Britain soars by more than 200,000 in ONE YEAR as one in six jobs are taken by foreigners

- Nearly 1 million Eastern Europeans are now working in the UK
- Overall EU total smashes 2 million barrier for first time in a calendar year
- The number of Romanian and Bulgarian workers rises by more than 40,000
- Overall unemployment rate remains at 10-year low of 5.1%.[23]

Prominent Brexiters sang the same tune. In a speech reproduced on the Vote Leave website, Iain Duncan Smith, who had been Cameron's Secretary of State for Work and Pensions, asserted:

the EU isn't working for over regulated small businesses and lower-paid and lower-skilled Britons. They now have to compete with millions of people from abroad for jobs and a wage rise. The Government's own Migration Advisory Committee reported that for every 100 migrants employed twenty-three UK born workers would have been displaced.[24]

Such claims ignored factual information, in the public domain, that immigration was beneficial for the economy overall, especially in the service sector.[25] The BBC's 'Reality Check' pointed out that Brexiters were misleadingly citing global numbers of migrant workers, giving the impression they were citing EU migrant workers only.[26] A study commissioned from Oxford Economics by the government itself in preparation for Brexit, found that both the average European migrant and the average non-European migrant would in 2016 make a *positive* net contribution to the UK's public finances compared to

---

[22] Wren-Lewis (2018), p. 171, citing Sayers (2016), available at https://yougov.co.uk/topics/politics/articles-reports/2016/04/28/campaign-memo-its-economy-versus-immigration.

[23] *MailOnline*, 17 February 2016, www.dailymail.co.uk/news/article-3450762/Unemployment-UK-stays-ten-year-low-earnings-edge-1-9.html.

[24] 'Iain Duncan Smith: Are we in this together?', *Why Vote Leave* website: www.voteleavetakecontrol.org/iain_duncan_smith_are_we_in_this_together.html.

[25] Petrongolo (2016).

[26] BBC News, 'Reality Check: "Do EU migrants take jobs from UK-born workers?"', www.bbc.co.uk/news/uk-politics-eu-referendum-36261966.

a UK-born citizen.[27] But more rhetorically powerful than talking employment statistics was to press emotional buttons and activate personal concerns and anxieties. It was easy to do this by appealing to the British population's sentimental attachment to the NHS. So, as with damage to the economy, it was the immigrants who were blamed for the visible deterioration of the NHS. But Cameron and his Conservative pro-Remain allies did little if anything to counter this line – perhaps they did not want to draw attention to the fact that was under Tory policies that the NHS had declined.[28]

What subsequently happened is that the Brexit demagogues exploited the absence of an effective Remain response. They were able to rhetorically link the idea of an immigrant threat to the NHS, by putting out unfounded warnings of a danger of massive immigration. And this was blamed on the EU, because, so it was asserted, the EU was allowing Turkey to join. It was already a well-established view that Turkey, which had started membership negotiations in 2005, was highly unlikely to accede in the foreseeable future. Cameron himself had taken care to say publicly in May of 2016 that Turkey's accession was 'not remotely on the cards'.[29] He was clearly anticipating Leavers' readiness to exploit a European Commission announcement that it would grant visa-free travel to Turkish nationals. This would have applied to travel only within the Schengen zone, of which the UK was not a member. Moreover, Turkey would not be admitted, unless numerous conditions were met, including the rule of law and human rights. In early 2016, EU leaders were well aware that the Turkish President was not following a democratic path, and they did not favour continuation of accession talks. The truth was that little progress had been made with the Turkey accession talks and officials in Brussels did not think Turkey would ever join.[30] By May 2016, the facts should surely have been known to UK government ministers, as well as to pro-Leave campaigners outside parliament. Indeed, the UK could have been pressing for closure of talks on Turkey's accession on human-rights grounds, as Germany had done in 2013. With Brexit in the offing, the UK government had presumably chosen not to bother.

Vote Leave nevertheless continued to assert that the EU was expanding by admitting Turkey and some Balkan states. A Vote Leave online poster read:

Turkey (population 76 million) Is Joining the EU.

This assertion is three-ways ambiguous. In order of likelihood the possible readings are as follows. It could be taken to mean that the decision has been

---

[27] Oxford Economics, www.oxfordeconomics.com/recent-releases/8747673d-3b26-439b-9693-0e250df6dbba.
[28] Wren-Lewis (2018), pp. 174–6.
[29] Reported by the BBC on 4 May 2016, www.bbc.co.uk/news/uk-politics-eu-referendum-36205844.
[30] Phinnemore and İçener (2016).

made and Turkey is about to join in the imminent future. It *could* be taken to mean that Turkey will join the EU at some unspecified time in the future. This was likely to have been the reading for EU-hating Brexiters. And it *could* – just possibly – be taken to mean that Turkey was (only) in the process of seeking to join. The latter is an improbable reading, given the context. What was possible, however, is that Brexiters might claim all three meanings at the same time. That is, they could intend readers to take it as a true statement that Turkey was actually going to join, while readying themselves to respond to any challenge by claiming they only meant Turkey was in the process of seeking to join in the future. Even that, though, could be read as a threat, and intentionally so. In any event, the phrase was a misrepresentation of the facts of Turkey's relationship with the EU.[31]

The idea this piece of propaganda sought to get across was that if the UK remained in the EU, then Turks would migrate to the UK in overwhelming numbers. Michael Gove, at that time Secretary of State for Justice and Lord Chancellor no less, and Penny Mordaunt, Minister of State for the Armed Forces, chose to propagate the same message. Both of them made factually misleading statements that had the potential to stir unfounded fears and anxieties.

On Friday 20 May 2016, Gove made a statement to press reporters, backed up the following Monday by an official Vote Leave campaign broadcast. In his statement he asserted that remaining in the EU would have 'huge consequences for the NHS', implying of course negative consequences. Such rhetoric may not conventionally count as lying, but it allowed the audience to make the assumption that they were being told all the sufficient, and all the relevant, facts – the default assumption of all verbal communication. Gove's assertions would also depend for their acceptance on hearers accepting his authority and status. He went on to suggest that Turkey and four other countries would be members of the EU by 2020, which would result in 5.2 million extra people coming into the UK, thanks to the EU's freedom of movement provisions:

> The idea of asking the NHS to look after a new group of patients equivalent in size to four Birminghams is clearly unsustainable. Free movement on that scale will have huge consequences for the NHS.[32]

This supposed 'threat' to the NHS was part of the general message that

> voting to remain in the EU means voting for more Europe, more power ceded to Brussels, more migration and more money from UK taxpayers to fund Europe's expansion.[33]

---

[31] Cf. Ball (2017), pp. 53–4.
[32] Quoted by *The Guardian*, 20 May 2016, www.theguardian.com/politics/2016/may/20/eu-immigrant-influx-michael-gove-nhs-unsustainable.
[33] Quoted by *Daily Express*, 20 May 2016, in an online article at www.express.co.uk/news/politics/672233/EU-referendum-Michael-Gove-Vote-Leave-UK-population-five-million-Brexit-EU-migration.

The way this message works involves, as propaganda messages generally do, triggering the background contextual knowledge that would be needed in order to make sense of the literal meanings of the words. Hearers were expected to know what the vague 'more Europe' meant, and that it was a bad thing. His list of 'more ... more ... more ... more' supposedly bad things was rhetorically designed to reinforce negative attitudes. Vague emotive prompts replace facts.

On Sunday 22 May, Penny Mordaunt followed in Gove's footsteps in a BBC interview with Andrew Marr.[34] Marr begins by asking about an earlier statement that a million people may come to the EU from Turkey in the next eight years. '[That's] strange', he says, 'because most people don't expect Turkey to join in the next eight years'.

MORDAUNT: I think it's very likely that they *will* in part because of the migrant crisis. It's escalating, speeding up, Turkey in particular but other accession countries coming in [...] [Theresa May] made a speech earlier in the campaign that pointed to, or questioning the merits of the EU expanding and having a land border with Syria, Iraq and Iran.

Marr's question has not been answered. He points out that her party leader, Boris Johnson, has said he was in favour of Turkey's joining.

MORDAUNT: Well I think you can't ... what is dishonest is to say, is to have a policy of expansion and then at the same time to deny member states what they need to mitigate the security risk that comes with it. Theresa May herself has pointed to the problems of terrorism and organised crime that is in these accession countries.

The EU, she goes on, is 'denying us the tools to keep us safe and secure'. And 'this referendum is going to be our last chance to have a say on that':

MORDAUNT: We're not going to be consulted or asked to vote on whether we think those countries or others should join [...] they are *going* to join ...

So Marr tries again, repeating that the UK has a veto against Turkey's accession.

MORDAUNT: No, it *doesn't*, we are not going to be able to have our say.

Flat denial of the facts. Marr doesn't let her off the hook, saying each country has a veto on new accessions. But she persists:

MORDAUNT: No, I do not think that the EU is going to keep Turkey out. I think [it] is going to join, I think the migrant crisis is pushing it more that way [...] if you're going to pursue that policy [of expansion], you've got to allow us the tools to protect our own interests, to protect our national security. That we do not have [...] if you are going to have these policies, if you're going to ever expand the EU, you have to allow us to mitigate the security risk that comes with that.

[34] BBC, *The Andrew Marr Show*, 22 May 2016, www.bbc.co.uk/programmes/p03vxlks.

More denial, more mentions of security. She then repeats her earlier distortion of the facts:

MORDAUNT: ... and I think it is quite wrong that the British people will not be asked their view on this in the future. The referendum is our only chance to say no, no we disagree with that.

Near the end of his interview Marr returns to his opening question:

MARR: I'm pretty sure that we do have a veto over stopping Turkey joining if we want to. Are you sure that we don't?

MORDAUNT: Well, we haven't, I think that with the current situation, the migrant crisis and other issues that are going on in Europe at the moment we will be unable to stop Turkey joining [...] and I think, I think that the British public, this is a matter for the British people to decide and the only shot that they will get expressing a view on this is in this referendum.

Marr tries one last time, saying 'But if we don't want Turkey in we can stop Turkey from coming in?'

MORDAUNT: I don't think that the UK will be able to stop Turkey joining.

Throughout, the awkward questions are stalled by 'well, I think' or 'I don't think'. Mordaunt's closing words betray either culpable ignorance of the EU's basic principles, or she is trying to deceive viewers by blanket assertions resting only on perceived authority. As always in Brexitism, opinion and blanket assertion substitutes for evidence and rational argument. Truth is not respected. Counter-evidence counts for nothing.

Many commentators, at the time and since, accused Mordaunt of barefaced lying. Later the same day, Mordaunt was explicitly contradicted by her own leader David Cameron, who stated the actual legal situation – that EU countries had a right of veto over the accession of a new state. Of course, this fact could be ignored, since Cameron was a 'remainer'. In any case, the propaganda aim was achieved – there was a threat to national security that the 'British people' could not prevent, because the EU was stopping them 'having a say'. It was a double threat: one came from Turkish immigrants and the other from being exposed to dangerous countries in the Middle East. All this duplicitous talk about Turkey by two government ministers was merely a prelude to a step change in the level of mendacity and manipulation. The 'influx' of immigrants was about to become an 'invasion'.

The day after Mordaunt's interview, Monday 23 May, Vote Leave beamed its referendum broadcast into UK homes on all five TV channels. At the same time, selected groups, identified by personal profiling, were targeted on a very large scale through social media.[35]

---

[35] BBC report of 26 July 2018. www.bbc.co.uk/news/uk-politics-44966969 Cf. Shaw (2018).

In its referendum broadcast, Vote Leave put out a five-minute video that included a migration map and a sequence performed by actors supposedly depicting scenes from an NHS hospital.[36] The video starts with, and later repeats, a map of Europe stretching from the UK to the Black Sea and Turkey. On it are superimposed red arrows coming out of Turkey, Albania and neighbouring countries, sweeping across Europe and arriving at the UK coastline. This is a military-style map, evoking folk memories of such maps from World War II, and what was at that time a genuine threat of invasion. The film switches to the playlet. Scene one is a white woman looking concerned about her mother's cough, as they sit drinking a cup of tea. Scene two finds them going to an NHS A&E. The screen splits into two. One half, labelled 'INSIDE THE EU', shows mother and daughter looking unhappy, with hostile-looking men behind them in a dingy lift area. The other half, labelled 'OUTSIDE THE EU' shows the same pair in a bright room, clean and clear of strangers. Words are not needed – these scenes do not in fact have any dialogue or voice-over. There is just some soft background guitar music. The film segues into the map graphic once more. Repeated in the new healthcare context, there is a powerful causal implication: the EU is bringing Turks through Europe to the UK, and this will cause a deterioration of the UK's health system and cause the elderly to suffer in overburdened NHS hospitals.

The visual similarities between the Vote Leave propaganda maps and military-style maps are striking. Consider, for example, the simplified map in Figure 6.3, which represents the lines of attack that were expected in the German Operation Sea Lion ('Unternehmen Seelöwe') – the German code name for the intended, but abandoned, invasion of Britain in 1940.

Arrows on maps have become a cartographic convention. Those maps intended for popular consumption generally have arrows that are red and tapered, as in Figure 6.3 – and also in the Vote Leave maps (Figures 6.4a and 6.4b). Such arrows on maps are not simply to denote directed movement from a starting point to a target. Contextual and background knowledge are involved in how viewers interpret them. Arrows are also understood deictically, that is, in relation to where viewers are expected to mentally locate themselves on the map. In this way, arrows can produce emotions of foreboding and fear. So in all the arrowed maps shown here, the arrowhead is taken to be aimed at 'us' in the UK by a distant force, a hostile enemy. What is particularly noteworthy is that cartographic arrows, which are by cultural habit taken to be military, are also conventionally used to map 'flows' ('floods', 'waves', 'swarms', etc.) of people. Migrations and invasions are easily conflated in this graphic mode of rhetoric.[37]

---

[36] Video no longer available on BBC website. Described by Brian Wheeler on BBC News website, www.bbc.co.uk/news/uk-politics-eu-referendum-36367247.
[37] On these points, see Cheshire and Kent (2023).

Invasion 143

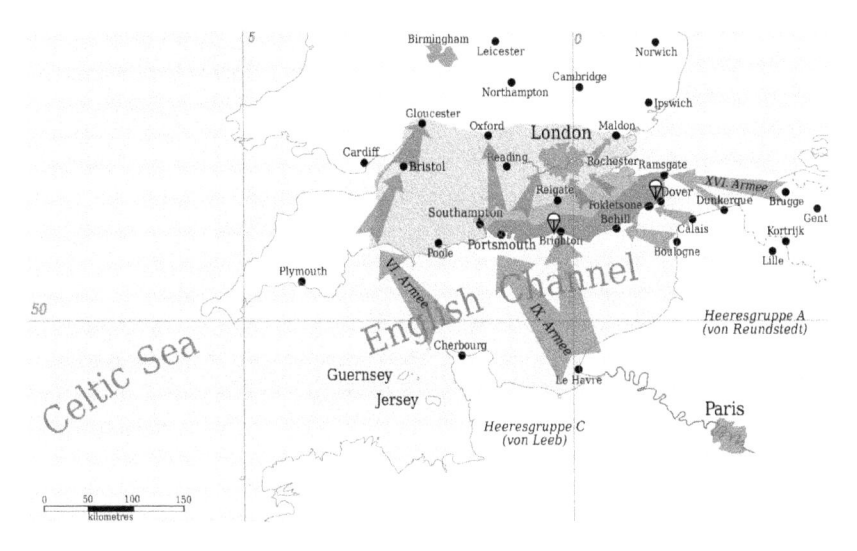

Figure 6.3 Invasion arrows (Operation Sea Lion).
Source: Wikimedia Commons.
https://commons.wikimedia.org/wiki/File:Sealion.svg

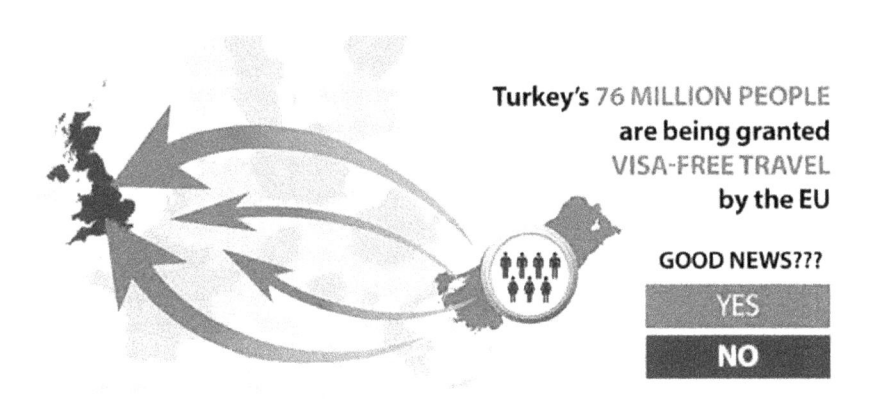

Figure 6.4a Invasion from Turkey.
Source: UK Parliament, Department of Culture, Media and Sport Committee (2018), p. 21, 2942.
www.parliament.uk/globalassets/documents/commons-committees/culture-media-and-sport/Fake_news_evidence/Vote-Leave-50-Million-Ads.pdf
Contains Parliamentary information licensed under the Open Parliament Licence v3.0

144 Fear of Foreigners Mobilised

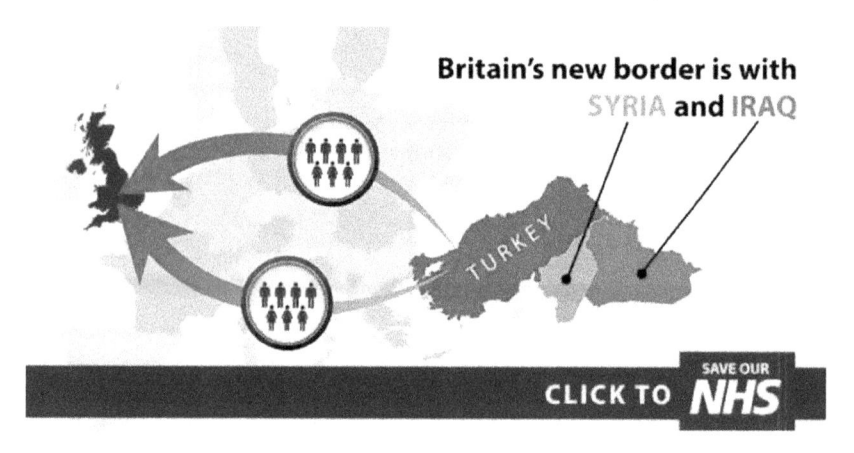

Figure 6.4b Border with Syria and Iraq.
Source: UK Parliament, Department of Culture, Media and Sport Committee (2018), p. 34, 2968.
www.parliament.uk/globalassets/documents/commons-committees/culture-media-and-sport/Fake_news_evidence/Vote-Leave-50-Million-Ads.pdf
Contains Parliamentary information licensed under the Open Parliament Licence v3.0

As well as on TV, map-and-arrow images figured widely on Vote Leave flyers, posters and, importantly, in social media ads. In the versions shown in Figures 6.4a and 6.4b, what grabs attention is the swooping red arrows penetrating the UK border. Only part of the message is conveyed through the literal meaning of the words displayed. The sentence in the top right-hand corner is a statement but the message is by implication, activated by the graphics and colour. One implication is the mendacious idea that the whole of Turkeys' population is coming partly to Europe but mainly (bigger arrows in Figure 6.4a) to the UK. The circle, with its seven human silhouettes representing Turkey, tells viewers that the Turks are coming *here*. The red words 'visa-free travel' indirectly evokes a certain frame of reference, that of the EU's fundamental freedom of movement principle, detested by Brexiters on the grounds that it stops Britain controlling its own borders. The military style of the maps coheres with the Brexiter references to immigration as 'invasion', and is used in several versions of this series of propaganda pictures.

The version in Figure 6.4b has two red arrows, both coming out of Turkey – a pincer movement targeting the UK. The graphics, again, needed no words, since they directly activate spatial intuitions and, potentially, fear reactions. The focus here is on UK borders, defending them being an *idée fixe* of the Brexiters.[38]

---

[38] See also Sykes (2018).

The invading arrows connect only Turkey with the UK, overflying the vague grey mass of the European mainland. The circles representing populations produce a conceptual blend of immigration movements and military penetration of borders. The worded message in the top right-hand corner draws viewers' attention to an entirely fallacious inference from the already manipulative visual material – that the EU is imposing on the UK a 'new border' with two dangerous countries. Furthermore, in the blue strip along the bottom, the intended inference is that the NHS is under threat from the falsely depicted population movements.

The images in Figures 6.4a and 6.4b work on the mind and the emotions because they suggest threat and danger. In addition to the emotive effects of red arrows, the depiction of bounded spaces being penetrated inevitably taps into the basic cognitive schemas CONTAINER, PATH, and FORCE. The CONTAINER schema is the spatial basis for concepts of 'inside' and 'outside' as well as 'boundary' or 'border'. Apart from the circles containing people and denoting geographical regions, countries stand out as bounded entities – particularly in the case of the UK. In Figure 6.4b, the caption makes sure of the cognitive effect. The arrows are based on the brain's generalised representation of physical motion, with a source and a goal, and movement in a particular direction (the PATH schema). Arrows also involve the FORCE schema, since they imply an impact on a target. The schemas CONTAINER, PATH and FORCE can be made deictic in particular contexts for particular purposes. That is, the target can be *us* and the source *they*, or vice versa.

Such manipulations of the mind are the stuff of demagoguery and propaganda. They are the graphic equivalent of lying and verbal scaremongering. Challenges can be dismissed on the grounds that any inferences are not explicitly intended and are even the responsibility of the viewers, who have been left to figure out possible meanings for themselves. In the stepped-up Brexit campaign, the falsifying verbiage of Gove and Mordaunt (among others) was all of a piece with Vote Leave's visuals. They exploited the different devices of language and graphics to trigger the same cognitive and emotive effects. The message was simple. There was a threat to national security from foreign population penetration, a danger to vulnerable British citizens, and a danger to the venerated National Health Service.

The number of migrant arrivals into the UK began to rise sharply around 1997, with another sharp rise just after 2004 that remained steady until yet another sharp rise around 2015. More or less concurrently, opinion polls showed increased numbers of people saying that immigration was the most important issue, but with particularly sharp increases in 2004 and 2016. We may ask what the relation is between objective immigrant increases and expressions of subjective concern by the public. The answer is complex, but it cannot be simply assumed that there is a straightforward causal relation. A large part of any answer must be the intervening factor of national populist propaganda, and its intensification around the 2016 referendum.

During the 1990s UKIP emerged and expanded its numbers right up to the referendum, exploiting as it went the existing undercurrent of British xenophobia, racism, and uncertainties about British identity. The Conservative Party, under political pressure from the rise of UKIP as well as from its own extreme Eurosceptics, also stepped up its public rhetoric around immigration to new heights. In an attempt to outpace UKIP, prime minister David Cameron misguidedly called the 2016 referendum. This did not halt the rightward drift of his party, nor the gradual erosion of democracy that went with it. On the contrary, with Brexit the Conservative Party increasingly espoused the nationalist and populist values of UKIP, a process that continued well beyond their referendum triumph. The most important and insidious aspect of this process was the shifting of political culture, its norms and its discourse, towards the abandonment of truthfulness and the tolerance of falsehoods of all kinds. Of course, politicians have always been suspected of manipulation and mendacity. But pro-Brexit leaders went further. Their methods were both direct and indirect, playing on irrationality and emotion. How exactly did that work in practice?

7   How Demagogues Do It

Political contexts are partly of the moment but they also have historic continuities. When political processes produce a situation where a major decision has to be made, politicians reach for ways to steer public opinion in the direction they want. The social and political pressures on the UK government in the early 2000s led to the referendum on EU membership. And the propaganda campaign for leaving the EU was implemented on a very large scale, across multiple platforms. This was the sort of context that was wide open to the devices of demagoguery.

The chronic wariness of democratic forms of government, handed down from ancient Athens, was driven by the fear that the crowds would be misled by demagogues. The demagogue was an individual who operated in the agora and the forum, speaking to the crowd live and face-to-face. Demagogues were expert in using the devices of rhetoric, which were classified by theorists and professional instructors, with the aim of manipulating thoughts and emotions. Today's populist demagogues are no different in that respect, but the channels of communication they use, and the devices they deploy, are immeasurably more sophisticated – and sophistical. As ever, the most powerful weapons in the demagogue's persuasive arsenal are words that trigger powerful emotions.[1] The classical knowledge of rhetorical devices provided some tools of critical analysis suitable for the times. But under today's conditions, more precise descriptive and analytical tools are needed to explain the capacity of strategic language to penetrate the brains of hearers and influence their political behaviour.

What Words Do to the Brain

As Arash Javanbakht, a medical researcher into fear and anxiety disorders, has noted, 'when demagogues manage to get hold of our fear circuitry, we often regress to illogical, tribal and aggressive human animals, becoming weapons ourselves – weapons that politicians use for their own agenda'.[2] The relevance

[1] Wirz (2018).   [2] Javanbakht (2019).

148 How Demagogues Do It

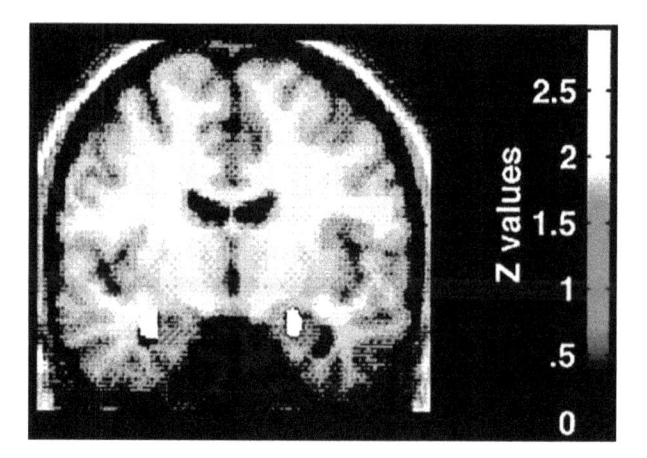

Figure 7.1 Response to threat words: activation of the amygdala.
Source: Nancy Isenberg et al. (1999), 96(18), p. 10457, with the permission of *Proceedings of the National Academy of Sciences of the USA*.
www.pnas.org/content/96/18/10456 Copyright (1999) National Academy of Sciences, U.S.A

of this claim to the Brexit context is clear. Neurological research provides empirical evidence that words are capable of triggering the fear responses in human brains, responses that are also involved in physical threat detection. This is evolutionarily part of one of the oldest systems (the limbic system) of the human brain and handles our fight-or-flight responses. It is a system of the brain that can be set off by language input; language is an integral part of the human environment. As Weisholtz and colleagues note, 'many of the threats humans encounter are nuanced and indirect, and can be conveyed adequately only via language'.[3] To which one should add that certain speech acts, such as warnings and threats, are *direct* signals in the human social environment. They can and do cause fear. Whatever the trigger, neural networks of the fear systems are connected with both threat detection and behavioural responses to threat. Demagogues have the skill of pressing the right linguistic buttons to stimulate fear. But it is important not to take a deterministic view. In humans, the emotional networks are connected to neocortical, later evolved structures where judgements, including ethical ones, and decisions are processed.

Is it really the case that mere words can produce ideas and feelings that the receivers would not have had without hearing or reading those words? It is only relatively recently that it has become possible to show much more directly the causal relationship between word selection and the brain's response. This

---

[3] Weisholtz et al. (2015), p. 12.

question has been investigated by Isenberg, Weisholtz and colleagues in an experiment using brain-imaging techniques. The experiment used a list of eighty English words that were judged by the experimenters to be 'neutral-valence' and eighty judged 'threat-valence' (see Appendix). The words were presented randomly to each subject, each word being randomly printed in one of five different colours. The subjects were all healthy native English speakers. Each was asked to name the colour of each word as it appeared on a computer screen.[4] While they did this, each person underwent a whole brain scan (PET), and later the images of their brain reactions (see Figure 7.1) were examined statistically. What the results showed was systematic activation of the main fear centres (the left and right amygdalae) for the threat-valence words but not for the neutral-valence words.[5]

These findings provide us with tools to explore the direct effects of words on the mind in real situations. As it happens, many of the words used in the experiment by Isenberg and colleagues were exactly the words that occur in the sort of demagogic oratory where the speaker is aiming to excite fear. The arch-demagogue Enoch Powell, in his 'rivers of blood' speech, deployed many of the words, or parts of those words, on experimenters' lists.[6]

The following words are the ones deployed by Powell and also found experimentally to trigger responses in the human brain:

persecute[d], destroy, attack[ed], [im]prison[er], evil[s], whip[cord], condemn[ed], betrayal, abuse[d], blood[stain], follow[ed], mislead, danger[ous].[7]

Of these words, the morpheme *evil* (in the form 'evils') is used four times, and the morpheme *danger* seven times (once in the form 'danger', six times in the form 'dangerous'). Not all the words in the experimental lists would be expected to be directly relevant to the speech, but that does not reduce the significance of the ones that do occur. Conversely, we can consider words and phrases in this speech that are not on the experimenters' list, but which are no less likely to trigger fear or anxiety. For example, the following:

extreme urgency, rising peril, curses, difficulties, troubles, alien, stranger, match on to gunpowder, dominate, weapons [even though it is metaphorical].

This is probably not a complete list. And there are also words in the speech that may not activate a fear response in isolation but which are highly likely to in their particular context. An example would be the verb 'take(n) over'.

---

[4] A modified Stroop design, to ensure that subjects were not looking for emotion content.
[5] Isenberg et al. (1999), Isenberg (2011). A similar experiment was conducted by Weisholtz et al. (2015). See also Maddock et al. (1997) and Maddock et al. (2003).
[6] See Chilton and Kopytowska (2018).
[7] In square brackets are parts of words differing between Powell's text and the list used by Isenberg et al.

The audience is told a story about an elderly white woman living in a 'respectable' street:

> Then the immigrants moved in. With growing fear, she saw one house after another taken over. The quiet street became a place of noise and confusion. Regretfully her white tenants moved out.[8]

The text of the speech links single lexical triggers to other items that may not, on their own, be fear-triggers – an important case would be the word 'immigrant(s)', which is frequently linked in all racist discourse with fear expressions. A further example involves a concentration of fear stimuli – a sentence that includes one of the words ('whip') on the list used by Isenberg and Weisholtz, and which Powell claimed was spoken to him by a constituent:

> In this country in 15 or 20 years' time the black man will have the whip hand over the white man.

In these extracts, the brain's reaction to threat and danger words involves the verbal context of what has been said as well as background knowledge and the circumstances of the utterance. The reaction can, of course, be modulated by the hearer's personality type and degree of critical verbal vigilance. Nonetheless, the results of the experiments are very relevant when political scientists and others ask about the actual effects of the 'rivers of blood' speech.

It is possible to trigger emotions linguistically even if trigger words are not actually being used. The way this is done is by using language that causes speakers to guess what is being hinted at by drawing on background knowledge. Here the theoretical idea of *implicature* comes in. Implicatures are a normal part of efficient communication. They occur when some expression is not expected in a particular context, and appears counter to the usual norms of communication. If an expression is not obviously relevant to the situation, for example, or is unusually obscure, or seems to give less information than needed – then an implied meaning, or implicature, is generated. Hearers draw on background knowledge to unconsciously figure out a meaning. The brain does this automatically and rapidly. Implicatures are normal, but they can be deployed strategically by demagogues and propagandists. And what is implicated can be something that causes an emotional response.

Implicature is a handy means for demagogues to affect an audience while avoiding responsibility for what they are doing: 'I didn't actually say that'.

---

[8] Powell (1968).

Sometimes speakers use implicature to set the alarm bells ringing and then follow up with a more explicit assertion. For example:

> In 15 or 20 years, on present trends, there will be in this country three and a half million Commonwealth immigrants and their descendants. That is not my figure. That is the official figure given to parliament by the spokesman of the Registrar General's Office.

On their own, these numbers are just numbers; they are not inherently 'fear words'. The words just have their literal meaning and are not in themselves alarming – until hearers' brains have, rapidly and beneath awareness, connected to context and background knowledge. Then the words will worry, frighten or anger some people in some places and at certain moments. Even if the numbers were correct, it is only in a particular context that they can be used to frighten indirectly, that is by automatic implicature. At the time of the Brexit campaigns the right-wing press used headlines that simply shouted numbers of immigrants.

Another kind of rhetorical insinuation involves semantic *presupposition*, which can bring a new referent into the context, or may serve to re-categorise or define something already mentioned. The commonest example is *the*. In the speech, presupposition combines with implicature:

> Already by 1985 the native-born would constitute the majority. It is this fact which creates the extreme urgency of action now, of just that kind of action which is hardest for politicians to take, action where the difficulties lie in the present but the evils to be prevented or minimised lie several parliaments ahead.

Here, 'the majority' and 'the native-born' are presupposed to exist in a hypothetical future. Hearers know from the preceding co-text that these are black people. The phrase 'the extreme urgency of action now' presupposes that a situation of urgency actually exists at the time of speaking. In the same way, the phrase 'the difficulties' presupposes that these difficulties do exist. And, given the context, 'the evils' presupposes that these 'evils' will exist in the future. By way of implicature, verbal context and background knowledge, hearers rapidly infer that these things are caused by an increase in British-born black people. Moreover, for hearers so inclined, there can be an implicature (by the principle of relevance) that black people are 'evil'. All these indirect statements, along with their emotional triggers, are rapidly processed in the brains of hearers.

By these routes, the brain may activate circuits connected to the perception of out-groups. The neuroscientist Antonio Damasio writes:

> ... the reactions that lead to racial and cultural prejudices are based in part on the deployment of social emotions evolutionarily meant to detect *difference* in others because difference may signal risk or danger, and promote withdrawal or aggression. That sort of reaction probably achieved useful goals in a tribal society but is no longer

useful, let alone appropriate, to ours. We can be wise to the fact that our brain still carries machinery to react in the way it did in a very different context years ago. And we can learn to disregard such reactions and persuade others to do the same.[9]

Which personality type or socio-economic groups are most likely to be swayed by racially and culturally antagonistic language? Some hypotheses are provided by political scientists and social psychologists. Sobolewska and Ford's explanation of Brexit proposes that the major factor in the socio-political polarisation of the UK in 2016 was the divide between the identity types 'identity conservative' and 'identity liberal'. The first type being closely related to sections of the population consisting of white early school-leavers, who are also more likely to be ethnocentric in worldview. At the time Powell's speech hit the headlines, a much larger proportion of the British population would have matched Sobolewska and Ford's definition of 'identity conservative' and it is likely that this was the group that was impacted. It is also likely that it was this group he was mainly targeting in his speeches – those he patronisingly referred to as 'ordinary English people', 'the ordinary, decent, sensible people'. Such language is almost identical to that of Farage and other national populists forty years later.

The targeted audiences also were similar. After 'rivers of blood', Powell received around 100,000 letters from individuals who were distressed by what they perceived as 'national' decline, and for whom he 'was a new leader who promised to remedy national follies and ills – to give voice to "ordinary people" and make Great Britain great once again'.[10]

Karen Stenner's empirical work in political psychology makes it possible to link ethnocentrism with the dynamics of the authoritarian personality.[11] Although there may be exceptions, this type of personality is markedly ethnocentric and sensitive to social difference and change. The authoritarian disposition is sensitive to normative threat, that is, threat to a group's social or cultural norms. One of the things that 'rivers of blood' did – and still does – is focus hearers' minds on a particular social change, stimulating the perception of threats to social order and stability. People with authoritarian personalities, who are prone to being aroused by such perceptions, are likely to be made more openly hostile to out-groups by national-populist rhetoric and propaganda, even if they have not previously seen out-groups in that way. Those with authoritarian dispositions are likely to be among the white identity-conservative parts of the population. Such people are not exclusively to be found among the early school-leavers of the urban working class, however. Middle- and upper-class authoritarian personalities, including actors in the political class, are also likely to succumb to national-populist discourse. Indeed, it is more accurate to say that they are more often than not its prime movers.

---

[9] Damasio (2003), p. 40.   [10] Whipple (2009), p. 720.   [11] Stenner (2005).

Vehicles of Untruth

The economic consequences of leaving the customs union and single market were obscured in the campaign by diverting attention to an alleged immigration threat and by claiming that immigrants over-used NHS resources. This strategy was effected by two specific propaganda claims. One was the idea that the money the UK paid to the EU (with significant rebate) deprived the NHS of financial resources, and the other was the implication that this money actually *would* be spent on the NHS if Britain left the EU. In other words, there were two speech acts – an inexplicit assertive speech act about a sum of money, and an inexplicit speech act of commitment concerning a future action. The propositional content of the assertion has been contested numerous times and shown to be untrue by agencies that by any rational standard are legitimate and authoritative – business leaders, financial analysts, economists and official statisticians.

These claims and commitments required careful verbal formulation, as well as an attention-grabbing means of visual communication. The most notorious expression of these elements of the campaign was displayed on the side of a bus (Figure 7.2a). A similar message (Figure 7.2b) was disseminated by way of a replicable digital format for use on several other sites – social media, billboards, handbills, and posters. This format came with slightly variant wordings but the same visual design. It was used in many contexts, often as

Figure 7.2a Taking voters for a ride.
Source: Jack Taylor/Stringer/Getty Images News/Getty Images.

Figure 7.2b Variation on the theme with Boris Johnson.
Source: Matt Cardy/Stringer/Getty Images News/Getty Image.

background for meetings, press conferences and the like. It was deployed in various publicity settings by Boris Johnson, Michael Gove and Priti Patel. The whole project ensured the attention of a wide range of people via different media and distribution patterns.

On the bus in Figure 7.2a, the top line is a simple sentence performing an assertive speech act. This assertion was in fact immediately called into question by critical journalists, scholars and social institutions of various kinds. The UK Statistics Authority, a non-ministerial government department with responsibility for maintaining national standards in public statistics, wrote to Vote Leave saying the claim was 'misleading and undermines trust in official statistics'. It pointed out, as did the scholars and journalists, that the slogan's number omitted the rebate from the EU received by the UK, as well as other payments received by the UK from the EU, and did not count in the contributions to the treasury from trade and business that would not have happened without the EU single market. In sum:

The UK Statistics Authority concluded on 21 April 2016 that the use of the £350 million figure, which is a gross figure which does not take into account the rebate or other flows from the EU to the UK public sector (or flows to non-public sector bodies), alongside the suggestion that this could be spent elsewhere, without further explanation, was potentially misleading.[12]

---

[12] 'UK Statistics Authority statement on the use of official statistics on contributions to the European Union', published 27 May 2016, https://uksa.statisticsauthority.gov.uk/news/uk-stat

One response from the Vote Leave side was that only a *gross* figure had actually been their intention. A similar response was to argue that it was *literally* true to say that £350 million was 'sent to', or 'taken by' the EU even though there was a subsequent rebate (negotiated by Margaret Thatcher in 1984). It was soon pointed out that in fact the rebate was deducted *before* the sum was transmitted.[13] And numerous economists and journalists corroborated the UK Statistics Authority's point that the EU's financial contributions to the UK must be factored into the equation. The Institute for Fiscal Studies estimated that in 2014 going forward the UK's net contribution to the EU was around £150 million per week.[14]

The second sentence of Figure 7.2a – 'let's fund our NHS instead' – is not an assertion. It can be read as enacting a proposal for action, or as a kind of imperative speech act urging hearers to act jointly with the speaker in a certain way. But the wording on the bus can also be read as implying a commissive act of promising or pledging. It was in fact read this way by many of those who saw it.

What do the first two sentences of Figure 7.2a mean, taken together? There is no *explicit* wording, other than the 'instead', that links the phrase 'fund the NHS' to the transferring of a specific EU payment, as mentioned in the first sentence. The processing of meanings is always indirect and context-dependent, so it was natural and normal for people to infer that the named sum would be used to fund the NHS, which from background knowledge was known to be underfunded. Because this meaning was not explicit, there was scope for people, especially the slogan's authors, to claim that it did not 'exactly say' that the precise sum mentioned would be used for the NHS – it only says 'let's fund our NHS'. Similarly, the slogan's defenders could claim, 'well, we never literally said we'd promise'.

The version in Figure 7.2b has the same content as the bus version and has much the same effect. However, it is packaged differently and tells us something about the tricks of demagoguery. Variant 7.2b packs the two sentences of 7.2a into one: 'Let's give our NHS the £350 million the EU takes every week.' The typographical layout gives prominence to the part of the sentence that may look like it is a commitment. The layout also makes visually salient the amount of money that the EU supposedly takes from the UK. And the two versions are different in another respect. On the bus, the agent of the transfer of the money is 'we' – 'we send [to] the EU'. On the poster, it is the EU that is the agent – 'the EU takes'. In this case, there is an implicated victim of the taking, and that is

---

istics-authority-statement-on-the-use-of-official-statistics-on-contributions-to-the-european-union/.
[13] See, for example, Henley (2016). [14] Emmerson et al. (2016), p. 2.

'us'. Furthermore, the 'the' in 'the £350 million', presupposes the existence of that precise amount of money as the thing transferred.

However, people do not take in every detail of a sentence in these circumstances – their brains will automatically construct a meaning. Messages like those in Figure 7.2a and 7.2b are typically scanned very briefly. The brain will in any case process key content words on the basis of background knowledge, and context-related inferences, including some implicatures and presuppositions.[15] The layout and typography of the messages is designed to prompt readers to pick out parts of the message – those parts the message-producers want people to attend to. Campaign utterances do not come in isolation, but as part of ongoing discourse that people may have already engaged in. By a certain stage in a campaign, merely glancing at the single large-print line could have been sufficient to bring to mind the whole conceptual package: Britain pays to the EU money that could be used for the NHS. Even at a rapid glance, many readers might infer that the wording amounts to a commissive speech act such as a promise or pledge. But if anyone were to challenge any supposed composer of the words, he or she could easily deny that any commitment was intended at all, or claim that some other meaning was intended. Here is an example.

In 2017, the pro-Brexit journalist and broadcaster Iain Dale complained on his website that Leave leaders were not taking on the Remainers' argument 'that the £350 million a week "promise" wasn't in any way a promise'. He then wheels out the literalistic device:

The words on the bus actually said 'We send the EU £350 million a week. Let's fund our NHS instead.' Now you can argue if you want that this is a promise to spend £350 million extra every week on the NHS, but it didn't actually say that, did it? 'Let's fund our NHS instead' certainly means more money for the NHS but it doesn't necessarily mean all of the £350 million would be spent on the NHS. And even if it did, Vote Leave was a campaign, it wasn't an alternative government.[16]

It would be natural and normal for any reader in a real communicative context to automatically interpret the 'let's' sentence as expressing a commitment, even a promise. Dale is deploying the literalistic manoeuvre in order to claim that Remainer readers wrongly interpreted the sentence as a promise – it is their fault.

Two days after Dale's website piece, there was a reply from the pro-EU analyst Jon Worth, who argued that the poster variant in particular made it reasonable to speak of a 'commitment' or a 'pledge' to NHS spending, on the ground that 'there was enough of a connection made between the £350 m figure

---

[15] Baggio (2022), p. 38. [16] Dale (2017).

and the NHS to imply that money would be spent on the NHS'.[17] James Ball made more detailed criticisms:

> The pledges were clearly defined – to insiders, they were never promises in the sense of manifesto, as only a potential government could make those. To the public, they could easily appear as firm pledges.[18]

This was a response to another pro-Brexit journalist, Isabel Oakeshottt, who had said on Twitter/X that the words on the bus and poster 'fell well short of the definition of that pledge'. This was another form of the literalistic manoeuvre: '"Let's" meant "we could"; not "we will".' But Ball points out that 'the average voter' cannot be expected to have the capacity to 'see a poster with a one-sentence slogan, or a snatch of an interview with a Cabinet minister, and correctly deduce that this isn't a pledge or a promise but instead a vague and unactionable suggestion'. This is fair point, consistent with what we know of ordinary language behaviour. Demagogues know this and exploit ambiguity and inexplicitness precisely to convey a meaning that they can later deny having intended. It is difficult to prove that this particular message was taken to be a promise, or that the sum of £350 million was accurate, and influenced voters' voting behaviour. But the hypothesis that it did is a reasonable one. Two years later, the claim that the UK was sending, or the EU was taking, £350 million a week was still believed by 42 per cent of those who had heard of the claim, while 36 per cent thought it was false, and 22 per cent were unsure, according to a joint Ipsos MORI and King's College London poll.[19]

Demagoguery certainly appears to have done its work. One political actor, instrumental in the design of the NHS pseudo-pledge posters, seems to have thought so. The director of Vote Leave's campaign and Boris Johnson's advisor, Dominic Cummings, wrote in *The Spectator* in 2017 that Vote Leave had to avoid discussing the economy directly. Rather, the campaign needed to let the economy as a serious issue in the referendum come in, if at all, in an emotionally charged context. Specifically, it needed to switch public focus onto two ideas: the supposed danger of immigration and the idea of the EU taking money from the nation's health care system:

> for millions of people, *£350 m/NHS was about the economy and living standards – that's why it was so effective*. It was clearly the most effective argument not only with the crucial swing fifth but with *almost every demographic*. Even with UKIP voters it was level-pegging with immigration. Would we have won without immigration? No. *Would we have won without £350 m/NHS? All our research and the close result strongly suggests No.* Would we have won by spending our time talking about trade and the Single Market? No way.[20]

---

[17] Worth (2017).   [18] Ball (2017), pp. 63–4.
[19] Research by King's College London Policy Institute in association with Ipsos MORI, www.kcl.ac.uk/policy-institute/research-analysis/the-publics-brexit-misperceptions. Cf. Stone (2018).
[20] Cummings (2017). Italics as in original text. Cf. Stone (2018).

Apparently, it did not matter to Cummings whether or not he misled people, or lied to them. It is likely that he did not really care about truth and falsity in any case. He was quite candid in admitting to the short-term strategy of provocation: 'Sometimes we said "we send the EU £350 m" to provoke people into argument.'[21] As Ball points out, Remain's counterarguments, however accurate when demonstrating that the figure was really more like £175 million, were psychologically ineffective. The public were still left feeling that the figure was a hell of a lot of money. In any case, the higher figure was so frequently and prominently repeated that it was the one that stuck in the memory.[22]

We could say that '£350 million a week for the NHS was the ultimate bullshit political claim'.[23] The moral philosopher Harry G. Frankfurt has written of what he refers to as 'bullshit' that it is 'never finely crafted, that in the making of it there is never the meticulously attentive concern with detail'.[24] That is not quite correct for Vote Leave propaganda – the wording was carefully chosen, as Cummings's remarks above indicate. The detailed analyses of wording in this section have tried to show how carefully chosen words worked in the Leave campaign's favour. But Frankfurt is right in several respects. The bullshitter does not *care* about the facts or the truth, they are *care-less* with respect to both facts and the people they are addressing – and in many instances they do not know the facts in any case. This is part and parcel of the 'post-truth' attitude of mind – the relativist scepticism regarding the knowability of facts, consistent with the idea that experts and expertise are irrelevant.[25] A consequence is that the bullshitter does not take any moral responsibility for their utterances, so long as the aims of the moment are achieved.

Breaking Point

A piece of propaganda that generated much controversy was the 'breaking point' poster adopted by UKIP (Figure 7.3a), which was launched by Farage on 14 June 2016, only a week before the referendum. It was subsequently justified by him after it was condemned by critics in the national press, online media and news conference platforms. The strategy behind UKIP's campaigning was brought out in a statement attributed to Arron Banks, major UKIP donor and founder of the national-populist campaign organisation Leave.EU. Speaking after the Leave referendum victory Banks stated:

The Remain campaign featured fact, fact, fact, fact, fact. It doesn't work. You've got to connect with people emotionally. It's the Trump success.[26]

---

[21] Cummings (2017). [22] Ball (2017), pp. 50–3. [23] Ball (2017), p. 52.
[24] Frankfurt (2005), pp. 21–2. [25] Frankfurt (2005), pp. 62–3. Cf. Cassam (2019).
[26] Bell (2016).

Breaking Point 159

Figure 7.3a UKIP's 'Breaking point' poster.
Source: UKIP via Twitter/X.
https://twitter.com/UKIP/status/743388676244176896

So, what are the exact means 'to connect with people emotionally', and which emotions were excited?

The image on the poster showed a column of people appearing to be moving towards the viewer. The meaning of the image and its capitalised caption, BREAKING POINT, was not spelled out explicitly. Once again, it was left to viewers to infer a meaning, drawing on context and background knowledge – in this case the ongoing discourse aimed at immigrants. In actual fact, the image was a photograph of refugees crossing the border from Croatia into Slovenia in 2015, escaping from conflict in Turkey and Syria.[27] Most voters who saw the poster would not have been able to fact-check the image, or would not have bothered to do so, and were quite likely influenced by it. However, soon after the appearance of UKIP's poster, critical commentators detected a close similarity between that poster and a Nazi propaganda film from 1941.[28]

Figure 7.3b is a screenshot from live footage from the weekly Nazi propaganda film *Deutsche Wochenschau*, screened in 1941, during the German invasion of the Soviet Union (Operation Barbarossa). Extracts were included in a BBC documentary in 2005.[29] UKIP's poster has the same visual structure as the clip from the Nazi film shown in Figure 7.3b. In the original film the

[27] Beaumont-Thomas (2016), Drainville (2016), Ball (2017), pp. 55–6.
[28] E.g. Bartlett (2016), Stewart (2016), Sykes (2018).
[29] *Auschwitz: The Nazis and 'The Final Solution'*, six episodes from 11 January 2005. Two screenshots were placed on Twitter/X on 16 June 2016 by Brandan Harkin and Indy100 published four shots. They were compared with the poster by van Houtum and Lacy (2017), pp. 91–3.

Figure 7.3b Nazi propaganda film.
Source: *Die Deutsche Wochenschau* (1941), Bundesarchiv, Koblenz. DW 570/33/1941

audience saw a winding line of Jewish people, captured by German troops, moving from the far distance in the top left of the screen down to close-up faces at the bottom left. The BBC added running text over the film that is a translation from the German voice-over. In the original, a German Nazi narrator refers to 'floods of Jews' (*Judenfluten*), saying that they have overwhelmed and foreignised (*überfremdet*) central and western Europe. The Jews, says the voice, are 'parasites' who 'threaten thousand-year-old cultures' and bring with them 'crime, corruption and chaos' wherever they appear. This is the kind of language all too familiar in the discourse of Powellite racism and far-right anti-immigrant Brexiters. It is impossible to know whether UKIP, Farage or the person who designed the poster intended or was in any way aware of the resemblances. This does not necessarily mean that the similarities were an insignificant coincidence. More disturbingly, one suspects that the equivalent visual techniques, and the accompanying language, reflect the same mentality. If they arise because the underlying thought patterns are similar, the implications are far-reaching and justifiably aroused strong objections.

UKIP's image could have influenced the minds of voters in several ways. The image alone, without the huge capitalised caption and suggestive strapline.

From a certain viewing distance, the basic image is understood as a crowd of non-white people in a line, a moving line, in which each person is facing the viewer and proceeding on foot in the same direction towards the viewer. This line of walking people goes across the picture field, to the viewer's right then to their left. The foreshortening and changing sharpness of the figures' outlines, together with the way the column of figures is cut off by the frame at the bottom left, suggest a continuing forward movement into the viewers' space. These ordinary pictorial devices are unconsciously interpreted by the viewing brain and are capable of triggering affective responses. It is part of the overall cognitive effect of the image that the figures are perceived as *coming towards me, into my space*.

Image schemas underlie the understanding of visual as well as verbal stimuli. There are several at work here. One is the basic-level cognitive schema PATH, with the endpoint oriented towards the self. This schema grounds familiar verbal metaphors for a moving mass of people: 'floods', 'flows', 'waves' and 'rivers'. The contour of the line of figures may evoke the curving course of a river. The directional movement of the line of figures was another version of the arrows used in the graphics that suggested invasion of the UK by Turkish migrants.

Another cognitive schema automatically activated in the 'breaking point' poster is CONTAINER, in which a boundary is a natural component. In the poster, the line of figures is 'overflowing' the border, or boundary, of the picture, coming into the containing space of the viewer. Given background knowledge, this is the containing space of sovereign Britain – the space of the 'us' and the 'we' in the small-print lines of the poster. Viewing space, personal space and socio-political space are merged in the mind. The likely emotional effects are fear, heightened vigilance and hostility. There was nothing new in activating these kinds of reaction. As one commentator on the 'breaking point' poster notes, 'This poster is the visual equivalent of Enoch Powell's "rivers of blood" speech.'[30]

What about the words? Suppose you come across the phrase 'breaking point' outside of any surrounding context, visual or verbal. Your memory (the part known as 'semantic' memory in psychology) holds the conceptual, context-less meanings of the words along with knowledge of how to combine them in sentences. The conceptual basis of *break* is the FORCE schema, linked to bodily experience and to the fracturing of objects under pressure. Thus, people too can have their 'breaking points' and can 'break under pressure'. As can physical containers and boundaries, as well as abstractions such as institutions and societies. In all such expressions, the sense of force and disintegration may remain, and this is why they are capable of activating emotions of anxiety and

---

[30] Jones (2016).

fear. By contrast, people also 'break free' from some restraining force – here both FORCE and CONTAINER are involved. So there may be two contrasting emotions activated in the small-print message. On the one hand, breaking free out of a containing space (the EU) has positive valence. On the other hand, breaking free necessarily implies not being free prior to the escape. The compressed double valence here may have unconscious emotional effect. The same is true of 'we must take back control'.

If you read the two words 'breaking point' in a real situation, and with the background of a campaign discourse centring on immigration, then you probably construct a meaning relevant to you in the present. The poster's originators can count on viewers using the principle of relevance to put two and two together. And they can also deny, if it suits them, that your interpretation was what was intended. Overall, the composite message of the poster comes to something like: 'we', as individuals or as a nation, are at 'breaking point', in some vague sense that combines physical and emotional meanings.

All the implicatures, presuppositions and invited inferences that are involved in a contextual reading of the poster – these technical terms come under the umbrella term 'dog whistles'.[31] They are an analyst's way of trying to explain how dog whistles actually work. They can be verbal or visual, or a combination of both. The key point about them is that they operate in demagogic practice by activating perfectly normal systems of linguistic processing in human brains: 'the brain must assign meaning to the input, using at least knowledge of word meanings but usually also syntax and externally available information about the speaker, the context, and the goals of the exchange'.[32] This does not mean the processes are conscious: usually they are not. The brain sometimes builds a meaning just on the basis of content words and context, subsequently checking against grammatical structure. Vigilant hearers might, consciously and critically, attend to speaker, context – and the speaker's goals. But the second phase may not happen when words are read or heard fleetingly, as with slogans. Moreover, 'language processing is open to influences from internal or external sources of multimodal information [...] Such information is typically used as soon as it becomes available, exploiting interactive, parallel processing in the brain.' These are exactly the unconscious processes that propagandists can exploit in their multimodal messaging, especially in those contexts when they can anticipate inattentive processing. They can also expect some at least of the verbal and visual content to activate the brain's emotional circuits, including the amygdala.

This is how dogwhistling demagogues do it. One of the reasons why Brexit campaigners were able to do it was the context in which they were operating. Immigration had been deliberately made the central element of the Leave

---

[31] Cf. Saul (2012, 2018). [32] Baggio (2022), p. 63–8.

campaigns. And immigration was dogwhistled racism. The strategy worked well, because there already existed a latent post-imperial racism. It had been rhetorically reignited by Powell fifty years before, and the Leave campaigners were easily able to do the same with modern techniques.

There was another reason why the dog whistle worked politically. British public attitudes and discourse had changed radically since Powell's day. In retrospect, his racist utterances seem shockingly overt. But the term 'racist' was not at that time current in the sense and contextual connections it has now. Racial discrimination movements were only just beginning to emerge. The taboos against using racial slurs did not exist in the society of the time. 'Racist!' was not an utterance of angry abuse (justified or not) for another decade or so. By the time of the Brexit campaigns, it was well established among large sections of the UK population that hostile language and other behaviours directed at non-white people was racist, and was unacceptable. This was a value not necessarily accepted by everyone, and prevailed mostly in identity-liberal sections, rather than identity-conservative ones. Among conservative individuals there were those who would not identify themselves as 'liberals' in socio-political terms, but would seek to avoid being accused of racism. And among populist demagogues, there were those who would seek to avoid the 'racist' label, and also knew how to exploit the surrounding anti-racist culture.

It is convenient for demagogues to accept, and to exploit, the widespread assumption that racism has to be overt to count as racism. However, as Martin Shaw notes, 'hostility or enmity may be covert, indirect, latent or concealed, as well as overt, direct, manifest or proclaimed. [...] As racism has been delegitimized over the last century, its most potent forms have often been those which are less obvious or openly designed.'[33] Brexit populist racism was indeed covert. The spread of anti-racism values had driven it underground, with the result that in public discourse it could, outside of openly fascist and neo-Nazi circles, only be done by the various techniques of dog whistling. But this situation provides the demagogue with opportunities to promote a cause. As Durrheim and colleagues put it, 'populist leaders know what kinds of arguments will attract the criticism of racism, and they are then able to use these accusations to build popular support' – while denying that that is what they are doing.[34] If opponents do make an accusation of racism, the reply is the familiar literalistic manoeuvre: 'I (or we) didn't actually say that'. That then provides the opportunity for the exploitation of three more tricks of populist discourse. One is that the demagogue can make a counter-accusation that the accuser is just one of the 'elite establishment'. No need for more to be argued when addressing predisposed audiences. The job of building an us-against-them identity among supporters is done. A second, and equally potent, device is

[33] Shaw (2022), p. 30.   [34] Durrheim et al. (2018), p. 401.

that the demagogue can deploy the populist claim that he or she speaks for 'the people', 'the ordinary decent people'. Thirdly, in doing all this they are able to make claims to moral authority and legitimacy as defenders of free speech, facts and reasonableness.

The Fear of Losing It

The phrase *take back control* was the masterstroke of Brexit demagoguery. It was carefully crafted to mobilise the properties of the English language together with the processes of interpretation that readers were likely to use. We know this because Dominic Cummings, Vote Leave's chief demagogue, publicly summarised the preparatory steps he went through. An important factor was Vote Leave's ability to spread the net extremely wide. According to Cummings, the organisation was able to implement 'the winning message' in approximately 125 million leaflets, and crucially, in 'nearly a billion targeted digital adverts regardless of all complaints'. The latter was a powerful way of making individuals attend to, and absorb a carefully thought out message that was endlessly iterated. Timing, he knew was important, because 'adverts are more effective the closer to the decision moment they hit the brain'.

What Cummings calls 'our story' rested on five 'simple foundations'. Top of his list is his slogan 'take back control'. Second is, in his words, 'The official bill of EU membership is £350 million per week – let's spend our money on our priorities like the NHS instead'. The third foundation was also about 'taking control', specifically of immigration policy. It included the danger of Turkey joining the EU, the claim that the UK did not have 'democratic control' over immigration or a vote over Turkey's accession, and the assertion that 'It's safer to take back control.' The fourth was about the euro and the EU economy, and again, '*It's safer to take back control*' (Cummings's emphasis). And fifth is the 'anti-establishment' line of the populists.

How did the various versions of the phrase work exactly? In its basic form 'take back control', each of the three words contributes to a tightly packed meaning. The combination of these elements results in an overall communication that is both cognitive and emotive. On the linguistic level the crucial content word is obviously *control*. Here too, the basic conceptual structure is the FORCE schema. A language user's memory stores associated concepts and typical objects of control. One of the linked concepts is indicated in the idioms *be under someone's control* and *have control over someone*. This suggests that the meaning of control also involves downward pressure and vertical hierarchy – concepts that become relevant in political contexts.

The simplest version, 'take control', generally occurred in the form 'Vote Leave, Take Control.' The more frequently used version illustrated in Figures 7.4a and 7.4b includes both *let's* and *back*: 'let's take back control'.

The Fear of Losing It   165

Figure 7.4a Take Back Control.
Source: Jack Taylor/Stringer/Getty Images News/Getty Images.

The *let's* implies a collective inclusive *we* clearly meant to be understood as the national *we*. And when *back* is attached to a verb like *take* it triggers a rich presupposition that pulls background context into the overall meaning. When you read 'let's take back control', you cannot but infer that you had control in the past, that you do not have it currently, and that you can, should or must take it back in the future. From where? Your background knowledge kicks in and you know that what is intended is 'from the EU', which currently holds control over you. It is part of the effect of using *back* that readers are likely to assume

166 How Demagogues Do It

> **Let's take back control**
> ☒ **Our Money** – Give the NHS millions more every week
> ☒ **Our Economy** – Create new jobs with new trade deals
> ☒ **Our Borders** – A new points-based immigration system
> ☒ **Our Security** – Deport dangerous foreign criminals
> ☒ **Our Taxes** – Cut VAT on household energy bills
> Vote Leave on 23 June

Figure 7.4b Control of what?
Source: Carl Court/Staff/Getty Images News/Getty Images.

that what is presupposed is actually true – that we once had control but no longer do.

Cummings knew what he was doing when he invented this campaign slogan. In his article in *The Spectator*, he says:

> 'Let's take back control'. The overall theme. When I researched opinion on the euro [in 1990–2002] the best slogan we could come up with was 'keep control'. I therefore played with variations of this. A lot of people have given me a lot of credit for coming up with it but all I really did was listen.

Cummings is claiming his slogan was based on discovering what people really wanted. But the main point is that he tells us how the Vote Leave slogan was cooked up. He had started with *keep control*, which wouldn't work in the context of Brexit, since *keep* presupposed that we currently had control, with a concurrent implication that we could lose it. Replacing *keep* with *take* performed the task that was needed for Vote Leave. He is aware of the strong emotive impact that this apparently simple slogan would have. The word *back* does indeed 'play into' an emotion-provoking fact. It does it by presupposing that we do not currently have control, and that someone else, the EU, has control over us. All that is processed unconsciously in the brain.

Take back control of what exactly? Campaigners did specify a bewildering number of areas over which the UK supposedly no longer had control. Figure 7.4b, for example, which was circulated on an enormous scale via Twitter/X, lists five areas over which Britain needed to regain control. The first four of these refer to items that repeat key Brexit themes already in circulation and which are loaded with emotional as well as political associations for many British citizens – the NHS, jobs, immigration, dangerous foreign criminals. The Vote Leave campaign had a 'briefing' entitled 'Taking back control from Brussels'.[35] The text of this document partly spells out the items of which control is allegedly being lost – these include control over 'UK law', 'trade, human rights and migration', the UK economy, 'how our intelligence services combat terrorism', and 'how we implement the vital 1951 Convention on refugees'. The issues involved are complex and require close examination that certainly was not provided by Vote Leave. The apparent aim, however, was to suggest a great quantity of alarming instances of domination by a malign power, 'Brussels'. As subsequent developments demonstrated, most conspicuously in the case of the border between Ireland and Northern Ireland, the solutions to alleged problems that Brexit was supposed to provide were either impractical or illogical. But listing issue areas over which the UK could regain control in any practical manner was not the main purpose of the campaign process. What mattered was to deploy structures of thought that would trigger emotional reactions.

Taking back control presupposes *having lost control* in a number of domains that the Leave campaigns sometimes specified. Vote Leave's 'briefing' makes the presupposition explicit, with several semantic and pragmatic effects, using some form of *lose* five times in its relatively short text:

- We've lost control of trade, human rights, and migration.
- Losing control costs a fortune – if you vote 'remain' you'll be paying for euro bailouts.
- Britain has lost control of many things that are fundamental to what Abraham Lincoln called 'government of the people, by the people, for the people' – our economy, trade, migration, human rights, and even the rules on things like the building of schools and hospitals (which add billions to taxpayer bills).
- *This loss of control is deeply damaging and undemocratic* ... [italics original].
- Every Treaty since the 1950s has given Brussels more power. The official plan involves another huge transfer of powers to Brussels including over taxes. [...] We have repeatedly given away control in the hope of 'influence'. The loss of control was real.

This is a list of situations, each of which has the potential to arouse somebody's 'loss aversion', their fear of losing things and control over their lives, which can reach pathological levels in individual psychology. The range is very

---

[35] www.voteleavetakecontrol.org/briefing_control.html.

wide – loss of control over money, migrants, trade and buildings, as well as abstractions with real-world effects such as human rights and democracy. The document's final paragraph is a list, not of areas over which 'we' must take control, but a list of control powers that 'we' have lost. The conceptual structure of *lose* is the opposite of that of *take*. Losing something is the movement of something away from the self, where the self has no agency. So, this piece of Vote Leave propaganda was concerned to bring the notion of loss to readers' minds.

Notwithstanding the versions of the slogan that listed domains of lost control, it was the three-word 'take back control' version that became ubiquitous, and was probably the most emotionally penetrating. It was designed, at least in a semi-conscious intuitive fashion, to switch on a subliminal feeling of fear. Because it did not specify a domain of control, it could apply to a range of personal reactions to loss of agency – loss of control over oneself, one's possessions, one's environment, one's freedom, and control over others. Can we be sure this was intentional? Once again, it is Cummings who gives an indication of what is going on in the background thinking. Following the passage quoted earlier, in parentheses, he adds the following:

NB 'back' plays into a strong evolved instinct – we hate losing things, especially control.

It is quite reasonable to think that the human nervous system has evolved an automatic fear of losing control over things, people and animals around them. In the modern world, this 'instinct' develops in some individuals into pathological obsession. He is also right to say, indirectly, that a single word – *back* – can 'play into' an emotional reaction, 'hate' of 'losing things'. Actually, what *back* does is stimulate the emotional reaction indirectly, by way of presupposition. It is all the more effective for being indirect. The emotion is fear, a fear contextually linked to losing agency. As we already saw at the beginning of this chapter, certain words have been shown experimentally to affect particular regions of the brain. In the case of words related to danger, it is the amygdalae that are stimulated. Loss of control is also a danger. Moreover, as levels of anxiety and fear increase, so the ability to think rationally and take rational decisions decreases. The demagogic masterstroke was to connect the fear response to remaining in the EU.

We shall never know for sure that it was the demagogic propaganda that finally swung the electorate, providing the Leave campaigners with their narrow majority for quitting the EU. But it is the missing link if one wants a full explanation of why the vote went the way it did. Many commentators in the UK and beyond have rightly said that Brexit was an irrational decision. This chapter has probed what that irrationality consisted of in terms of what was going on in the minds, that is, the brains, on the receiving end of the rhetoric of Brexiter demagogues.

Demagogues can be defined in terms of two main characteristics: fearmongering and mendacity. These are closely related to one another in practice, because fear is intended to be aroused by false narratives, such as the invention of enemies and stories of invading hordes. Fearmongering is highly effective because humans evolved to attend to danger and reported danger, so sensitivity to verbal and pictorial representation of danger is hard-wired in our brains. It can be, and is, weaponised in 'psychological warfare'. There are specialists in both the military and among professional advisors to politicians who know how to press the most effective linguistic buttons – whether intuitively or by exploiting scientific research. It is also important to recognise that accepting plain lies and being susceptible to fear arousal does not just affect isolated individuals. It can be collective. Whole sections of populations may manifest fear and delusion, which can be induced simultaneously by modern mass media and most powerfully by the interpersonal contagion afforded by social media. These are the modern forms of classic crowd gullibility and hysteria stoked up by demagogic orators. Among the psychological effects of collective fear can be a susceptibility to populist narratives of protectors of 'the people', a path that leads to the decline of democracy and a turn towards authoritarianism. Brexit and the demagogic devices it rested on was not simply about leaving the EU. It was an erosion of democratic deliberation and democratic institutions that proved difficult to undo.

Conclusion: Brexitspeak, Demagoguery, Decline of Democracy

In her account of the Brexit process, the former French ambassador to the UK, Sylvie Bermann, writes:

Ceux qui ont écouté les sirènes des tribuns du Brexit ont accepté d'être plus pauvres, mais pour combien de temps? (Those who have listened to the siren voices of the Brexit demagogues have accepted being poorer, but for how long?)[1]

In due course, the negative consequences of the referendum started to penetrate the minds of a significant number of Leavers. Within three years of 'getting Brexit done' in 2020, polls of British voters were showing a sustained upward trend in the number of voters who thought it had been wrong to leave the EU.[2] More erstwhile Leavers were changing their minds and shifting to Remain than vice versa. An important factor in this is the new generation of voters, mostly opposed to Brexit, who are replacing the older voters who predominantly supported it. A hard core remained, however, who still believed – yes, *believed* in faith-like fashion – that Brexit was right and had been betrayed.

Numerous independent analysts and commentators charted the economic, social and political changes appearing in the aftermath of the referendum, changes that could reasonably be attributed to Brexit when they were not explained away by the COVID-19 pandemic or by the subsequent war in Ukraine. The economies of different parts of the UK had begun to shrink. Economic growth was down, inflation was increasing, and the cost of living was going up, because of the UK's withdrawal from the EU single market and customs union. Exports to the rest of the world fell, despite the grand visions of a globally trading Britain. In May 2022, the Office for Budget Responsibility was forecasting a reduction in long-run productivity, a decline of 15 per cent in exports and imports, and warning that new trade deals with non-EU countries would 'not have material impact'.[3] On the eve of the sixth anniversary of the referendum, the investment management company Bloomberg UK reported

---

[1] Bermann (2021), p. 253. Author's translation. [2] See Kellner (2023).
[3] 'Brexit analysis', Office for Budget Responsibility, updated 26 May 2022, https://obr.uk/forecasts-in-depth/the-economy-forecast/brexit-analysis/-assumptions.

that the Resolution Foundation had found evidence for the decline of advanced manufacturing, especially in northern England.[4] Since 2019, total trade as a share of GDP had fallen by 8 percentage points. The Resolution Foundation report noted that, allowing for the impact of the pandemic, 'we should expect the lasting impact of reduced openness to be substantial and widespread productivity [shocks] and real income shocks – much of which has already taken place'.[5]

Beyond the economic decline, there were further negative effects of Brexit for the UK. The NHS did not benefit from the Brexit lie and instead lost money and staff. The socio-economic divisions underlying much of the referendum's voting patterns persisted. The ideological divisions spawned by the referendum – between Brexitspeakers and non-Brexitspeakers – marked the entire social spectrum. The xeno-racism generated by the Brexit campaign was reinforced. Social tensions increased – attacks against migrants, against established ethnic communities, and against European residents spiked following Brexit. Government policy continued to have adverse consequences for minorities.[6] Government also looked like reneging on the Northern Ireland Protocol that had been negotiated in 2019 to resolve the problem of the new border between the UK and the EU, risking a trade war with the EU, and damaging the UK's international standing. To observers beyond the UK, the country seemed likely to decline, with the degrading of democratic and ethical norms at home, together with a disregard for international law and for obligations abroad.

Brexitspeak managed to override economic self-interest and the UK's interest in maintaining its role in international relations. In the years following, the damaging consequences of Boris Johnson's 'hard Brexit' became increasingly evident, not least for businesses, services and the economically vulnerable. That demagoguery was a major factor has been one of the principal claims of this book. Somehow, 'we' were talked into quitting the EU. While the UK was not alone in having national-populist movements, most European democracies managed to keep them at bay at that time, whereas decisive portions of the UK electorate were persuaded by Leaver demagoguery, and continued to be persuaded long enough for the Brexiter hardliners to get the extreme separation from the EU that they wanted. Given the evidence and arguments, why did 'we' do it? This is a question that can be approached by investigating what was *said* about it by those who wanted it, and *how* they said it, and what the *consequences* were for the politics and society of the UK.

---

[4] Atkinson (2022), www.bloomberg.com/news/articles/2022-06-21/brexit-has-made-uk-less-open-and-competitive-study-finds.
[5] Dhingra et al. (2022), p. 15, https://economy2030.resolutionfoundation.org/reports/the-big-brexit/.
[6] Shaw (2022), pp. 197–203.

Identity

British identity was one of the fundamental problems behind the rise of the anti-EU movement, stirred up by conservative politicians and the right-wing press. The wave of identitarian populist movements elsewhere was not a mere backdrop, but an active Europe-wide and American network with which Britain's Brexit leaders interacted. This provided the national-populist terrain in which the Eurosceptic project was seeded in the UK. It did not matter that the referendum result was marginal. Brexit fed back into Europe's identitarian movement and provoked talk of 'Frexit', 'Grexit', 'Italexit', and more. In subsequent years, this theme faded into the background, with EU voters wary of destabilisation, and the spectacle of the impact of Brexit on the UK before their eyes. Nonetheless, the ultra-right continued to make gains across the EU, from Finland to Greece. This drift to the right had the overall effect of 'centrifying' parties and movements that had been marginalised since World War II. In the UK as well as on the mainland, national-populist discourse became normalised and entered mainstream politics – even in Germany. In Poland and Hungary, the conservative national populists headed towards authoritarian government. Electorates veered towards the extreme parties in the polling booths, apparently motivated by issues of national identity, and antipathy towards globalisation and multiculturalism.

Generalising somewhat, national identities are largely fabrications emanating from national elites and propagated to the population through public ceremonies, education systems, religious institutions, and sections of press and media. This was the case in the Brexit period, when tailored national narratives appeared among pro-Brexit politicians and agitators, and in order to appease them also in the Conservative Party leadership. Within the referendum electorate, semi-fictional stories of Britain's greatness appealed to 'identity conservatives', distinguished from 'identity liberals' in terms of socio-economic status, educational level, geographic and age characteristics. Brexiter rhetoric reflected this divide in its constant opposing of the 'ordinary people' to the 'establishment', the 'elite' and 'experts'. Even though it was some of the degree-holding members of the British social hierarchy that propagated the most extreme national-populist myths, and there were a large number of elite-educated Leavers whose influence was considerable. Nonetheless, it is probable that educational level – that is to say, educational deprivation – played a part in the referendum campaign. The evidence is that higher levels of education do yield greater inter-group contact, mutual knowledge, cooperation and tolerance of difference. It is also possible that individuals with higher levels of education had a more critical stance with respect to Brexitspeak.

There is a germ of hope in all this. Younger generations, whether identity conservative or identity liberal, are less concerned with national identity and more oriented to opportunities in continental Europe as well as further afield. If educational opportunity continues to expand and remains relatively liberal, the worldviews that motivated a significant number of Leave voters may also diminish. Personal identities are never fixed. But predictions are risky and Brexit has not isolated Britain from the continued advance of far-right parties across the continent. The normalisation of national-populist and anti-immigrant discourse that Brexit brought about may only embolden the far right.

Sovereignty

In the national-populist perspective, and specifically in the perspective proclaimed by the Brexit advocates, the world is seen as a collection of hermetically sealed independent nation states – an exaggerated version of the Westphalian concept of absolute national sovereignty. In this sovereigntist worldview one nation is in competition with another. Balance of power and coalitions are in the picture, but conflict is the fundamental assumption. And the cooperative interaction and shared sovereignty exemplified by the EU are outside the frame.[7] Brexitism is anti-globalisation. It has a rigid and simplistic understanding of international relations among sovereign nations. It is oblivious to the realities of an emergent multipolar world and to the EU's own interest in its relationship with the US. Brexiters pinned their hopes for trade expansion on the supposed 'special relationship' with the United States. They overlooked the possibility that Brexit could undermine that relationship. It should also have been clear that the US had to turn its attention southwards and eastwards.

The Brexit view of the world has its roots in the problem of British national identity, at a point in history where the political culture of the country *still* recalls its empire and the loss of that empire. The nationalist Eurosceptics talked in a fashion that harked back to a golden Elizabethan and Jacobean age of buccaneering and global domination of trade. In 2020, as the UK prepared to leave the single market, the still-influential Brexiter Iain Duncan Smith enthused:

I just wish I was 21 again, frankly, my goodness what prospects lie ahead of us for young people now. To be out there buccaneering, trading, dominating the world again.[8]

Brexitism's fixation on an anachronous idea of national sovereignty went hand in hand with the populists' notion of 'the sovereignty of the people'. As it happens, this meshes with a British discourse strand going back in one simplified form or another to Buchanan and Hobbes – not to mention the continental input from Rousseau onwards. Brexit ideologues seemingly share a crude Hobbesian view of the world as one of competing individuals and isolated national units vying for dominance. It is a world of individual sovereignties

---

[7] Cf. Krasner (2004), pp. 1085–6. [8] Quoted by Shaw (2022), p. 112.

over territorially bounded entities, with ethnically homogeneous contents, and a fear of some hostile Other. One can glimpse a nightmarish realisation of Hobbesian theory in the national-populist tendency generally.[9] In the 2000s, the drift towards forms of authoritarianism became evident in the isolationist abandoning of international organisations, regulation and law that was central to the Brexit idea and continued under the Johnson regime. In its extreme manifestation – Trump and Putin – the Hobbesian nightmare takes shape in forms of personalised power claiming to represent the sovereignty of the people and refusing to recognise any international constraint or international community.

Hobbes's line of thought can result in imagining the collective abstraction 'the people' as the sovereign source of legitimacy. This kind of political discourse comes out in various guises at critical moments of national life, as was the case for Hobbes's generation. Similarly, Hobbes's forebear George Buchanan also developed a notion of a sovereign people, though he was extremely wary of giving free rein to this 'beast with many heads'. Yet both thinkers contributed to the laying down of the conceptual basis for a continuous national form of talk revolving around competing notions of political authority and 'the people', or claims about 'the people' by political actors. In the context of today's political movements, 'the people' do not have to be em-bodied or in-corporated (with or without an imaginary contract) in an absolutely powerful monarch. The populists' drift is to imagine the multitude as an individual actor. Contract theories, and arguments and slogans based on them, depend on metaphorically imagining 'the people' as a single individual person – as the Brexit Party was in effect doing in offering a so-called 'contract with the people'. One of the upshots of this way of thinking is that the populist demagogues can claim that 'the people' has a single 'will'. In a further step, the multitude may be seen as incorporated in a single leader. Such an individual, or set of individuals, generally claims to know 'the will of the people' without consulting them, and may claim to have a 'contract with the people'. Importantly for the referendum result of 2016, populist leaderships also maintain that they have the people's 'mandate'. A single will, a single leadership – this conceptual framing points in the direction of a monolithic authoritarian state.

Foreigners

Elements of xenophobia cut across the social and political spectrum and can be exploited to create the sentiment of a unified national popular identity. As shown exhaustively by Martin Shaw (2022), during the 2016 referendum

---

[9] On Trumpism as a Hobbesian nightmare, see Bose (2020).

xenophobia manifested itself as racism, and was found not only in UKIP and far-right campaign propaganda but also in that of the cross-party Vote Leave organisation. It was a racism that was communicated in a variety of indirect forms that could be denied or dismissed if critical individuals objected. But the point was that like-minded racist individuals, and individuals partially so inclined, would be reinforced in their disposition – and all this could work consciously or unconsciously. Such strategies were crucial in swinging the popular vote. An important question that arises with respect to the racism of the anti-EU campaign is: Why was it so easy to mobilise it?

Anti-black attitudes arose in, and were cultivated and embedded in British society during the Empire. After World War II, the liberal British Nationality Act of 1948 produced alarm in successive governments at the number of migrants that it had unexpectedly encouraged. By the 1960s, pro-white anti-black attitudes were expressed openly by governments, politicians and the public. That Enoch Powell is a crucial figure in post-World War II British political culture is accepted by a number of writers on Brexit. Powell's demagogic powers go a long way towards explaining how British racism was reinforced, disseminated and perpetuated right into the twenty-first century. His activities contributed significantly to the latent xenophobia and racism that Leave propaganda re-activated and exploited. Powell*ism* has remained an active current in British culture, perpetuating itself linguistically, whether in the obscene slang of the murderers of Stephen Lawrence or in the polite but vicious dog whistles of politicians.

Powell embodied the post-war psychological confusion concerning national identity. He was a product of the imperial bureaucracy and of an internalised worldview based on British superiority, perhaps racial superiority. In the 1940s and 1950s, that worldview became less realistically tenable, and for some its loss may have left psychological damage linked with personal identity. This was reflected in the fact that Powell opposed Britain's formal membership of the Empire's successor, the Commonwealth of Nations, which would have placed Britain on an equal footing with other members. It is clear from his rhetoric that he did not abandon a deep-seated belief in a naturally given and naturally superior British race. Powell could not have been alone among his generation. Many other Britons had been through similar socialisation and education processes up to the 1960s. In the period following World War II, with the disappearance of the imperial story of greatness, the predominant identity narrative was one in which Britain had stood alone against chaos in Europe and defeated a continental enemy. A generalised suspicion of 'foreigners' persisted. Post-war British society did not produce a narrative of reconciliation (one exception was Coventry's partnering with Dresden). British schools did not teach the history of nationalism, Nazism and the Holocaust in the way in which Germany, of necessity, and other European nations did. There was no basis for any narrative of the formation of the EEC, and then of the EU, in which these new economic and political unions were understood as a pacifying and restorative process.

Demagoguery and Propaganda

It was the demagogues who won Brexit. Today's demagogues have resources that those of the twentieth century, including Powell, could not have imagined, and propaganda has entered a new dimension. The printed press and traditional mass media have not stopped exerting their influence, but digital channels are capable of influencing minds in far more insidiously powerful ways. Furthermore, we need to think now in terms of entrepreneurial demagoguery, not only of the individual skilled orator. The demagogic entrepreneurs often include extremely wealthy individuals who are ideologically motivated and financially driven, or they may be narrowly focused IT specialists, or some mix of all these. The agents of demagoguery include already existing data management companies, 'political consultancies' and 'election management' firms, such as Cambridge Analytica and its network of subsidiaries and proxies. Both the official Vote Leave campaign and Farage's Leave.EU engaged the services of Cambridge Analytica (indirectly in the case of Vote Leave), its database (illegally drawn from Facebook), and its expertise in targeting different types of voters. Operations of this kind rest on massive funding, which has to be hidden or disguised in order not to infringe electoral laws that limit campaign spending. There is evidence to indicate such laws were broken.[10]

Across the political spectrum the new communication strategists took manipulation of the electoral mind well beyond the intuitive resources of classic orators. They influenced party and governmental structures in the roles of 'consultants' and 'special advisors' ('spads'), while often occupying positions in private campaign companies that they had themselves set up. Demagogic organisations had the funding and organisational structures to implement what has been learned about the mental and social mechanisms of 'messaging'. As well as drawing on Cambridge Analytica, Vote Leave employed its own technocratic demagogues in the shape of Matthew Elliott and Dominic Cummings, who had co-founded Vote Leave. Elliott was a libertarian lobbyist who had already found funding, mostly from obscure sources, for several successful campaigning organisations on the right. Both Elliott and Cummings adopted the selective online targeting of potential voters, and also had the demagogue's talent for crafting messages to match the target.

Vote Leave's rival organisation, Leave.EU, was founded, funded and managed by Arron Banks, whose donations came from a near-impenetrable

---

[10] Wylie (2019), Geoghegan (2020).

network of insurance and other businesses around the world. The money financed digital manipulation on social media and the acquiring of personal data of potential Brexit supporters. Banks also supported Nigel Farage and UKIP financially on an unprecedented scale. Ideologically, Banks expressed approval for authoritarian leaders around the world, including Vladimir Putin, and had close links with Donald Trump and Trump's alt-right advisor Steve Bannon. Banks was an intuitive demagogue in his own right: he was responsible for the most extreme of Leave.EU's verbal and visual propaganda, which was focused almost entirely on immigration.[11] Vote Leave, Leave.EU, and organisations connected to them in effect bought the UK's core democratic processes – free electorates, free elections and, from time to time, referendums. The laws and regulations that were in place to protect these processes, and thus to protect representative democracy itself, were insufficient and insufficiently clear.

The Brexit campaign of 2016 drew on technical expertise behind the scenes. It was not only a matter of new digital communication channels and vast data analysis. The new demagogic operators are now able to think in terms of the direct effects on the brain of propaganda 'messages'. Brexit campaign organisers were fully aware of the power of fear arousal – fear of anything that was politically relevant to the goals of the Leave campaigns. Neuroscience can now show how words can stimulate the particular emotion of fear. The demagogue's intuitive grasp of this goes back many centuries, as Enoch Powell knew, and as individual pro-Leave orators also knew. Such mind-bending strategies need to be well timed. This was certainly the case for the carefully targeted social-media messages launched by Leave.EU and Vote Leave three days before the vote. The intention was to boost the idea of an 'invasion' by immigrants from Turkey, supposedly brought about by the EU. And the invasion metaphor is still being used to trigger a military mental frame and a fear of territorial encroachment – notably by Conservative Home Secretary Suella Braverman, telling the House of Commons for example that 'The British people deserve to know which party is serious about stopping the invasion on our southern coast'.[12]

What about Remainer propaganda? The Labour Remain campaign, Labour In for Britain, was weak and made no appeal to popular sentiment. It focused on economic issues, reasonably enough, but failed to counter the exploitation of the topic of immigration by the Leave campaigns. Their largest handicap was their seeming half-heartedness about the UK remaining in the EU, together with the electorate's awareness of Jeremy Corbyn's previous Eurosceptic stance. The official Remain campaign, Britain Stronger In Europe, was more prominent and had access to very large amounts of funding and to extensive data about the electorate. But it did not reach those parts of the electorate that

[11] Geoghegan (2020), p. 65.   [12] Hansard, 31 October 2022: Column 641.

the Leave campaigns managed to influence. The Stronger In campaign, like Labour In, made the mistake of focusing on the economic risks of leaving the EU, without tackling Leave.EU's aggressive anti-migrant messaging. Stronger In spent large amounts on traditional messaging methods, such as leafleting every household. It did not take the opportunities for getting appropriately worded propaganda into the personal, if not entirely private, space of individual digital devices. By focusing mainly on the negative consequences of leaving the EU, rather than promoting a positive attitude towards membership, Stronger In risked merely arousing alarm. The Leave campaigns, by contrast, strategically mobilised fear, using targeted messages harnessed specifically to their campaign goals.

In democracies, demagoguery is now deeply embedded in political structures and processes. Democratic freedom of expression – as the ancient philosophers feared – has an inherent potential for demagoguery. Modern democracies have developed political communication systems that have magnified the scope of verbal persuasion, facilitated oligarchic monopolisation of media, and made possible the manipulation of whole populations. This ongoing transformation amounts to a threat to freedom of thought. It is the demagogisation of democracy that is at issue, giving rise to what we might call *demagocracy*. In totalitarian regimes, there is just one centralised demagogic structure pouring out propaganda. A demagocracy is characterised by competition between two or more demagogic organisations, and it is the demagogic organisation that is the best funded and best equipped that wins.

Lies and Post-truth Politics

The post-truth condition is characterised by the questioning of the distinction between the true and the false. It tends towards a generalised relativism, including scientific enquiry and findings. In a popularised form, and often in political contexts, concern for truth diminishes. 'Post-truth' can lead to abandoning logic and evidence in favour of emotional justification, ideological commitment and religious belief. A consequence of this in public life is that falsification and 'fake news' no longer matter, which means that the ethical norms against lying are less and less observed. 'Alternative facts' can be constructed *ad libitum*. At the extreme, the cooperative principle that underlies human communication simply breaks down. The degradation of language use in politics is the first sign of the degradation of democracy. It is not possible for democracies to function if truth and truthfulness become unstable.

The blatant inaccuracy of Vote Leave's bus slogan – 'We send the EU £350 million a week' – was denounced by Remain politicians and independent commentators in advance of the referendum. The slogan was passed off as rhetorical exaggeration, a 'truthful hyperbole'. But the facts were easy to check, and demonstrated that the slogan was a lie. Some Brexiters more or less admitted the £350 million claim was not accurate. In a *Telegraph* article of September 2017, Boris Johnson rephrased the slogan's wording, writing about 'taking back control' of the fictitious £350 million extra money that the country would have after leaving the EU.[13] He still did not specify how his figure was arrived at, and still implied that it would be spent on public services, particularly the NHS. When David Norgrove, the head of the UK Statistics Authority, challenged Johnson on the basis of the bus slogan's original assertion, Johnson responded by asserting that Norgrove's criticism was a 'wilful distortion of the text of my article' and demanded it be withdrawn.[14] This response was the demagogue's standard defence: 'that isn't what I meant, it's your fault for misinterpreting me'.

Falsehoods and duplicitous statements, even if objectively debunked, may nonetheless be believed by the original audience, and Brexiters knew that their lie about the UK's contribution to the EU would be effective. A survey conducted by King's College London in 2018 showed that 42 per cent of people who had heard about the £350 million claim still believed it to be true, despite the evidence.[15] The justification of lies and misleadings became less of a felt moral requirement. Telling untruths became normalised.

National-populist movements thrive in post-truth environments where truth is not an epistemic requirement and fictions and falsehoods are legitimate. They have the potential to shift polities towards types of regime incompatible with the principles of authentic representative models of democracy based on information, equality, diversity and justice. The American historian, Timothy Snyder, commenting on the assault on the Capitol Building in January 2021, noted that 'post-truth is pre-fascism'.[16] The main danger of populist movements consists in their dependence on 'the leader'. Populist theorists, where they exist, often insist on the importance of having a 'leader' as the unifier of the diverse demands of 'the people'. Such a political turn depends on communicative capacity of a *non*-deliberative kind – in short, on demagoguery and on an electorate audience swayable by public performers. A strong populist leader does not have to resemble a stereotypical authoritarian leader, the fascist leaders of historical memory. But a populist leader with authoritarian

---

[13] John Lichfield, 'Boris Johnson's £350m claim is devious and bogus. Here's why', *The Guardian*, 18 September 2017, www.theguardian.com/commentisfree/2017/sep/18/boris-johnson-350-million-claim-bogus-foreign-secretary.

[14] Anushka Asthana, 'Boris Johnson left isolated as row grows over £350m post-Brexit claim', *The Guardian*, 17 September 2017, www.theguardian.com/politics/2017/sep/17/boris-johnson-slapped-down-statistics-chief-fresh-350m-brexit-claim.

[15] 'Public wrong on key facts around Brexit and impact of EU membership', News Centre, King's College London, 28 October 2018, www.kcl.ac.uk/news/public-wrong-on-key-facts-around-brexit-and-impact-of-eu-membership. See also Stone (2018).

[16] Snyder (2021).

inclinations will play fast and loose with the truth, the law, the constitution, and the institutions of representative democracy.

There are several types of lying. One is the simple case of knowing facts you genuinely believe to be true but making public statements that are contrary or inconsistent with that belief. There is an ancient justification for this: the claim that the lie is 'a noble lie'. Plato argued that the noble lie is needed to ground the good society. Religions and ideologies argue in the same way. This a justification that always begs the question 'what justifies the cause you are lying for'? Political myths are also lies. Brexitspeak rested on a myth of insular greatness, occasionally supplemented by the myth that the Turks are about to 'invade' Europe.

Another kind of lying is the barefaced lie, where an individual believes he knows the facts, publicly says the opposite, but has no concern whether their public believes their utterance or not. This kind of lie, especially if constantly repeated, can make the false claim stick in the hearers' minds, and whether or not that happens it can be an assertion of the speaker's dominance. Brexitspeak was replete with easily verifiable falsehoods, half-truths and vague claims – the most absurd example being the claim in some tabloids that the EU would abolish the royal family.

A further kind of lying incorporates a 'couldn't care less' attitude towards truth, factuality and evidence – the stance that can be called 'epistemic insouciance'. This is a kind of lying that can affect a whole culture, whether a localised body of people such as a government leadership or a whole society.

We may never know what goes on in a liar's mind. But in the instance of intense adherence to a cause, there is a complicated cognitive adjustment on the part of the liar. Orwell captures this mental state in his description of 'doublethink' in *Nineteen Eighty-Four*:

> To know and not to know, to be conscious of complete truthfulness while telling carefully constructed lies, to hold simultaneously two opinions which cancelled out, knowing them to be contradictory and believing in both of them, [...] to forget whatever it was necessary to forget, then to draw it back into memory again at the moment when it was needed, and then promptly to forget it again ...

Undoing Democracy

British political culture and institutions rested on, and maintained, ideas and attitudes that could be exploited by those who rejected existing representative democratic institutions.[17] Brexit has not rescued or reinvigorated or reformed democracy, as some of its supporters claimed it would, but undermined it and

---

[17] On the global erosion of democracy, see for example Mounk (2018), Runciman (2018), Levitsky and Ziblatt (2019).

forestalled improvement and progress where they were needed. True, the existing form of representation and the electoral voting system have not increased the inclusion of the politically alienated. Nor have they enhanced the processes of rational participatory deliberation that are the bedrock of the very idea of democracy. Some of these tendencies – the socio-economic divisions, the decline of party representation, the deterioration of ethical norms in public communication – were already in train. Brexit exploited and solidified them.

The referendum process itself held serious implications for constitutional soundness and for the political norms of representative democracy. The UK has no constitutional requirement to implement the results of referendums. Neither the European Union (Referendum) Bill 2013–14 nor the European Referendum Act 2015 included such a requirement. Further, the UK constitution does not provide for a vote threshold in referendums, and the two Acts did not provide one either. Despite the lack of a constitutional requirement, both a threshold and a statement on whether the result was binding on the government or not should have been expected, given the historical significance of withdrawing from the EU. In the face of all this, and a ministerial statement that the result was to be advisory, Cameron's own government declared that result would be implemented. The omissions and the inconsistencies left the constitutional role of referendums in the UK unstated. Theoretically, this leaves the way open for internal political conflict with the possibility of a populist coup.

As for the voting figures, because no thresholds were set, a simple majority could be used in arguments based on populist assumptions, in which 'the people' is an emotionally qualitative concept, not a quantitative one. Naturally, drawing attention to the relative proportions of votes and their relation to electoral make-up was avoided. The much flaunted 51.89 per cent was the percentage of votes actually cast. Was it representative? The number of individuals eligible to vote was 46,500,001, the number of valid Leave votes 17,410,742, and the number of valid Remain votes 16,141,241. On that basis, the Leave percentage was 37.44 per cent, Remain 34.71 per cent, showing an even smaller margin. Of course, one does not expect full turnout, but this is one of the instances where a supermajority threshold should become relevant. The fact remains that on official figures the percentage difference between the Leave and the Remain votes was only 3.78 per cent. In effect, the failure to set a threshold percentage left political pressures and rhetoric in charge of deciding whether 3.78 per cent was a reasonable margin to take as the basis for subsequently dividing a whole democratic population.

The referendum campaign propaganda had developed the essential article of populist faith: 'the will of the people' automatically hands an imperative mandate to the government. The distinction between *imperative* mandates and *free* mandates is key to elucidating the drift away from representative democracy towards a type of governance in which, it is imagined, the people are direct participants. Imperative mandates bind governments, but at the same time give them the chance to act as they wish in the name of 'the people'. Free mandates leave elected representatives to follow their own judgement, conscience and processes of deliberation. But they still require representatives to be accountable at election time and to justify their relatively free decisions in office. However, for populists this is not 'democratic' because 'the people' has not been directly involved.[18] Populists favour referendums with simple binary questions, since the results can be claimed to be the voice of 'the people'. The populist fantasy of 'direct' democracy expressing an idealised 'will of the people' logically implies the dismissal of the framework of democratic pluralism, elections, parliamentary process, and undermines the separation of powers. It leads to the denial of an election's legitimate outcome. The ambiguous and dishonest claim to be *truly* 'democratic' enables populists to enter government via existing representative structures, and once inside, to erode it from within. After the referendum, the crucial question of whether the result was advisory or mandatory received little serious debate. The government perfunctorily argued that the referendum was indeed mandatory, despite the fact that the Leave majority was marginal, and proceeded to act on that basis. This position was in part driven by the shift to a populist mindset that obscured what should have been a constitutional question concerning the conditions on referendums in the UK. In a short time, the matter was passed over in silence.

The assumption of mandatory powers was of doubtful constitutional and democratic validity, and it paved the way for further undermining of democratic principles. Following the referendum, the Conservative premiership moved to the right, pushing as far as it could Westminster's inherent executive dominance – that is, 'elective dictatorship'. The constitutional principle that the prime minister be no more than *primus inter pares* was also eroded, as was the principle of collective responsibility of government ministers. The premiership became more personalised. Johnson tried to cling on to power, declaring that he was holding on to his office in order to fulfil his duty to his electors. He invoked 'the mandate' of 'the British people', making it appear as if 'the people' had mandated him personally.

Immediately after the referendum, the then prime minister Theresa May, succeeding David Cameron, had announced that she intended to invoke Article 50 of the Treaty on European Union, in order to initiate the process of withdrawal. But only 24 per cent of MPs had supported Leave.[19] In 2019, after protracted argument and uncertainty in the House of Commons, the

---

[18] Müller (2016), pp. 12–13.
[19] 'Brexit: The People vs. Parliament', House of commons Library, 8 July 2016, https://commonslibrary.parliament.uk/brexit-the-people-vs-parliament/.

government attempted to use prerogative powers to bypass further parliamentary debate. Subsequently, the Supreme Court ruled that parliamentary approval was required before Article 50 could be invoked. Conservative MPs were, however, 'whipped' into supporting the government. When Boris Johnson succeeded May, he attempted to prorogue Parliament for the longest period since 1930, in the face of criticism from constitutionalists. Like May, he was seeking to evade scrutiny of his government's EU withdrawal proposals. Some commentators thought his actions amounted to an internal coup. The Supreme Court again ruled that the government's move was unlawful, and prorogation was annulled. From the other side of the Channel, these goings-on were viewed as politically extreme. In the German newspaper *Die Zeit*, one of their journalists wrote, with only a dash of irony:

Es ist ein Staatsstreich. Der Regierungschef hat gegen das Parlament geputscht. Das Parlament stand dem Premierminister im Weg, daraufhin hat er es weggeräumt. So enden Demokratien. (It's a coup d'état. The head of government has mounted a putsch against Parliament. Parliament stood in the way of the Prime Minister, so he moved it aside. That's how democracies end.)[20]

It is not just that the withdrawal from the EU had damaging consequences, social, economic and political, for the UK. It was also the *processes* – the twisting of truth, of electoral processes, of the constitution – that had serious implications for the nature of British democracy. The years following the referendum bequeathed an electorate divided into two ideological tribes: those who did and those who did not speak Brexitspeak. The UK lost international standing and influence. French, German and other EU observers looked on with incredulity and even alarm. The country was left socially divided, and deeply split in culture and values. Brexit solidified that division. After the referendum, and following Johnson's fall from grace, the Brexit post-truth demagogues still had their practitioners and their audiences. The force of pro-Brexit voices continued, even after public opinion began to recognise the impoverishment they had been persuaded to accept. These voices blocked, or at least delayed, the return of rational debate on membership of the EU. Given the logic of the UK's electoral system and the persistent effects of the Brexit movement, even the Leader of the Opposition felt obliged to announce, in June 2022, that his party would never seek to rejoin the EU, not even the single market or the customs union.

But there was at least the *potential* for change. The ill effects of Brexit were beginning to be felt in the hard realities of everyday life. And this was reflected

---

[20] Imke Henkel, *Die Zeit*, 28 August 2019. Author's translation.

in the polls. In the long term, any demagogic figure is vulnerable to swings of public opinion motivated by forces beyond their control. Over time, demographic change will increasingly transform the values and attitudes of the audience that the Brexit demagogues depended on. The new generation will in growing numbers ask the question, 'how on earth could such a decision as Brexit have happened?' And this will be in a radically altered national and geopolitical context. Already we are at a turning point for Europe and beyond, one which could, and should, lead to seeing Brexit in a very different perspective.

Appendix A   Experimental Threat Words (Isenberg et al. 1999)

Words (or parts of words) in bold are present in Powell's 'rivers of blood' speech; number of occurrences present in Powell is in parentheses; form in which word appears in Powell is in square brackets, if different from word list.

threat words			
persecute (1) [persecuted, adjective]	assassinate	conspiracy	mutilate
threat	bruise	loathe	**blood**stain (1) [blood]
destroy (1)	hijack	assault	injure
whisper	gun	harass	hate
slaughter	**pursue (1)**	investigation	contaminate
death	rape	trap	torture
bludgeon	suffocate	capture	hostage
hit	wound	damage	suspicion
attack (1) [attacked, verb past participle]	abhor	beat	**follow (1)** [followed, verb past participle]
spy	failure	suspect	**blind**fold (2) [blind]
prisoner (1) [prison]*	kidnap	annihilate	im**prison***
distrust	suspicious	deceive	**whip (1)****
bully	poison	bullet	**mislead (1)**
torment	molest	kill	blame
evil (4) [evils]	knife	corruption	strangle
execute	disturb	arrest	**danger (6)** [danger (1), dangerous (5)]
whipcord**	**betrayal (1)**	**suffer (1)**	intrude
condemn (1) [condemned, verb past participle]	stab	chase	conspire
opposition	**abuse (1)** [abused, verb past participle]	punish	stare
steal	sinister	overthrow	accuse

* The word 'prison' occurs once in Powell; the word list has two instances of this morpheme.
** The word 'whip' occurs once in Powell; the word list has two instances of this morpheme.

185

Appendix B Experimental Threat Words (Weisholtz et al. 2015)

Words in bold are present in Powell's 'rivers of blood' speech.

accused	whisper	**pursue**
danger	**persecute**	harass
blame	distrust	**blind**fold
sinister	poison	spy
deceive	injure	torment
attack	**betray**ed	threat
corrupt	investigation	steal
abuse	mislead	**evil**

Appendix C Words and Phrases That Are Plausible Fear-Activating Words Present in Powell's 'Rivers of Blood' Speech But Not on the Above Lists

grave	resentment
troubles	pillory
gravity	ominous
curses	reprisals
execration	penalties
inflame	risk [verb]
extreme urgency	fear [verb, also noun]
without delay	afraid
difficulties	taken over
alien	windows are broken
stranger	excreta
agent provocateur	overawe
insane	dominate
mad	fragmentation
delusion	divisive
funeral pyre	agitate against
rising peril	campaign against
confront	canker
deprivation	weapons
throwing a match on to gunpowder	foreboding
alarm	horror

References

Adorno, Theodor W. (1950). 'Democratic leadership and mass manipulation', in A. W. Gouldner (ed.), *Studies in Leadership: Leadership and Democratic Action*. New York: Harper & Row, pp. 418–38.
Adorno, Theodor W., Else Frenkel-Brunswick, Daniel J. Levinson and R. Nevitt Sanford (1950). *The Authoritarian Personality*. New York: Wiley.
Albertazzi, Daniele M. and Duncan McDonnell (eds.) (2008). *Twenty-First Century Populism: The Spectre of Western European Democracy*. New York: Palgrave Macmillan.
Alessio, Dominic and Kristen Meredith (2014). 'Blackshirts for the twenty-first century? Fascism and the English Defence League', *Social Identities*, 20(1), pp. 104–18.
Altemeyer, Bob (1981). *Right-Wing Authoritarianism*. Winnipeg: University of Manitoba Press.
Altemeyer, Bob (1988). *Enemies of Freedom: Understanding Right-Wing Authoritarianism*. San Francisco, CA: Jossey-Bass.
Altemeyer, Bob (1996). *The Authoritarian Specter*. Cambridge, MA: Harvard University Press.
Anderson, Benedict ([1983] 2006). *Imagined Communities: Reflections on the Origin and Spread of Nationalism*. London: Verso.
Applebaum, Anne (2020). *Twilight of Democracy: The Failure of Politics and the Parting of Friends*. London: Allen Lane.
Arendt, Hannah (1951). *The Origins of Totalitarianism*. London: Penguin.
Arendt, Hannah (1967). 'Truth and politics', *The New Yorker*, 25 February.
Arendt, Hannah (1971). 'Lying in politics: Reflections on the Pentagon papers', *New York Review*, 18 November.
Aristotle (1981). *The Politics*. Translated by T. A. Sinclair and revised by T. J. Saunders. London: Penguin.
Art, David (2020). 'The myth of global populism', *Perspectives on Politics*, 20(3), pp. 999–1011.
Ashcroft, Richard T. and Mark Bevir (2021). 'Brexit and the myth of British national identity', *British Politics*, 16(2), pp. 117–32.
Atkinson, Andrew (2022). 'Brexit has made UK less open and competitive, study finds', Bloomberg UK, 22 June, www.bloomberg.com/news/articles/2022-06-21/brexit-has-made-uk-less-open-and-competitive-study-finds.
Atkinson, Max (1984). *Our Masters' Voices: The Language and Body Language of Politics*. London: Routledge.
Austin, John L. ([1962] 1975). *How to Do Things with Words*. Oxford: Clarendon Press.
Ayer, A. J. (1936). *Language, Truth and Logic*. London: Victor Gollancz.

References

Baggio, Giosuè (2022). *Neurolinguistics*. Cambridge, MA: MIT Press.
Bale, Timothy (2017). 'Truth to tell: Populism and the immigration debate', London School of Economics, 1 March, http://blogs.lse.ac.uk/politicsandpolicy/truth-to-tell-brexit-will-not-reduce-migration/.
Bale, Timothy (2018). 'Who leads and who follows? The symbiotic relationship between UKIP and the Conservatives – and populism and Euroscepticism', *Politics*, 38(3), pp. 263–77.
Ball, James (2017). *Post-Truth: How Bullshit Conquered the World*. London: Biteback Publishing.
Banks, Kathryn (2009). 'Interpretations of the body politic and of natural bodies in late sixteenth-century France', in A. Musolff and J. Zinken (eds.), *Metaphor and Discourse*, pp. 205–18. London: Palgrave Macmillan.
Barker, Stephen (2011). 'Speech-acts', in P. C. Hogan (ed.), *The Cambridge Encyclopedia of the Language Sciences*, pp. 786–9. Cambridge: Cambridge University Press.
Bartlett, Evan (2016). 'People are calling out Ukip's anti-EU poster for resembling "outright Nazi propaganda"', *Indy100*, 16 June, www.indy100.com/news/people-think-ukip-s-new-antieu-poster-resembles-outright-nazi-propaganda–7299841.
Bat Ye'or (2001). *Islam and Dhimmitude: Where Civilizations Collide*. Madison, NJ: Fairleigh Dickinson University Press.
Bat Ye'or (2005). *Eurabia: The Euro-Arab Axis*. Madison, NJ: Fairleigh Dickinson University Press.
BBC News (2020). '"Happy Brexit Day" signs at Norwich flats say "only speak English"'. BBC News, 1 February, www.bbc.co.uk/news/uk-england-norfolk-51341735.
Beaumont-Thomas, Ben (2016). 'Jeff Mitchell's best photograph: "These people have been betrayed by Ukip"', *The Guardian*, 22 June, www.theguardian.com/artanddesign/2016/jun/22/jeff-mitchells-best-shot-the-column-of-marching-refugees-used-in-ukips-brexit-campaign.
Beauzamy, Brigitte (2013). 'Explaining the rise of the Front National to electoral prominence: Multi-faceted or contradictory models?', in R. Wodak, M. KhosraviNik and B. Mral (eds.), *Right-Wing Populism in Europe: Politics and Discourse*, pp. 177–90. London: Bloomsbury.
Bell, Emily (2016). 'The truth about Brexit didn't stand a chance in the online bubble', *The Guardian*, 7 July, www.theguardian.com/media/2016/jul/03/facebook-bubble-brexit-filter.
Berend, Iván T. (2020). *A Century of Populist Demagogues*. Budapest: Central European University Press.
Bermann, Sylvie (2021). *Goodbye Britannia: Le Royaume-Uni au défi du Brexit*. Paris: Éditions Stock.
Bhatia, Tej K. (2011). 'Bilingualism and multilingualism', in P. C. Hogan (ed.), *The Cambridge Encyclopedia of the Language Sciences*, pp. 125–8. Cambridge: Cambridge University Press.
Blackledge, Adrian (2002). 'The discursive construction of national identity in multilingual Britain', *Journal of Language, Identity and Education*, 1(1), pp. 67–87.
Blunkett, David (2002). 'What does citizenship mean today?', *The Guardian*, 15 September, www.theguardian.com/world/2002/sep/15/race.thinktanks.

Bose, Joydeep (2020). 'Trump's Americana was a Hobbesian nightmare, but not to the cynic', *The Free Press Journal*, 9 November, www.freepressjournal.in/analysis/trumps-americana-was-a-hobbesian-nightmare-but-not-to-the-cynic.

Brooke, Peter (2007). 'India, post-imperialism and the origins of Enoch Powell's "rivers of blood" speech', *The Historical Journal*, 50(3), pp. 669–87.

Brown, Penelope and Stephen C. Levinson (1987). *Politeness: Some Universals in Language Usage*. Cambridge: Cambridge University Press.

Brown, Roger W. and Albert Gilman (1960). 'The pronouns of power and solidarity', in T. A. Sebeok (ed.), *Style in Language*, pp. 253–76. Cambridge, MA: MIT Press.

Browning, Christopher S. (2019). 'Brexit populism and fantasies of fulfilment', *Cambridge Review of International Affairs*, 32(3), pp. 222–44.

Buchanan, George (1579). *De Jure Regni apud Scotos Dialogus*, www.philological.bham.ac.uk/scotconst/text.html.

Buchanan, George ([1680] 1689). *Dialogus de jure regni apud Scotos. Or, A Dialogue, Concerning due Priviledge of Government in the Kingdom of Scotland. Betwixt George Buchanan and Thomas Maitland, By the said George Buchanan. Translated out of the Original Latine into English*. London: Richard Baldwin.

Buckledee, Steve (2018). *The Language of Brexit: How Britain Talked Its Way Out of the European Union*. London: Bloomsbury.

Bull, Peter (2003). *The Microanalysis of Political Communication: Claptrap and Ambiguity*. London: Routledge.

Bull, Peter (2006). 'Invited and uninvited applause in political speeches', *British Journal of Social Psychology*, 45(3), pp. 563–78.

Bulman, May (2019). 'Austerity measures and hostile environment "entrenching racism" in UK, Says UN', *The Independent*, 15 June, www.independent.co.uk/news/uk/home-news/austerity-racism-hostile-environment-xenophobia-un-report-rapporteur-immigration-bame-a8959866.html.

Busher, Joel (2018). 'Why even misleading identity claims matter: The evolution of the English Defence League', *Political Studies*, 66(2), pp. 323–38.

Cain, Sian (2018). 'British "linguaphobia" has deepened since Brexit vote, say experts', *Guardian*, 28 May, www.theguardian.com/books/2018/may/28/british-linguaphobia-has-deepened-since-brexit-vote-say-experts.

Canovan, Margaret (1981). *Populism*. New York: Harcourt Brace Jovanovich.

Canovan, Margaret (1999). 'Trust the people: Populism and the two faces of democracy', *Political Studies*, 47(1), pp. 2–16.

Canovan, Margaret (2004). 'Populism for political theorists?', *Journal of Political Ideologies*, 9(3), pp. 241–52.

Canovan, Margaret (2005). *The People*. Cambridge: Polity Press.

Cap, Piotr (2019). 'Britain is full to bursting point', in V. Koller, S. Kopf and M. Miglbauer (eds.), *Discourses of Brexit*, pp. 69–85. London: Routledge.

Cassam, Quassim (2019). *Vices of the Mind: From the Intellectual to the Political*. Oxford: Oxford University Press.

Ceaser, James W. (2007). 'Demagoguery, statesmanship and the American presidency', *Critical Review*, 19(2–3), pp. 257–98.

Charteris-Black, Jonathan (2006). 'Britain as a container: Immigration metaphors in the 2005 election campaign', *Discourse and Society*, 17(5), pp. 563–81.

Cheshire, James and Alexander J. Kent (2023). 'Getting to the point? Rethinking arrows on maps', *The Cartographic Journal*, Taylor and Francis Online, https://doi.org/10.1080/00087041.2023.2178134.
Chilton, Paul (1996). *Security Metaphors*. New York: Peter Lang.
Chilton, Paul (2004). *Analysing Political Discourse: Theory and Practice*. London: Routledge.
Chilton, Paul and Monika Kopytowska (2018). '"Rivers of blood": Migration, fear and threat construction', *Lodz Papers in Pragmatics*, 14(1), pp. 133–61.
Chilton, Paul and Monika Kopytowska (2022). 'Political dialogue across time, space and genres', *International Review of Pragmatics*, 14(2), pp. 226–51.
Churchill, Winston S. (1964). *The Island Race*. London: Cassell.
Collings, Rex (ed.) (1991). *Reflections of a Statesman: The Writings and Speeches of Enoch Powell*. London: Bellew.
Cosmides, Leda (1989). 'The logic of social exchange: Has natural selection shaped how humans reason? Studies with the Wason selection task', *Cognition* 31(3), pp. 187–276.
Cosmides, Leda and John Tooby (1992). 'Cognitive adaptations for social exchange', in J. Barkow, L. Cosmides and J. Tooby (eds.), *The Adapted Mind: Evolutionary Psychology and the Generation of Culture*, pp. 162–228. New York: Oxford University Press.
Cosmides, Leda and John Tooby (2000). 'Consider the source: The evolution of adaptations for decoupling and metarepresentations', in D. Sperber (ed.), *Metarepresentation: A Multidisciplinary Perspective*, pp. 53–116. Oxford: Oxford University Press.
Cowley, Jason (2017). 'Nigel Farage: The arsonist in exile', *New Statesman*, 8 December.
Crines, Andrew, Tim Heppell and Michael Hill (2016). 'Enoch Powell's "rivers of blood" speech: A rhetorical political analysis', *British Politics*, 11(1), pp. 72–94.
Crines, Andrew and Tim Heppell (2017). 'Rhetorical style and issue emphasis within the conference speeches of UKIP's Nigel Farage 2010–2014', *British Politics*, 12(2), pp. 231–49.
Croft, William and D. Alan Cruse (2004). *Cognitive Linguistics*. Cambridge: Cambridge University Press.
Crosby, Lynton (2016). 'Out campaign must make its case more relevant to voters', The Telegraph, 19 April.
Crouch, Colin (2020). *Post-Democracy after the Crises*. Cambridge: Polity.
Cummings, Dominic (2017). 'How the Brexit referendum was won', *The Spectator*, 9 January, www.spectator.co.uk/article/dominic-cummings-how-the-brexit-referendum-was-won/.
Dale, Iain (2017). 'Leave politicians told us exactly what we'd be voting for – it's a shame Remain leaders didn't, but we all know why', *Iain Dale* [website], 19 February, www.iaindale.com/articles/leave-politicians-told-us-exactly-what-we-d-be-voting-for-it-s-a-shame-remain-leaders-didn-t-but-we-all-know-why.
Damasio, Antonio (2003). *Looking for Spinoza: Joy, Sorrow and the Feeling Brain*. London: Vintage Books.
D'Ancona, Matthew (2017). *Post-Truth: The New War on Truth and How to Fight Back*. London: Penguin.

Da Silva, Renato Rodrigues (2021). 'The uses of the "Anglo-Saxon" past between revolutions, imperialism and racism', *Práticas da História*, 12, pp. 129–60.
de Benoist, Alain (2004a). 'Nous et les autres: problématique de l'identité', *Eléments*, 113, pp. 1–61.
de Benoist, Alain (2004b). 'On identity'. Translated by Kathy Ackerman and Julia Kostova, *Telos*, Summer, pp. 9–64.
de Benoist, Alain (2006). *Nous et les autres. Problématique de l'identité*. Paris: Éditions Krisis.
de Cillia, Rudolf, Martin Reisigl and Ruth Wodak (1999). 'The discursive construction of national identities', *Discourse and Society*, 10(2), pp. 149–73.
Dhingra, Swati, Emily Fry, Sophie Hale and Nigyuan Jia (2022). 'The Big Brexit: An assessment of the scale of change to come from Brexit', *The Economy 2030 Inquiry*, The Resolution Foundation, June, https://economy2030.resolutionfoundation.org/reports/the-big-brexit/.
Dorling, Danny and Sally Tomlinson (2019). *Rule Britannia: Brexit and the End of Empire*. London: Biteback.
Dornbusch, Rüdiger and Sebastian Edwards (eds.) (1992). *The Macroeconomics of Populism in Latin America*. Chicago: University of Chicago Press.
Drainville, Ray (2016). 'The visual propaganda of the Brexit Leave campaign', *Hyperallergic*, https://hyperallergic.com/310631/the-visual-propaganda-of-the-brexit-leave-campaign/.
Durrheim, Kevin, Mukadder Okuyan, Michelle Sinayobye Twali, Efraín García Sánchez, Adrienne Pereira, Jennie Sofia Portice, Tamar Gur, Ori Wiener-Blotner and Tina F. Keli (2018). 'How racism discourse can mobilize right-wing populism: The construction of identity and alliance in reactions to UKIP's Brexit "Breaking Point" campaign', *Journal of Community and Applied Social Psychology*, 28(6), pp. 385–405.
Eatwell, Roger and Matthew Goodwin (2018). *National Populism: The Revolt against Liberal Democracy*. London: Pelican.
Ebner, Julia (2020). *Going Dark: The Secret Social Lives of Extremists*. London: Bloomsbury.
Emmerson, Carl, Paul Johnson, Ian Mitchell and David Phillips (2016). *Brexit and the UK's Public Finances*. IFS Report 116. London: Institute for Fiscal Studies, https://ifs.org.uk/sites/default/files/output_url_files/r116.pdf.
Enos, Ryan D. (2014). 'Causal effect of intergroup contact on exclusionary attitudes', *Proceedings of the National Academy of Sciences of the United States of America*, 111(10), pp. 3699–704.
Erskine, Caroline (2016). 'George Buchanan, English Whigs and Royalists, and the canon of political theory', in C. Erskine and R. A. Mason (eds.), *George Buchanan: Political Thought in Early Modern Britain and Europe*, pp. 229–47. London: Routledge.
Esteves, Olivier (2019). 'An international press review of the Powell moment (1968–1973)', in O. Esteves and S. Porion (eds.), *The Lives and Afterlives of Enoch Powell*, pp. 65–80. London: Routledge.
Esteves, Olivier and Stéphane Porion (eds.) (2019). *The Lives and Afterlives of Enoch Powell: The Undying Political Animal*. London: Routledge.
Evans, Geoffrey and Jonathan Mellon (2019). 'Immigration, Euroscepticism, and the rise and fall of UKIP', *Party Politics*, 25(1), pp. 76–87.

Fallis, Don (2012). 'Lying as a violation of Grice's first maxim of quality', *Dialectica*, 66(4), pp. 563–81.
Farage, Nigel (2011). *Flying Free*. London: Biteback.
Farage, Nigel (2013a). Speech to UKIP Conference, 23 March, www.youtube.com/watch?v=bAR0bOdY1mU.
Farage, Nigel (2013b). Speech to UKIP Conference, 19 September, UKPOL.CO.UK, www.ukpol.co.uk/nigel-farage-2013-speech-to-ukip-conference/.
Farage, Nigel (2014). Speech to UKIP Conference, 28 February, www.youtube.com/watch?v=A6JgyJp_QJw.
Fauconnier, Gilles (1994). *Mental Spaces*. New York: Cambridge University Press.
Fauconnier, Gilles and Mark Turner (2002). *The Way We Think: Conceptual Blending and the Mind's Hidden Complexities*. New York: Basic Books.
Faye, Guillaume (2000). *La Colonisation de l'Europe: discours vrai sur l'immigration et l'Islam*. Paris: L'Æncre.
Faye, Guillaume (2016). *The Colonisation of Europe*. Translated by Roger Adwan. Budapest: Arktos.
Fekete, Liz (2001). 'The emergence of xeno-racism', Institute of Race Relations, 28 September, https://irr.org.uk/article/the-emergence-of-xeno-racism/.
Ferguson, Niall (2004). 'The way we live now: 4-4-04; Eurabia', *New York Times*, 4 April.
Fillmore, Charles J. (1977). 'Scenes-and-frames semantics', in A. Zambolli (ed.), *Linguistic Structure Processing*, pp. 55–82. Amsterdam: North Holland.
Fillmore, Charles J. (1982). 'Frame semantics', in *Linguistics in the Morning Calm*, pp. 111–37. Seoul: Hanshin Publishing Company.
Ford, Robert (2019). 'Powell and after: Race, immigration and politics in Britain 1964–1979', in O. Esteves and S. Porion (eds.), *The Lives and Afterlives of Enoch Powell*, pp. 13–31. London: Routledge.
Ford, Robert and Matthew Goodwin (2014a). *Revolt on the Right: Explaining Support for the Radical Right in Britain*. London: Routledge.
Ford, Robert and Matthew Goodwin (2014b). 'Understanding UKIP: Identity, social change and the left behind', *Political Quarterly*, 85(3), pp. 277–84.
Ford, Robert, Will Jennings and Will Somerville (2015). 'Public opinion, responsiveness and constraint: Britain's three immigration policy regimes', *Journal of Ethnic and Migration Studies*, 41(9), pp. 1391–411.
Foxley, Rachel (2013). *The Levellers: Radical Political Thought in the English Revolution*. Manchester: Manchester University Press.
Frankfurt, Harry G. ([1986] 2005). *On Bullshit*. Princeton, NJ: Princeton University Press.
Gallie, Walter Bryce (1964). 'Essentially Contested Concepts', in W. B. Gallie, *Philosophy and the Historical Understanding*, pp. 157–91. London: Chatto & Windus.
Gentleman, Amelia (2017). '"I can't eat or sleep": The woman threatened with deportation after 50 years in Britain', *The Guardian*, 28 November, www.theguardian.com/uk-news/2017/nov/28/i-cant-eat-or-sleep-the-grandmother-threatened-with-deportation-after-50-years-in-britain.
Gentleman, Amelia (2019). *The Windrush Betrayal: Exposing the Hostile Environment*. London: Faber.

Geoghegan, Peter (2020). *Democracy for Sale: Dark Money and Dirty Politics*. London: Apollo.
Goffman, Erving (1967). *Interaction Ritual: Essays on Face-to-Face Behavior*. York: Anchor Books.
Goodhart, David (2017). *The Road to Somewhere: The Populist Revolt and the Future of Politics*. London: Hurst.
Goodman, Simon and Amrita Narang (2019). '"Sad day for the UK": The linking of debates about settling refugee children in the UK with Brexit on an anti-immigrant news website', *European Journal of Social Psychology*, 49(6), pp. 1161–72.
Goodwin, Matthew (2011). *New British Fascism: Rise of the British National Party*. London: Routledge.
Goodwin, Matthew and Oliver Heath (2016). 'Brexit vote explained: Poverty, low skills, and lack of opportunities', Joseph Rowntree Foundation, 31 August, www.jrf.org.uk/report/brexit-vote-explained-poverty-low-skills-and-lack-opportunities.
Grayling, Anthony Clifford (2001). *The Meaning of Things*. London: Weidenfeld & Nicolson.
Grayling, Anthony Clifford (2016). 'The reply A. C. Grayling got when he wrote to Parliament (and how he reacted)', *The New European*, 23 November, www.theneweuropean.co.uk/brexit-news-the-reply-a-c-grayling-got-when-he-wrote-to-15604/.
Grayling, Anthony Clifford (2018). *Democracy and Its Crisis*, updated edition. London: Oneworld.
Grice, Herbert Paul (1975). 'Logic and conversation', in P. Cole and J. Morgan (eds.), *Syntax and Semantics 3: Speech Acts*, pp. 41–58. London: Academic Press.
Grice, Herbert Paul (1989). *Studies in the Way of Words*. Cambridge, MA: Harvard University Press.
Guild, Elspeth, Steve Peers and Jonathan Tonkin (2019). *The EU Citizenship Directive: A Commentary*, second edition. Oxford: Oxford University Press.
Hamilton, Alexander, James Madison and John Jay (2009). 'Federalist No. 10', in *The Federalist Papers*, pp. 49–54. New York: Palgrave Macmillan.
Hann, Michael (2016). '"Fashwave": Synth music co-opted by the far right', *The Guardian*, 14 December, www.theguardian.com/music/musicblog/2016/dec/14/fashwave-synth-music-co-opted-by-the-far-right.
Hansen, Randall (2000). *Citizenship and Immigration in Post-war Britain*. Oxford: Oxford University Press.
Harsin, Jayson (2019). 'Post-truth and critical communication studies', in D. L. Cloud (ed.), *Oxford Research Encyclopedia of Communication and Critical Cultural Studies*. Oxford: Oxford University Press.
Hart, Christopher (2011a). 'Legitimizing assertions and the logico-rhetorical module: Evidence and epistemic vigilance in media discourse on immigration', *Discourse Studies*, 13(6), pp. 751–69.
Hart, Christopher (2011b). 'Force-interactive patterns in immigration discourse: A cognitive linguistic approach to CDA', *Discourse and Society*, 22(3), pp. 269–86.
Hart, Christopher (2013). 'Argumentation meets adapted cognition: Manipulation in media discourse on immigration', *Journal of Pragmatics*, 59(B), pp. 200–9.
Hattenstone, Simon (2018). 'Why was the scheme behind May's "Go Home" vans called Operation Vaken?', *The Guardian*, 26 April, www.theguardian.com/commentisfree/2018/apr/26/theresa-may-go-home-vans-operation-vaken-ukip.

Hawkins, Kirk A., Rosario Aguilar, Bruno Castanho Silva, Erin K. Jenne, Bojana Kocijan and Cristóbal Rovira Kaltwasser (2019). 'Measuring populist discourse: The Global Populism Database', paper presented at the 2019 EPSA Annual Conference in Belfast, UK, June 20–22, https://populism.byu.edu/App_Data/Public ations/Global%20Populism%20Database%20Paper.pdf.

Heffer, Simon (1998). *Like the Roman: The Life of Enoch Powell*. London: Weidenfeld & Nicolson.

Henkel, Imke (2019). 'So enden Demokratien', *Die Zeit*, 28 August, www.zeit.de/poli tik/ausland/2019-08/eu-austritt-parlamentspause-unterhaus-boris-johnson-grossbri tannien-brexit.

Henley, Jon (2016). 'Why Vote Leave's 350m weekly EU cost claim is wrong', *Guardian*, 10 June, www.theguardian.com/politics/reality-check/2016/may/23/doe s-the-eu-really-cost-the-uk-350m-a-week.

Heritage, John. and David Greatbach (1986). 'Generating applause: A study of rhetoric and response at party political conferences', *American Journal of Sociology*, 92(1), pp. 110–57.

Hidalgo-Tenorio, Encarnación, Miguel-Ángel Benítez-Castro and Francesca De Cesare (eds.) (2019). *Populist Discourse: Critical Approaches to Contemporary Politics*. London: Routledge.

Hillman, Nicholas (2008). 'A "chorus of execration"? Enoch Powell's "Rivers of Blood" forty years on', *Patterns of Prejudice*, 42(1), pp. 83–104.

Hobbes, Thomas ([1651] 2012). *Leviathan*, ed. N. Malcolm. The Clarendon Edition of the Works of Thomas Hobbes. Oxford: Oxford University Press.

Hogan, Patrick Colm (ed.) (2011). *The Cambridge Encyclopedia of the Language Sciences*. New York: Cambridge University Press.

Hogg, Quintin (1976). 'Elective dictatorship', *The Listener*, 21 October, pp. 496–500.

Huang, Yan (2007). *Pragmatics*. Oxford: Oxford University Press.

Hume, Mick (2018). 'They are all in contempt of the people', *sp!ked*, 6 December, www.spiked-online.com/2018/12/06/they-are-all-in-contempt-of-the-people/.

Huntington, Samuel P. (1996). *The Clash of Civilizations and the Remaking of World Order*. New York: Simon & Schuster.

Ingram, Mike (2001). 'British Conservative Party exposes its racist underbelly', World Socialist Web Site, 3 April, www.wsws.org/en/articles/2001/04/hag-a03.html.

Isenberg, Nancy B. (2011). 'Amygdala', in P. C. Hogan (ed.), *The Cambridge Encyclopedia of the Language Sciences*, pp. 96–7. New York: Cambridge University Press.

Isenberg, N. B., D. A Silbersweig, A. Engelien, S. Emmerich, K. Malavade, B. Beattie, A. C. Leon and E. Stern (1999). 'Linguistic threat activates the human amygdala', *Proceedings of the National Academy of Sciences USA*, 96(18), pp. 10456–9, www .pnas.org/doi/10.1073/pnas.96.18.10456.

Javanbakht, Arash (2019). 'The politics of fear: How fear goes tribal, allowing us to be manipulated', *The Conversation*, 11 January, https://theconversation.com/the-polit ics-of-fear-how-fear-goes-tribal-allowing-us-to-be-manipulated-109626.

Johnson, Mark (1987). *The Body in the Mind: The Bodily Basis of Meaning, Imagination, and Reason*. Chicago: Chicago University Press.

Jones, Jonathan (2016). 'Farage's poster is the visual equivalent of Enoch Powell's "Rivers of Blood" speech', *The Guardian*, 16 June, www.theguardian.com/commen

tisfree/2016/jun/16/farage-poster-enoch-powell-rivers-of-blood-racism-ukip-european-union.

Kanai, Ryota, Tom Feilden, Colin Firth and Geraint Rees (2011). 'Political orientations are correlated with brain structure in young adults', *Current Biology*, 21(8), pp. 677–80, www.ncbi.nlm.nih.gov/pmc/articles/PMC3092984/.

Kassam, Raheem (2016a). 'Second Peaceful PEGIDA UK March Takes Place in Birmingham', *Middle East Forum*, 2 April, www.meforum.org/5941/pegida-uk-march.

Kassam, Raheem (2016b). 'Interview with PEGIDA founder Lutz Bachmann', *Middle East Forum*, 5 April, www.meforum.org/5942/interview-lutz-bachmann.

Kassam, Raheem (2018). *Enoch Was Right: Rivers of Blood 50 Years on*. Raheem Kassam [self-published].

Kellner, Peter (2023). 'Anti-Brexit Britain has reached the point of return', *The New European*, 21 June, www.theneweuropean.co.uk/anti-brexit-britain-has-reached-the-point-of-return/.

KhosraviNik, Majid (2019). 'Populist digital media? Social media systems and the global populist right discourse', *Public Seminar*, 26 October, https://publicseminar.org/2019/10/populist-digital-media-social-media-systems-and-the-global-populist-right-discourse/.

Koller, Veronika, Susanne Kopf and Marlene Miglbauer (eds.) (2019). *Discourses of Brexit*. London: Routledge.

Kopytowska, Monika (2022). 'Proximization, presumption and salience in digital discourse: On the interface of social media communicative dynamics and the spread of populist ideologies', *Critical Discourse Studies*, 19(2), pp. 144–60.

Krasner, Stephen D. (2004). 'The hole in the whole: Sovereignty, shared sovereignty, and international law', *Michigan Journal of International Law*, 25(4), pp. 1075–101.

Krulic, Brigitte (2007). 'Le peuple français chez Maurice Barrès: une entité insaisissable entre unité et diversité', *Sens public*, www.sens-public.org/articles/384/.

Kuper, Simon (2019). 'How Oxford University shaped Brexit – and Britain's next prime minister', *Financial Times*, 18 September, www.ft.com/content/85fc694c-9222-11e9-b7ea-60e35ef678d2.

Laclau, Ernesto (2005). *On Populist Reason*. London: Verso.

Lakoff, George (1987). *Women, Fire, and Dangerous Things: What Categories Reveal about the Mind*. Chicago: University of Chicago Press.

Lakoff, George (2008). *The Political Mind*. New York: Penguin.

Lakoff, George and Mark Johnson (1980). *Metaphors We Live By*. Chicago: University of Chicago Press.

Lane, Melissa (2012). 'The origins of the statesman-demagogue distinction in and after ancient Athens', *Journal of the History of Ideas*, 73(2), pp. 179–200.

Larsen, Jeppe Fuglsang (2022). 'The identitarian movement and fashwave music: The nostalgia and anger of the new far right in Denmark', *Popular Music*, 41(2), pp. 152–69. www.cambridge.org/core/journals/popular-music/article/abs/identitarian-movement-and-fashwave-music-the-nostalgia-and-anger-of-the-new-far-right-in-denmark/760C530AA964F3E3A86B95C335A56598.

Lawton, Chris and Robert Ackrill (2016). 'Hard evidence: How areas with low immigration voted mainly for Brexit', *The Conversation*, 8 July, https://theconversation

.com/hard-evidence-how-areas-with-low-immigration-voted-mainly-for-brexit–62138.
Levitsky, Steven and Daniel Ziblatt (2019). *How Democracies Die: What History Reveals about our Future*. London: Penguin.
Levy, David A. L., Billur Aslan and Diego Bironzo (2016). *UK Press Coverage of the EU Referendum*. Oxford: Reuters Institute for the Study of Journalism, https://reutersinstitute.politics.ox.ac.uk/sites/default/files/2018-11/UK_Press_Coverage_of_the_%20EU_Referendum.pdf.
Lewis, Bernard (1993). *Islam and the West*. New York: Oxford University Press.
Lindop, Fred (2001). 'Racism and the working class: Strikes in support of Enoch Powell in 1968', *Labour History Review*, 66(1), pp. 79–100.
MacDonald, Alex (2013). 'EDL leader, Tommy Robinson, claims common ground with UKIP on immigration and Islam', *Backbencher*, 3 April, https://thebackbencher.co.uk/english-defence-league-leader-tommy-robinson-backs-ukip-on-immigration-and-islam/.
Macdonald, Ian, Reena Bhavnani, Gus John and Lily Khan (1989). *Murder in the Playground: Report of the Macdonald Inquiry into Racism and Racial Violence in Manchester Schools*. London: Longsight Press.
Macpherson, William (1999a). *The Stephen Lawrence Inquiry: Report of an Inquiry by Sir William Macpherson of Cluny*, February, reference Cm 4262-I, https://assets.publishing.service.gov.uk/government/uploads/system/uploads/attachment_data/file/277111/4262.pdf.
Macpherson, William (1999b). *The Stephen Lawrence Inquiry: Appendices*. London: Stationery Office.
Maddock, Richard. J. and Michael H. Buonocore (1997). 'Activation of left posterior cingulate gyrus by the auditory presentation of threat-related words: An fMRI study', *Psychiatry Research*, 75(1), pp. 1–14.
Maddock, Richard, Amy S. Garrett and Michael H. Buonocore (2003). 'Posterior cingulate cortex activation by emotional words: fMRI evidence from a valence decision task', *Human Brain Mapping*, 18(1), pp. 30–41.
Madison, James (1787). *The Federalist Papers*, No. 10, 22 November.
Manzoor, Sarfraz (2008). 'Black Britain's darkest hour', *The Observer*, 24 February, www.theguardian.com/politics/2008/feb/24/race.
McDougall, Gay (2021). 'The International Convention on the Elimination of All Forms of Racial Discrimination', United Nations Audiovisual Library of International Law. New York: United Nations, https://legal.un.org/avl/pdf/ha/cerd/cerd_e.pdf.
Meibauer, Jörg (2005). 'Lying and falsely implicating', *Journal of Pragmatics*, 37(9), pp. 1373–99.
Meibauer, Jörg (2014). *Lying at the Semantics-Pragmatics Interface*. Berlin: De Gruyter.
Meibauer, Jörg (2018). 'The linguistics of lying', *Annual review of linguistics*, 4(1), pp. 357–75.
Mény, Yves and Yves Surel (eds.) (2002). *Democracies and the Populist Challenge*. New York: Palgrave.
Merrick, Rob (2017). 'Ukip: A timeline of the party's turbulent history', *The Independent*, 29 September, www.independent.co.uk/news/uk/politics/ukip-time

line-party-westminster-alan-sked-nigel-farage-conference-key-events-brexit-leader ship-a7974606.html.
The Migration Observatory (2023). 'Commonwealth migrants arriving before 1971, year ending June 2017', University of Oxford, https://migrationobservatory.ox.ac.uk/commonwealth-migrants-arriving-1971-year-ending-june–2017/.
Mills, Claudia (1995). 'Politics and manipulation', *Social Theory and Practice*, 21(1), pp. 97–112.
Montesquieu, Charles de Secondat, baron de ([1748] 1973). *De l'esprit des lois*. Paris: Garnier.
Moore, Martin and Gordon Ramsay (2017). *UK Media Coverage of the 2016 EU Referendum Campaign*. King's College London, Centre for the Study of Media, Communication and Power, www.kcl.ac.uk/policy-institute/assets/cmcp/uk-media-coverage-of-the-2016-eu-referendum-campaign.pdf.
Mounk, Yascha (2018). *The People vs. Democracy: Why Our Freedom Is in Danger and How to Save It*. Cambridge, MA: Harvard University Press.
Mudde, Cas (2004). 'The populist zeitgeist', *Government and Opposition*, 39(4), pp. 527–40.
Mudde, Cas (2007). *Populist Radical Right Parties in Europe*. Cambridge: Cambridge University Press.
Mudde, Cas and Cristóbal R. Kaltwasser (2014). 'Populism and political leadership', in R. A. W. Rhodes and Paul't Hart (eds.), *The Oxford Handbook of Political Leadership*, pp. 376–88. Oxford: Oxford University Press.
Mudde, Cas and Cristóbal Rovira Kaltwasser (2017). *Populism: A Very Short Introduction*. New York: Oxford University Press.
Müller, Jan-Werner (2003). *A Dangerous Mind: Carl Schmitt in Post-war European Thought*. New Haven, CT: Yale University Press.
Müller, Jan-Werner (2016). *What Is Populism?* Philadelphia: University of Pennsylvania Press.
Murray, Douglas (2013). 'Census that revealed a troubling future', *Standpoint*, 25 February, https://standpointmag.co.uk/features-march-13-census-that-revealed-a-troubling-future-douglas-murray-immigration-multiculturalism-race-ethnicity/.
Murray, Douglas (2017). *The Strange Death of Europe*. London: Bloomsbury.
Musolff, Andreas (2010). *Metaphor, Nation and the Holocaust*. London: Routledge.
Musolff, Andreas (2011). 'How (not) to resurrect the *body politic*: The racist bias in Carl Schmitt's theory of sovereignty', *Patterns of Prejudice*, 45(5), pp. 453–68.
Musolff, Andreas (2012). 'Immigrants and parasites: The history of a bio-social metaphor', in M. Messer, R. Schroeder and R. Wodak (eds.), *Migrations: Interdisciplinary Perspectives*, pp. 249–58. Vienna: Springer.
Musolff, Andreas (2016). *Metaphor and Political Discourse: Analogical Reasoning in Debates about Europe*. Basingstoke: Palgrave Macmillan.
Musolff, Andreas (2017). 'Truths, lies and figurative scenarios: Metaphors at the heart of Brexit', *Journal of Language and Politics*, 16(5), pp. 641–57.
Noiriel, Gérard (1988). *Le creuset français: histoire de l'immigration (XIXe–XXe siècles)*. Paris: Éditions du Seuil.
Oakley, Todd (2010). 'Image schemas', in D. Geeraerts and H. Cuycken (eds.), *The Oxford Handbook of Cognitive Linguistics*, 214–35. Oxford: Oxford University Press.

Oborne, Peter (2021). *The Assault on Truth: Boris Johnson, Donald Trump and the Emergence of a New Moral Barbarism*. London: Simon & Schuster.

Oliver, Tim and Michael John Williams (2016). 'Special relationships in flux: Brexit and the future of the US-EU and US-UK relationships', *International Affairs*, 92(3), pp. 547–67.

O'Neill, Brendan (2019a). 'Parliament vs. the people', *sp!ked*, 28 March, www.spiked-online.com/2019/03/28/indicative-votes-parliament-vs-the-people/.

O'Neill, Brendan (2019b). 'The silencing of the people', *sp!ked*, 10 September, www.spiked-online.com/2019/09/10/the-silencing-of-the-people/.

Orellana, Pablo de and Nicholas Michelsen (2019a). 'The New Right: How a Frenchman born 150 years ago inspired the extreme nationalism behind Brexit and Donald Trump', *The Conversation*, 3 July, https://theconversation.com/the-new-right-how-a-frenchman-born-150-years-ago-inspired-the-extreme-nationalism-behind-brexit-and-donald-trump–117277.

Orellana, Pablo de and Nicholas Michelsen (2019b). 'Reactionary Internationalism: The philosophy of the New Right', *Review of International Studies*, 45(5), pp. 748–67.

Orwell, George ([1949] 2004). *Nineteen Eighty-Four*. London: Penguin.

Orwell, George ([1946] 2013). *Politics and the English Language*. London: Penguin.

O'Toole, Fintan (2018). *Brexit: Heroic Failure*. London: Head of Zeus.

Owen, David (1995). *Ethnic Minorities in Great Britain: Patterns of Population Change, 1981–91*, 1991 Census Statistical Paper no. 10, Centre for Research in Ethnic Relations, University of Warwick, https://warwick.ac.uk/fac/soc/crer/research/publications/nemda/nemda1991sp10.pdf.

Padilla Gálvez, Jesús (2017). 'Democracy in times of ochlocracy', *Synthesis*, 32(1), pp. 167–78.

Patapan, Haig (2019). 'On populists and demagogues', *Canadian Journal of Political Science*, 52(4), pp. 743–59.

Pavlenko, Aneta (ed.) (2006). *Bilingual Minds: Emotional Experience, Expression and Representation*. Toronto: Multilingual Matters.

Pavlidou, Theodossia-Soula (ed.) (2014). *Constructing Collectivity: 'We' across Languages and Contexts*. Amsterdam: Benjamins.

Pelinka, Anton (2013). 'Right-wing populism: Concept and typology', in R. Wodak, M. KhosraviNik and B. Mral (eds.), *Right-wing Populism in Europe: Politics and Discourse*, pp. 3–22. London: Bloomsbury.

Pelinka, Anton (2018). 'Identity politics, populism and the far right', in R. Wodak and B. Forchtner (eds.), *The Routledge Handbook of Language and Politics*, pp. 618–29. London: Routledge.

Petersoo, Pille (2007). 'What does 'we' mean? National deixis in the media', *Journal of Language and Politics*, 6(3), pp. 419–38.

Petrongolo, Barbara (2016). 'Do immigrants harm the job prospects of UK-born workers?' LSE, 19 October, https://blogs.lse.ac.uk/brexit/2016/10/19/do-immigrants-harm-the-job-prospects-of-uk-born-workers/.

Pettigrew, Thomas F. (1998). 'Intergroup contact theory', *Annual Review of Psychology*, 49(1), pp. 65–85.

Pettigrew, Thomas F. and Linda R. Tropp (2005). 'Allport's Intergroup Contact Hypothesis: Its history and influence', in J. F. Dovidio, P. Glick and L. A. Rudman (eds.), *On the Nature of Prejudice: Fifty Years on after Allport*, pp. 262–77. Malden: Blackwell.

Pettigrew, Thomas F. and Linda R. Tropp (2006). 'A meta-analytic test of intergroup contact theory', *Journal of Personality and Social Psychology*, 90(5), pp. 751–83.

Pettigrew, Thomas F. and Linda R Tropp (2008). 'How does intergroup contact reduce prejudice? Meta-analytic tests of three mediators', *European Journal of Social Psychology*, 38(6), pp. 922–34.

Phinnemore, David and Erhan İçener (2016). 'Never mind Brexit scaremongering – Turkey is a long way from joining the EU', *The Conversation*, 10 May, https://theconversation.com/never-mind-brexit-scaremongering-turkey-is-a-long-way-from-joining-the-eu-58958.

Pilkington, Hilary (2016). *Loud and Proud: Passion and Politics in the English Defence League*. Manchester: Manchester University Press.

Pipes, Daniel (1990). 'The Muslims are coming! The Muslims are coming!', *National Review*, 19 November, www.danielpipes.org/198/the-muslims-are-coming-the-muslims-are-coming.

Plato (2007). *The Republic*. Translated by D. Lee, with an Introduction by Melissa Lane. London: Penguin.

Polybius ([1922] 2010). *The Histories*. Translated by W. R. Paton, revised by F. W. Walbank and C. Habicht, Loeb Classical Library. Cambridge, MA: Harvard University Press.

Polybius ([1889] 2020). *The Histories of Polybius*. Translated by E. S. Shuckburgh. Kyiv: Strelbytskyy Multimedia Publishing.

Porion, Stéphane (2019a). 'The end of an intellectual journey: How Alfred Sherman's ideas on immigration and the British nation were framed by Powellism', in O. Esteves and S. Porion (eds.), *The Lives and Afterlives of Enoch Powell*, pp. 128–46. London: Routledge.

Porion, Stéphane (2019b). '"Enoch was right" – the Powell effect on the National Front in the 1970s', in O. Esteves and S. Porion (eds.), *The Lives and Afterlives of Enoch Powell*, pp. 147–63. London: Routledge.

Portes, Jonathan (2019). 'Scruton is part of an intellectual culture giving respectability to racism', Politics.co.uk, 5 April, www.politics.co.uk/comment-analysis/2019/04/25/scruton-is-part-of-an-intellectual-culture-giving-respectabi.

Powell, Enoch (1968). 'Speech at Birmingham, 20th April, 1968', www.enochpowell.net/fr-79.html.

Powell, Enoch (1973). 'Mr Powell on "earthquake" when main aim is attainable only from party's enemies', *The Times*, 9 June, p. 3.

Powell, Enoch (1974). *The Speeches of John Enoch Powell*. POLL 4/1/9 Speeches, January 1973–February 1974, 4 files, POLL 4/1/9 File 1, November 1973–February 1974, http://enochpowell.info/wp-content/uploads/Speeches/Nov%201973-Feb%201974.pdf.

Powell, Enoch (1977). *Wrestling with the Angel*. London: Sheldon Press.

Powell, Enoch (1982). 'Speech by the Rt. Hon. J. Enoch Powell, M.P., to the Ilford S. Conservative Association's Annual Dinner', *The Speeches of John Enoch Powell*. POLL 4/1/15 File 3, January–May, http://enochpowell.info/wp-content/uploads/Speeches/Jan-May1982.pdf.

References

Reid, Mary (2013). '"Go Home" vans to go home', *Liberal Democrat Voice*, 22 October, www.libdemvoice.org/go-home-vans-to-go-home-36877.html.
Renwick, Alan (2016). 'What happens if we vote for Brexit?', The Constitution Unit, University College London, https://constitution-unit.com/2016/01/19/what-happens-if-we-vote-for-brexit/.
Rheindorf, Markus and Ruth Wodak (eds.) (2020). *Sociolinguistic Perspectives on Migration Control: Language Policy, Identity and Belonging*. Bristol: Multilingual Matters.
Rising, Lord Howard of (ed.) (2012). *Enoch at 100: A Re-evaluation of the Life, Politics and Philosophy of Enoch Powell*. London: Biteback.
Rohrer, Tim (2005). 'Image schemata in the brain', in B. Hampe and J. Grady (eds.), *From Perception to Meaning: Image Schemas in Cognitive Linguistics*, pp. 165–96. Berlin: De Gruyter Mouton.
Rosanvallon, Pierre (2020). *Le siècle du populisme. Histoire, théorie, critique*. Paris: Éditions du Seuil.
Rousseau, Jean-Jacques (1962). *Du contrat social, ou, Principes du droit politiques*. Paris: Garnier.
Runciman, David (2018). *How Democracy Ends*. London: Profile Books.
Šarić, Ljiljana and Mateusz-Milan Stanojević (eds.) (2019). *Metaphor, Nation and Discourse*. Amsterdam: Benjamins.
Saul, Jennifer (2012). *Lying, Misleading, and What Is Said*. Oxford: Oxford University Press.
Saul, Jennifer (2018). 'Dog whistles, political manipulation, and the philosophy of language', in D. Fogal, D. Harris and M. Moss (eds.), *New Work on Speech Acts*, pp. 360–83. Oxford: Oxford University Press.
Saunders, Robert (2019). 'Myths from a small island: The dangers of a buccaneering view of British history', *New Statesman*, 9 October, www.newstatesman.com/politics/uk/2019/10/myths-small-island-dangers-buccaneering-view-british-history.
Sayer, Duncan (2017). 'Why the idea that the English have a common Anglo-Saxon origin is a myth', *The Conversation*, 15 December, https://theconversation.com/why-the-idea-that-the-english-have-a-common-anglo-saxon-origin-is-a-myth-88272.
Sayers, Freddie (2016). 'Campaign memo: It's the economy versus immigration', YouGov, 28 April, https://yougov.co.uk/topics/politics/articles-reports/2016/04/28/campaign-memo-its-economy-versus-immigration.
Schierup, Carl-Ulrik (2006). 'The "migration crisis" and the genesis of Europe's new diversity', in C.-U. Schierup, P. Hansen and S. Castles (eds.), *Migration, Citizenship, and the European Welfare State: A European Dilemma*, pp. 21–47. Oxford: Oxford University Press.
Schiffels, Stephan, Wolfgang Haak, Pirita Paajanen, Bastien Llamas, Elizabeth Popescu, Louise Loe, Rachel Clarke, Alice Lyons, Richard Mortimer, Duncan Sayer, Chris Tyler-Smith, Alan Cooper and Richard Durbin (2016). 'Iron Age and Anglo-Saxon genomes from East England reveal British migration history', *Nature Communications*, 7 (article number 10408), pp. 1–9, www.nature.com/articles/ncomms10408#citeas.
Schiffrin, Deborah (ed.) (1984). *Meaning, Form, and Use in Context: Linguistic Applications*. Washington DC: Georgetown University Press.
Schiffrin, Deborah (1994). *Approaches to Discourse*. Oxford: Blackwell.

Schmid, Monika (2020). 'English in England: We should celebrate different languages, not write hate mail about them', *The Conversation*, 4 February, https://theconversation.com/english-in-england-we-should-celebrate-different-languages-not-write-hate-mail-about-them-131108.

Schmitt, Carl ([1932] 2007). *The Concept of the Political*. Translated by G. D. Schwab. Chicago: University of Chicago Press.

Schofield, Camilla (2013). *Enoch Powell and the Making of Postcolonial Britain*. Cambridge: Cambridge University Press.

Scruton, Roger (2006). 'Should he have spoken?', *The New Criterion*, 39(10). Reprinted in *American Renaissance*, 15 September, https://archive.is/OxCld.

Searle, John R. (1969). *Speech Acts: An Essay in the Philosophy of Language*. Cambridge: Cambridge University Press.

Searle, John R. (1995). *The Construction of Social Reality*. New York: Simon & Schuster.

Searle, John R. (1998). *Mind, Language and Society*. New York: Basic Books.

Searle, John R. (2010). *Making the Social World: The Structure of Human Civilization*. New York: Oxford University Press.

Sebba, Mark (2017). 'English a foreign tongue', *Journal of Language and Politics*, 16(2), pp. 264–84.

Sedgwick, Mark J. (ed.) (2019). *Key Thinkers of the Radical Right: Behind the New Threat to Liberal Democracy*. New York: Oxford University Press.

Seeman, Mary V. (2016). 'Bilingualism and schizophrenia', *World Journal of Psychiatry*, 6(2), pp. 192–8.

Shaw, Martin (2018). 'Truly Project Hate: The third scandal of the official Vote Leave campaign headed by Boris Johnson', *openDemocracy*, 30 August, www.opendemocracy.net/en/dark-money-investigations/truly-project-hate-third-scandal-of-official-vote-leave-campaign-headed-by-/.

Shaw, Martin (2022). *Political Racism: Brexit and Its Aftermath*. Newcastle upon Tyne: Agenda Publishing.

Signer, Michael (2009). *Demagogue: The Fight to Save Democracy from Its Worst Enemies*. New York: Palgrave Macmillan.

Sivanandan, Ambalavaner (2001). 'Poverty is the new black', *Race and Class*. 43(2), pp. 1–5, https://journals.sagepub.com/doi/abs/10.1177/0306396801432001?journalCode=racb.

Snyder, Timothy (2021). 'The American abyss', *The New York Times Magazine*, 9 January, www.nytimes.com/2021/01/09/magazine/trump-coup.html.

Sobolewska, Maria and Robert Ford (2020). *Brexitland: Identity, Diversity and the Reshaping of British Politics*. Cambridge: Cambridge University Press.

Sparrow, Andrew (2014). 'Nigel Farage: Parts of Britain are "like a foreign land"', *The Guardian*, 28 February, www.theguardian.com/politics/2014/feb/28/nigel-farage-ukip-immigration-speech.

Sperber, Dan, Fabrice Clément, Christophe Heintz, Olivier Mascaro, Gloria Origgi and Deirdre Wilson (2010). 'Epistemic vigilance', *Mind and Language*, 25(4), pp. 359–93.

Sperber, Dan and Deirdre Wilson (2002). 'Pragmatics, modularity and mind-reading', *Mind and Language*, 17(1–2), pp. 3–23.

Stanley, Jason (2015). *How Propaganda Works*. Princeton, NJ: Princeton University Press.

Stenner, Karen (2005). *The Authoritarian Dynamic*. New York: Cambridge University Press.
Stenner, Karen and Jonathan Haidt (2018). 'Authoritarianism is not a momentary madness but an eternal dynamic within liberal democracies', in C. Sunstein (ed.), *Can It Happen Here? Authoritarianism in America*, pp. 175–220. New York: Harper Collins.
Stewart, Heather and Rowena Mason (2016). 'Nigel Farage's anti-migrant poster reported to police', *The Guardian*, 16 June, www.theguardian.com/politics/2016/jun/16/nigel-farage-defends-ukip-breaking-point-poster-queue-of-migrants.
Stone, Jon (2018). 'British public still believe Vote Leave "£350 million a week to EU" myth from Brexit referendum', *The Independent*, 28 October, www.independent.co.uk/news/uk/politics/vote-leave-brexit-lies-eu-pay-money-remain-poll-boris-johnson-a8603646.html.
Sykes, Olivier (2018). 'Post-geography worlds, new dominions, left behind regions, and "other" places: Unpacking some spatial imaginaries of the UK's "Brexit" debate', *Space and Polity*, 22(2), pp. 137–61, www.tandfonline.com/doi/pdf/10.1080/13562576.2018.1531699?needAccess=true.
Taggart, Paul (2000). *Populism*. Buckingham: Open University Press.
Talmy, Leonard (1988). 'Force dynamics in language and cognition', *Cognitive Science*, 12(1), pp. 49–100.
Tannen, Deborah, Heidi E. Hamilton and Deborah Schiffrin (eds.) (2015). *The Handbook of Discourse Analysis*. Chichester: Wiley Blackwell.
Taylor, Charlotte (2020). 'Representing the Windrush generation: Metaphor in discourses then and now', *Critical Discourse Studies*, 17(1), pp. 1–21.
Taylor, Charlotte (2021). 'Metaphors of migration over time', *Discourse and Society*, 32(4), pp. 463–81.
Thatcher, Margaret (1995). *The Path to Power*. London: HarperCollins.
Thom, Martin (1995). *Republics, Nations and Tribes*. London: Verso.
Todd, John (2015). *The British Self and Continental Other: A Discourse Analysis of the United Kingdom's Relationship with Europe*. Oslo: ARENA Report No 1/15.
Tomba, Massimiliano (2018). 'Who's afraid of the imperative mandate?', *Critical Times*, 1(1), pp. 108–19.
Tomlinson, Sally (1988). 'Clarifying the Macdonald Report', Letters, *The Independent*, 2 July.
Tomlinson, Sally (1990). *Multicultural Education in White Schools*. London: Batsford.
Tomlinson, Sally (2018). 'Enoch Powell, empires, immigrants and education', *Race, Ethnicity and Education*, 21(1), pp. 1–14.
Tomlinson, Sally (2019). *Education and Race from Empire to Brexit*. Bristol: Policy Press.
Tournier-Sol, Karine (2019). 'The ambivalence of UKIP towards Enoch Powell's legacy', in O. Esteves and S. Porion (eds.), *The Lives and Afterlives of Enoch Powell*, pp. 162–75. London: Routledge.
Uberoi, Elise (2015). *European Referendum Bill 2015–16*, Briefing Paper, Number 07212, 3 June, House of Commons Library, https://researchbriefings.files.parliament.uk/documents/CBP-7212/CBP-7212.pdf.
UKIP (2017). *Britain Together. UKIP 2017 Manifesto*, https://d3n8a8pro7vhmx.cloudfront.net/ukipdev/pages/3944/attachments/original/1495695469/UKIP_Manifesto_June2017opt.pdf.

UK Parliament, Department of Culture, Media and Sport Committee (2018). *Vote Leave / 50 Million Ads*, www.parliament.uk/globalassets/documents/commons-committees/culture-media-and-sport/Fake_news_evidence/Vote-Leave-50-Million-Ads.pdf.

United Nations (1965). *International Convention on the Elimination of All Forms of Racial Discrimination*. New York: United Nations Audiovisual Library of International Law, https://treaties.un.org/doc/publication/UNTS/Volume660/v660.pdf.

Urbinati, Nadia (2014). *Democracy Disfigured: Opinion, Truth, and the People*. Cambridge, MA: Harvard University Press.

Urbinati, Nadia (2019). *Me the People: How Populism Transforms Democracy*. Cambridge, MA: Harvard University Press.

van Houtum, Henk and Rodrigo Bueno Lacy (2017). 'The political extreme as the new normal: The cases of Brexit, the French state of emergency and Dutch Islamophobia', *Fennia* 195(1), pp. 85–101.

Vucetic, Srdjan (2011). *The Anglosphere: A Genealogy of a Racialized Identity in International Relations*. Palo Alto, CA: Stanford University Press.

Wallace, Henry A. (1942). 'The century of the common man', speech delivered 8 May, Commodore Hotel, New York, American Rhetoric Online Speech Bank, www.americanrhetoric.com/speeches/henrywallacefreeworldassoc.htm.

Wallace, Henry A. (1943). *The Century of the Common Man*. New York: Reynal & Hitchcock.

Weale, Albert (2018). *The Will of the People: A Modern Myth*. Cambridge: Polity.

Weisholtz, Daniel S., James C. Root, Tracy Butler, Oliver Tüscher, Jane Epstein, Hong Pan, Xenia Protopopescu, Martin Goldstein, Nancy Isenberg, Gary Brendel, Joseph LeDoux, David A. Silbersweig and Emily Stern (2015). 'Beyond the amygdala: Linguistic threat modulates peri-sylvian semantic access cortices', *Brain and Language*, 151, pp. 12–22.

Wenzl, Nora (2019). '"This is about the kind of Britain we are": National identities as constructed in parliamentary debates about EU membership', in V. Koller, S. Kopf and M. Miglbauer (eds.), *Discourses of Brexit*, pp. 32–47. London: Routledge.

Wheeler, Brian (2016). 'Ad breakdown: Vote Leave EU referendum broadcast', *BBC News* website, 24 May, www.bbc.co.uk/news/uk-politics-eu-referendum-36367247.

Whipple, Amy (2009). 'Revisiting the "Rivers of Blood" Controversy: Letters to Enoch Powell', *Journal of British Studies*, 48(3), pp. 717–35.

Williams, Wendy (2020). *Windrush Lessons Learned Review*. London: Crown copyright, https://assets.publishing.service.gov.uk/government/uploads/system/uploads/attachment_data/file/876336/6.5577_HO_Windrush_Lessons_Learned_Review_LoResFinal.pdf.

Winder, R. (2004). *Bloody Foreigners: The Story of Immigration to Britain*. New York: Little, Brown.

Winlow, Simon, Steve Hall and James Treadwell (2017). *The Rise of the Right: English Nationalism and the Transformation of Working-Class Politics*. Bristol: Policy Press.

Wirz, Dominique S. (2018). 'Persuasion through emotion? An experimental test of the emotion-eliciting nature of populist communication', *International Journal of Communication*, 12, pp. 1114–38.

Wodak, Ruth (2015). *The Politics of Fear: What Right-Wing Populist Discourses Mean*. London: Sage.

Wodak, Ruth (2016). '"We have the character of an island nation": A discourse-historical analysis of David Cameron's "Bloomberg speech" on the European Union', European University Institute Working Paper, series RSCAS 2016/36, http://cadmus.eui.eu/bitstream/handle/1814/42804/RSCAS_2016_36.pdf?sequence=1&isAllowed=y.

Wodak, Ruth (2017). 'The "establishment", the "élites", and the "people"', *Journal of Language and Politics*, 16(4), pp. 551–65.

Wodak, Ruth, Rudolf de Cillia, Martin Reisigl and Karin Liebhart (2009 [first edition 1999]). *The Discursive Construction of National Identity*. Edinburgh: Edinburgh University Press.

Wodak, Ruth, Majid KhosraviNik and Brigitte Mral (eds.) (2013). *Right-wing Populism in Europe: Politics and Discourse*. London: Bloomsbury.

Worth, Jon (2017). 'The two versions of the £350 million for the NHS slogan', *Jon Worth Euroblog*, 21 February, https://jonworth.eu/the-two-versions-of-the-350-million-for-the-nhs-slogan/.

Wren-Lewis, Simon (2018). *The Lies We Were Told: Politics, Economics, Austerity and Brexit*. Bristol: Bristol University Press.

Wright, David and Gavin Brookes (2019). '"This is England, speak English!": A corpus-assisted critical study of language ideologies in the right-leaning British press', *Critical Discourse Studies*, 16(1), pp. 56–83.

Wylie, Christopher (2019). *Mindf*ck: Inside Cambridge Analytica's Plot to Break the World*. London: Profile Books.

Yorke, Barbara (1999). 'Alfred the Great: The most perfect man in history?', *History Today*, 49(10), www.historytoday.com/archive/alfred-great-most-perfect-man-history.

Ziem, Alexander (2008). *Frames und sprachliches Wissen: Kognitive Aspekte der semantischen Kompetenz*. Berlin: De Gruyter.

Index

Adorno, Theodor, 8, 83, 105
Altemeyer, Bob, 106
Alternative for Germany, 26
ambiguity, ambiguous, 1, 16, 43, 53, 55, 73, 87, 101, 104, 138, 157, 182
amygdala, 19, 148, 149, 162, 168
Anderson, Benedict, 86, 87
anglophone, 49, 66, 75, 81
Anglo-Saxonism, 88, 89, 133
Anti-Federalist League (AFL), 127, 128, 129, 130
apartheid, 108
Applebaum, Anne, 106
Arendt, Hannah, 11, 105
Aristotle, 10, 62, 64, 77
arrows, 142, 143, 144, 145, 161
Article 50, 70, 71, 182, 183
Athens, Athenian
  and democracy, 9
  and the demagogues, 8, 147
  and the demos, 62, 63
  and the sophists, 9
authoritarian personality, 105, 106, 152
authoritarianism/authoritarian, 27, 28, 94, 95, 105, 106, 134, 152, 169, 172, 174, 177, 179
Ayer, A. J., 1

Ball, James, 11, 14, 139, 157, 158, 159
Banks, Arron, 68, 158, 176, 177
Bannon, Steve, 121, 122, 177
Barrès, Maurice, 28, 29
Bermann, Sylvie, 170
bilingualism, 44, 47, 48
Birmingham, 110, 111, 114, 123, 133, 139
Blair, Tony, 132
Blunkett, David, 46, 47, 48
Bodin, Jean, 66, 74
Bolton, Henry, 87, 88
borders, boundaries, 4, 7, 19, 23, 24, 35, 39, 41, 43, 46, 51, 69, 76, 79, 86, 92, 121, 132, 140, 144, 145, 159, 161, 167, 171

Boston (UK), 32
brain, 1, 15, 18, 19, 20, 73, 145, 147–52, 156, 161, 162, 164, 166, 168, 169, 177
brain imaging, 19, 149
Brexit Party, 26, 44, 61, 71, 72, 82, 92, 93, 128, 174
Britain First, 118, 119
Britain Stronger in Europe, 132, 177
British Empire, 85–91, 107, 108, 110, 120
British National Party (BNP), 27, 113, 118, 126, 127, 128, 130
British Nationality Act, 91, 107, 108, 113, 114, 175
Brixton riot, 114
Brothers of Italy (Fratelli d'Italia), 26
Bruges Group, 127
Buchanan, George, 66, 73, 74, 75, 76, 77, 173, 174
bullshit, 11, 158
Burke, Edmund, 79
Burnage (Manchester), 115

Cambridge Analytica, 176
Cameron, David, 4, 36, 47, 49–54, 55, 56, 57, 58, 59, 60, 91, 99, 129, 130, 131, 132, 134, 136, 137, 138, 141, 146, 181, 182
  Bloomberg speech, 50, 51, 54, 55, 56, 57, 59, 91, 128, 136
Camus, Renaud, 29, 121
Canovan, Margaret, 4, 5, 61, 65, 81, 93
Carney, Mark, 131
Cassam, Quassim, 8, 9, 11, 158
Chilton, Brendan, 97
Clegg, Nick, 58
clusivity, 43
cognition
  cognitive linguistics, 19, 25, 86
  cognitive science, 18
conceptual blend, 101, 145
conservative, 4, 20, 25, 28, 29, 47, 49, 52, 55, 56, 59, 65, 70, 79, 85, 90, 97, 99, 101, 105, 106, 109, 110, 111, 112, 114, 119, 121,

Index

122, 123, 125, 128, 129, 130, 131, 132, 133, 134, 138, 152, 163, 172, 182, 183
Conservative Party, 4, 28, 37, 46, 54, 55, 59, 60, 101, 108, 110, 111, 113, 122, 127, 132, 146, 172
Conservative People's Party of Estonia (Eesti Konservatiivne Rahvaerakond (EKRE)), 26
conspiracy theory, 29
control, loss of, 123, 167, 168
Cox, Jo, 118, 119
Cromwell, Oliver, 75, 76
Crosby, Lynton, 37, 38, 136
Cummings, Dominic, 157, 158, 164, 166, 168, 176
customs union, 153, 170, 183

Dale, Iain, 156
Damasio, Antonio, 151, 152
Danish People's Party (Dansk Folkeparti (DF)), 26
de Benoist, Alain, 29, 30, 31
deictics (deixis), 43, 145
demagocracy [sic], 178
demagogue, demagoguery, 1–21, 24, 25, 35, 40, 42, 61, 63, 64, 78, 80, 101, 103, 106, 109, 125, 126, 128, 131, 135, 137, 138, 145, 147–69, 170–84
democracy, democratic
  decline of, 64, 106, 169, 170–84
  direct democracy, 8, 10, 29, 71, 72, 79, 93, 95, 96, 98, 101
  representative democracy, 7, 8, 26, 29, 59, 65, 67, 71, 72, 93, 94, 95, 96, 97, 98, 101, 134, 177, 179, 180, 181, 182
discourse, 2, 3, 4, 5, 6, 7, 11, 13, 14, 15, 19, 20, 23, 24, 25, 29, 30, 36, 39, 40, 41, 44, 46, 50, 52, 54, 56, 59, 60, 61, 62, 63, 64, 65, 66, 67, 69, 72, 73, 75, 77, 80, 81, 82, 83, 84, 85, 86, 87, 89, 91, 101, 103, 107, 108, 111, 112, 113, 114, 115, 116, 121, 125, 126, 127, 129, 130, 136, 146, 150, 152, 156, 159, 160, 162, 163, 172, 173, 174
dog whistle, 116, 124, 133, 162, 163, 175
doublethink, 180
Duncan Smith, Iain, 119, 137, 173

economy, economic, 3, 6, 12, 15, 20, 33, 34, 35, 37, 38, 39, 42, 45, 54, 80, 83, 84, 89, 90, 100, 106, 107, 108, 112, 114, 115, 116, 123, 130, 131, 132, 133, 134, 136, 137, 138, 153, 157, 164, 167, 170, 171, 172, 176, 177, 178, 181, 183
education, 1, 8, 9, 11, 33, 63, 71, 88, 89, 105, 119, 121, 172, 173, 175

'elite', 5, 7, 12, 29, 39, 55, 65, 67, 71, 72, 80, 83, 85, 89, 98, 101, 107, 109, 111, 116, 119, 125, 132, 134, 163, 172
Elliott, Matthew, 176
Ellsberg, Daniel, 11
emotion
  emotion triggers, 3, 7, 57, 102, 147, 150, 151, 167
  emotional valence, 162
empire, 10, 22, 41, 62, 103, 109, 130, 173, 175
  British, 85–91, 107, 108, 110, 120
Empire Windrush, 91, 107
English Civil War, 69, 72, 75
English Defence League (EDL), 27, 121, 126, 127
English language, 29, 30, 43, 44, 45, 46, 47, 48, 49, 50, 58, 60, 61, 62, 63, 64, 66, 69, 72, 73, 74, 75, 77, 80, 83, 84, 86, 88, 89, 101, 116, 120, 121, 149, 152, 164
Enlightenment, 8, 51, 66, 77, 102, 120
'establishment', 6, 7, 12, 13, 23, 30, 56, 65, 71, 74, 78, 79, 83, 101, 107, 113, 114, 131, 132, 138, 163, 171, 172
ethnocentrism, ethnocentric, 4, 5, 6, 59, 103–6, 109, 111, 113, 121, 122, 124, 126, 128, 130, 136, 152
Europe of Nations and Freedom (*Europe des nations et des libertés*), 26
European Commission, 95, 127, 138
European Research Group (ERG), 49, 90, 119, 132, 134, 136
Euroscepticism, Eurosceptic, 26, 28, 49, 50, 51, 53, 56, 58, 84, 99, 101, 122, 126, 129, 131, 132, 136, 146, 172, 173, 177
'experts', 9, 11, 65, 83, 98, 131, 133, 134, 147, 158, 172

Facebook, 27, 28, 176
face-threatening acts, 15, 52
fact-check, 12, 159
'fake news', 39, 178
Farage, Nigel, 8, 28, 44, 46, 47, 54–60, 61, 71, 72, 82, 83, 100, 112, 121, 127, 128, 129, 152, 158, 160, 176, 177
Faye, Guillaume, 29
fear, 3, 7, 9, 19, 20, 22, 24, 36, 38, 40, 47, 49, 63, 76, 77, 80, 92, 103–46, 147, 148, 149, 150, 151, 161, 162, 164–9, 174, 177, 178, 187
Ferguson, Niall, 30
Finns Party (Perussuomalaiset (PS), 26
Flemish Interest (Vlaams Belang (VB)), 26
Ford, Robert, 25, 45, 105, 106, 109, 111, 112, 113, 123, 130, 152
Fox, Claire, 72

Fox, Liam, 90
frame, 6, 13, 14, 17, 18, 20, 22, 26, 29, 39, 40, 43, 50, 58, 63, 64, 65, 66, 67, 71, 73, 74, 77, 79, 80, 82, 83, 86, 87, 98, 100, 101, 144, 161, 173, 177
Frankfurt, Harry G., 11, 158
free movement, 35, 36, 39, 40, 104, 134, 139
Freedom and Direct Democracy (Svoboda a přímá demokracie (SPD)), 26
Freedom Party of Austria (Freiheitliche Partei Österreichs (FPÖ)), 26
French Revolution, 68, 78, 79
Fromm, Erich, 105

Gallie, W.B., 61
Generation Identity, 27, 28, 121
Glorious Revolution, 68, 69, 76
Gove, Michael, 139, 140, 145, 154
Grayling, A. C., 70, 76, 78, 86, 95
Great Replacement, 29, 118, 121
Grice, Herbert Paul, 16
　cooperative principle, 16
　maxims, 16, 17
Griffin, Nick, 126, 127

Hague, William, 132, 133
Heath, Edward, 110, 111, 123
Herder, Johann Gottfried von, 31
Hobbes, Thomas, 66, 67, 68, 73, 173, 174
Hogg, Quintin, 70
Humboldt, Wilhelm von, 31

identitarianism, 4, 22, 25, 26–31, 41, 42, 46, 50, 172
　identitarian movements, 23, 27, 31, 121, 172
identity
　identity conservative, 25, 105, 106, 109, 129, 130, 131, 132, 152, 163, 172
　identity liberal, 25, 105, 152, 172
　national identity, 4, 22, 23, 26, 31, 43, 50, 51, 56, 57, 58, 60, 68, 85, 86, 87, 101, 102, 103, 105, 107, 113, 126, 172, 173, 175
Identity and Democracy movement, 26
Identity Movement (Identitäre Bewegung), 26, 27
if clause, 91
image schema
　CONTAINER, 18, 19, 25, 39, 51, 52, 57, 69, 145, 161, 162
　FORCE, 18, 19, 145, 161, 162, 164
　PATH, 18, 19, 112, 145, 161
immigration
　and EU, 3, 26, 32, 34, 35, 36, 37, 38, 39, 41, 105, 113, 132, 133, 134, 135, 136, 138, 157, 164

low immigration, 32, 33, 34
implicature, implicate, 16, 17, 150, 151, 155, 156, 162
Institute for Fiscal Studies, 155
Institute of Race Relations, 117
Isenberg, Nancy, xi, 20, 148, 149, 150, 185
Islam, 29, 30, 87, 89, 120, 121

Jackson, Andrew, 81
Jamaica, 91, 107
Javanbakht, Arash, 147
Jefferson, Thomas, 77, 78, 89
Jewish, Jews, 115, 117, 160
Jobbik, 46
Johnson, Boris, 8, 21, 28, 70, 72, 90, 92, 96, 97, 132, 140, 154, 157, 171, 174, 179, 182, 183
Jordan, Colin, 108
Joseph Rowntree Foundation, 33

Kassam, Raheem, 121, 122
Kopytowska, Monika, 117

Labour Party, 46, 133
　Labour Leave, 97
language, 1–21, 23, 24, 29, 31, 39, 42, 43, 44, 46, 47, 48, 49, 60, 61, 62, 64, 65, 66, 70, 82, 86, 87, 88, 89, 98, 104, 113, 116, 121, 122, 133, 136, 145, 147, 148, 150, 152, 157, 160, 162, 163, 164, 178
Law and Justice Party (Prawo i Sprawiedliwość), 27
Lawrence, Stephen, 116, 117, 119, 121, 175
League (Lega Nord, or more fully, Lega Nord per l'Indipendenza della Padonia), 26
League of Empire Loyalists, 108
Leave.EU, 9, 103, 119, 125, 158, 176, 177, 178
Les Identitaires, 26, 29
Levellers, 75, 76
Liberal Democrats, x, 49, 128, 134
lies, lying
　barefaced lie, 141, 180
　noble lie, 120, 180
Littman, Gisèle. *see* Ye'or, Bat
Locke, John, 66, 77, 78
London, 49, 89, 111, 116, 119, 121, 122, 135

Maastricht Treaty, 56, 104, 127
Macdonald, Ian, 115
Macpherson, William, 116
　Macpherson Report, 116
Madison, James, 78
Mair, Thomas, 118
Major, John, 112

Index

mandate
  imperative mandate, 94, 95, 96, 181, 182
  mandatory referendum, 97, 101
maps, 40, 120, 142, 144
Maurras, Charles, 28, 29
May, Theresa, 70, 71, 91, 92, 95, 96, 135, 136, 140, 182, 183
metaphor, metaphorical
  concept of, 40, 86
  flood, 41, 161
  flow, 41, 161
  human body, 46
  infection, 46
  invasion, 117, 177
  parasite, 46
  poison, 46
  swamp, 112, 113
  swarm, 41
Monday Club, 108, 119
monolingualism, monolingual, 31, 44–9, 60
Montesquieu, Charles de Secondat, 77, 78
Mordaunt, Penny, 139, 140, 141, 145
Mosley, Oswald, 108
Müller, Jan-Werner, 82, 94, 95, 182
multilingualism, multilingual, 31, 44, 46, 48, 89, 123
Murray, Douglas, 30, 121
Muslim, 29, 127

nation, 2, 4, 7, 19, 22, 23, 25, 26, 27, 28, 31, 32, 36, 38, 41, 43, 45, 46, 47, 48, 50, 51, 52, 55, 56, 57, 58, 59, 60, 61, 68, 69, 83, 84, 85–91, 92, 94, 95, 101, 102, 103, 105, 106, 107, 110, 113, 114, 122, 123, 126, 129, 132, 138, 140, 141, 145, 146, 152, 154, 157, 158, 162, 165, 171, 172, 173, 174, 175, 179
National Front (France). *see* National Rally
National Front (UK), 108, 113, 114, 115, 119
National Rally (Rassemblement national (RN)), 26, 28
nationalism, nationalist, 4, 24, 29, 31, 42, 45, 51, 55, 58, 59, 60, 84, 85, 87, 89, 99, 100, 101, 113, 114, 117, 120, 121, 122, 124, 126, 129, 132, 134, 136, 146, 173, 175
Nazism, Nazi, 24, 46, 47, 51, 105, 135, 159, 160, 175
neo-Nazi, 108, 113, 117, 118, 163
neural networks, 148
New Labour, 129, 130
news media
  BBC, x, 38, 44, 70, 72, 92, 100, 137, 138, 140, 141, 142, 159, 160
  Breitbart News, 122
  Channel 4, 38

Daily Express, 38, 39, 48, 96, 139
Daily Mail, 36, 38, 39, 40, 49, 71, 91, 116, 137
Daily Mirror, 38
Daily Star, 38
Daily Star Sunday, 38
Daily Telegraph, 38, 49
Financial Times, 38
Guardian, x, 32, 38, 46, 48, 82, 110, 119, 131, 135, 139, 179
Independent, x, 38, 58, 115
ITV, 38
Lincolnshire Reporter, 71
Mail on Sunday, 38
New Statesman, 38
Observer, 38
Sky, 38
sp!ked [sic], 71, 72
Spectator, 38, 157, 166
Sun, 38, 39
Sunday Express, 38
Sunday Telegraph, 38
Sunday Times, 38
TalkRadio [sic], 87
Times, 38, 114, 131
Vice News, 38
NHS, 136, 138, 139, 142, 145, 153, 155, 156, 157, 158, 164, 167, 171, 179
Norgrove, David, 179
Northern Ireland Protocol, 171
Norwich poster, 44, 46, 60
Notting Hill, 108, 109
Nottingham, 108, 109
Nouvelle Droite, 29

ochlocracy, 63, 64, 65, 76, 78, 79
Office for Budget Responsibility, 170
oligarchy, 64, 65, 178
Operation Vaken, 135
Orbán, Viktor, 8, 27, 65, 121
Orwell, George, 1, 2, 3, 81, 180

passive construction, 18
Patriotische Europäer gegen die Islamisierung des Abendlandes (Patriotic Europeans against the Islamisation of the West). *see* Pegida
Pegida, 27, 121
people, the people
  the British people, 4, 26, 44, 49, 53, 54, 85–102, 123, 141, 177, 182
  the common people, 61, 65, 73–84
  contract with, 92, 93, 174
  mandate of the people, 94–9, 101. *see also* imperative mandate

people, the people (cont.)
    ordinary people, 6, 61, 80–4, 85, 102, 152, 172
    will of the people, 6, 61, 78, 91–4, 95, 96, 100, 101, 174, 181, 182
Plato, 10, 62, 64, 74, 77, 120, 180
Plutarch, 10
Polybius, 63, 64, 65, 77, 79
populism, 4, 5–8, 9, 11, 28, 29, 50, 61, 64, 67, 71, 72, 75, 83, 84, 85, 95, 102, 103, 109, 122
    national populism, 28, 50, 61, 84, 85, 102, 103, 122
post-truth, 10–13, 158, 178–80, 183
Powell, Enoch
    'rivers of blood' speech, 110, 111, 113, 117, 118, 122, 130, 149, 150, 152, 161, 185, 186, 187
    and Euroscepticism, 122
Powellism, 112, 113–18, 119, 120, 121, 122, 124, 129, 175
presupposition, presuppose, 16, 91, 133, 151, 156, 166, 167
'project fear', 38, 132
pronouns, 15, 52, 59, 60
proroguing of parliament, 14
Putin, Vladimir, 174, 177

Race Relations Act, 110
racism, racist, 4, 5, 22, 44, 46, 59, 88, 103–6, 108, 110, 111, 113, 114, 115, 116, 117, 118, 119, 121, 122, 124, 126, 128, 133, 146, 150, 151, 152, 160, 163, 171, 175
Rainsborough, Thomas, 76
refugees, 35, 36, 37, 39, 41, 64, 104, 159, 167
relativism, relativist, 10, 12, 31, 158, 178
Resolution Foundation, 171
Robinson, Tommy, 27, 121, 127
Roosevelt, Franklin D., 81
Rousseau, Jean-Jacques, 28, 66, 78, 93, 173
Russell, Bertrand, x, 1

Saunders, Robert, 90
Scarman, Leslie, 114
    Scarman Report, 114
schema, image schema
    CONTAINER, 18, 19, 25, 39, 51, 52, 57, 69, 145, 161, 162
    FORCE, 18, 19, 145, 161, 162, 164
    PATH, 18, 19, 112, 145, 161
Schmitt, Carl, 24, 30
Scruton, Roger, 119, 120, 121
Searle, John, 14, 93
Self and Other, 19

Sellner, Martin, 27
Shaw, Martin, x, 116, 119, 141, 163, 171, 173, 174
Single market, 89, 92, 131, 153, 154, 157, 170, 173, 183
Sked, Alan, 127, 128, 129
Sleaford, 71
Snyder, Timothy, 179
Sobolewska, Maria, 25, 45, 105, 106, 109, 111, 113, 130, 152
social contract, 67, 77, 93, 94
social media, 2, 9, 117, 119, 124, 141, 144, 153, 169, 177
sovereignty, sovereign, 8, 10, 19, 22, 23, 24, 26, 50, 51, 61, 66–72, 73, 75, 76, 77, 80, 86, 91, 92, 97, 105, 122, 123, 134, 161, 173–4
speech acts
    assertives, 14, 15, 153, 154
    commissives (promise, pledge), 14, 15, 155, 156
    face-threatening acts, 15, 52
    threats, threaten, 14, 15
Stanley, Jason, 9
Stenner, Karen, 83, 106, 152
Stockport, 124
Straw, Jack, 116
Stuart, Gisela, 96
Suárez, Francisco, 66, 74
Syria, 36, 140, 144, 159

Telegram, 28
Thatcher, Margaret, 112, 113, 114, 155
they, them, their, theirs, 50, 54, 55, 56, 59, 104, 145
threat, 3, 14, 15, 19, 22, 23, 24, 30, 36, 39, 41, 53, 56, 63, 69, 87, 91, 105, 106, 121, 138, 139, 141, 142, 145, 148, 149, 150, 152, 153, 160, 178
threat words, 148, 185–6
Tice, Richard, 158
Tomlinson, Sally, x, 33, 34, 89, 107, 109, 115, 116
Townsend, John, 122, 133
Trades Union Congress, 108
Truman, Harry S., 81
Trump, Donald, 4, 8, 10, 158, 174, 177
truth claim, 15, 50
truth, truthfulness, 1, 10, 11, 12, 14, 15, 17, 31, 35, 47, 120, 122, 138, 141, 146, 158, 178, 179, 180, 183
Turkey, Turkish, Turk, 26, 36, 39, 138–46, 159, 161, 164, 177, 180
Tyndall, John, 113
typographical layout, 155

Index

Ugandan Asians, 111, 113
Ukraine, 170
Ulster Unionist Party, 114, 123
Union Movement, 108

vigilance, 3, 8, 20, 24, 150, 161
Volk, das, 61, 65, 66, 67, 82, 93
Vote Leave, 9, 37, 39, 52, 90, 96, 103, 119, 125, 137, 138, 139, 141, 142, 144, 145, 154, 155, 156, 157, 158, 164, 166, 167, 168, 175, 176, 177, 178
Vox, 26

Wallace, Henry, 81
Walsall, 110
we, *us*, *our*, *ours*, 15, 43, 44–60, 104, 145, 165
Westphalia, Peace of, 68
White Defence League, 108

Whorf, Benjamin Lee, 31
Wilders, Geert, 8, 30
Wilson, Harold, 123
Windrush scandal, 91, 136
Withdrawal Agreement, 97
Wodak, Ruth, x, 20, 24, 46, 51, 71, 86
Wolverhampton, 110, 111
Wren-Lewis, Simon, 131, 136, 137, 138

xenophobia, 3, 6, 28, 46, 64, 103–9, 124, 126, 128, 129, 131, 134, 135, 136, 146, 174, 175
Xurious website, 117

Yaxley-Lennon, Stephen. *see* Robinson, Tommy
Ye'or, Bat, 30
YouTube, 28, 44, 117

www.ingramcontent.com/pod-product-compliance
Ingram Content Group UK Ltd.
Pitfield, Milton Keynes, MK11 3LW, UK
UKHW021032170125
453800UK00012B/56